Jordan's Guide
British Steam Locomotives

As we rush, as we rush in the train,

The trees and the houses go wheeling back,

But the starry heavens above the plain

Come flying on our track.

In the Train: James Thomson (1834–1882).

After the first powerful plain manifesto

The black statement of pistons, without more fuss

But gliding like a queen, she leaves the station.

The Express: Stephen Spender (1933).

She's a picture of the Age of Steam

You represent my wildest dream,

But it's farewell, to the *Mallard*, and You ...

The Mallard: Michael Chapman (1995).

Jordan's Guide to British Steam Locomotives

by
Owen Jordan

The King's England Press
2003

ISBN 1 872438 70 9

Jordan's Guide to British Steam Locomotives
is typeset in Century Scoolbook 11pt, and published by
The King's England Press, Cambertown House,
Commercial Road,
Goldthorpe, Rotherham, S63 9BL

Printed and bound in Great Britain by

Woolnough Bookbinding
Irthlingborough
Northamptonshire

Foreword:

The Revolution that drove the Revolution

At the end of the eighteenth century, after several thousand years of selective breeding, the horse remained mankind's prime mobile power source. Around the equine family's speed and tractive effort had been constructed transport systems that made the most of the power available from four hooves. Goods traffic on road or canal proceeded to its destination at about three miles per hour. Passengers travelling by coach or on horseback could muster ten miles per hour or a trifle more, but only on the new fangled turnpikes. The nineteenth century's first four decades comprehensively blew away those limiting top speeds, as the steam railway locomotive moved from outlandish fantasy to runaway commercial success.

Steam power on the 'iron road' defined the course and pace of (almost) all things in Britain, and much of the western world, for the seventy years to the outbreak of the First World War. The pace of the industrial revolution stepped up from a stately dance to a frantic whirl, with steam named king and tyrant in consecutive breaths. Journey times on this small island were cut from days to hours. The minute as a unit of travel time was invented, literally overnight. Predictions that mankind could not survive speeds in excess of sixty miles an hour were rapidly overhauled by events. The future had arrived, and it was going to be *different*. One hundred miles an hour may take a little while to achieve, but in a few short years everyone believed it would happen.

The steam locomotive post-1830 bestrides the literal cutting edge of technology, creating demand for better materials made and formed with more accurate machines. Thousands found employment as priests and servers at the altar of speed; millions came to worship. Transforming slow and cumbrous prototypes into a sleek and shiny racehorse, was the work of one man's inspiration, but within a decade all the inventive brainpower of a nation was bent to the task of hastening the locomotive's flight.

This then is the story, from cradle to grave, of the steam railway locomotive in Britain; from the unrewarded genius of Richard Trevithick, through the drawing of the final fires one hundred and sixty four years later, to life, of a sort, after death. This is mostly a British tale, but the effect was global.

The shrinking of the world started here.

Owen Jordan
Pengwaunsarah
Ochrywaun

January 2001

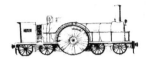

Introduction:

'Slower Than The Angels'

Two hundred years ago mankind, and the inhabitants of Britain in particular, stood on the edge of a revolution. Industrial Britain, as we understand it today, had set-to in earnest during the middle of the eighteenth century, and the transport demand this busy-ness had generated was solved with water-borne movement of goods along the canals, rivers and coasts of this island. The canal, however, proved not as efficient or seamfree a transport network as its proponents would have wished, particularly when it came to crossing hills, and especially when those hills were of porous chalk or limestone. Smooth and efficient transport of goods left unanswered the issue of movement of people; canals, despite a serious effort, had not succeeded in competing with transport on *terra firma*. Introduction of passenger boats, and their description as 'Fly Boats', belied the fact that these boats 'flew' at a speed well below the stalling speed of even the most sluggish bluebottle. Partial relief of these frustrations had come via construction of turnpike roads, raising coach and 'post' (travel on hired horses) speeds to the maximum the horse could sustain. Patently this was just more of the same, and not even remotely a revolution.

The problem was age-old; on foot, a fit man could cover upwards of thirty miles a day; on the back of a good horse, regularly changed, well over a hundred. These speeds had determined man's existence, set the limits of parish, country and empire for millennia, but at ten miles an hour maximum, and a sore posterior as reward, this was quite clearly less than ideal. Coach travel, prior to the turnpikes' rise, was so slow and unreliable as to be virtually useless. It was the accepted status quo in 1820 to wait two or more days for news from London to reach Newcastle, just as it had been half a millennium earlier.

If the problem was age old, then it was also true that mankind on the whole had resigned itself to a fate of being both lower than the angels and slower than most of the larger mammals. Mary Shelley, writing in 1824 of a future two hundred and fifty years ahead, could conceive no form of land transport faster than the horse, no air carriage beyond the balloon, and no ship beyond the combined steam/sail arrangements which the 1820's had to offer. Likewise the grand works of her hero (a thinly disguised latter-day Lord Byron) extended no further than more canals, as far as transport was concerned. One wonders, after three centuries of canal building, just how narrow the banks between these competing waterways would have been. Of the promise of tram and rail road, or indeed any fanciful alternative, there is no mention.

Society as a whole in 1820 seems to have had no better concept of the future than the sceptics who had poured scorn on Trevithick's vision fifteen years earlier. A few men with foresight and ambition saw opportunities in the industrial revolution's products, even if those well aquainted with wealth and privilege, and the intellectual elite, did not. Unfortunately, the future as a technological concept, invented by Leonardo da Vinci in the fifteenth century, had been notoriously fickle about arriving. Now the tools and materials of the age of the stationary steam engine made a transport take-off no mere pipe dream. The phrase 'go faster' captured the imagination in 1829 as no other concept has done since the dawn of time. Only at the start of the twenty-first century has mankind, facing the twin realities of a finitely shrunk Earth, and an infinitely expanding Universe, framed the response 'why?'

The solution to the conundrum of more and faster travel two hundred years ago came as two technologies were welded together in the first three decades of the nineteenth century: the rail or tram road, and the steam engine. Both tram road and steam engine were developed technologies at the start of the nineteenth century, but the twain had yet to meet, and railway and steam locomotive emerge from their union. The evidence of the four decades after 1780 suggests that the need for speed was high on society's agenda; turnpikes, being built by the hundred mile in this period (and still commemorated in pub names like the 'Bristol Flyer', on the Bristol and Gloucester turnpike, now the A38) had, after all, little else to offer. Unable to compete with canals for long distance goods traffic, roads were the obvious starting point for developing fast land transport. The centre of that development remained the horse, the best available mobile power unit.

As with any problem, throwing a lot of weight at existing 'solutions' is more likely to result in damaged foreheads than dents in brick walls. The breakthrough, when it finally came, appears to have taken both inventor and society completely by surprise, blowing away all previous conceptions about the limits of human experience. A transport revolution, based upon the emerging technology of steam, was, or so it seemed, too improbable in 1810 to be credible. Yet the infant railway was better than was needed, the locomotive almost beyond imagination; the union changed the world.

The tale,then, is of the marriage of steam to rail, how Trevithick cast the stone that put the stars to flight; how Robert Stephenson (not George, as the Bank of England would have it) conceived, *and built*, the hitherto inconceivable, and how the baton of progress was taken up and passed on in a hundred and twenty five years of frantic development. It is a tale of endless fascination. Samuel Smiles, first of the professional narrators, threw his moral and intellectual weight into the fray almost before the echoes of the first steam whistle had faded. E. L. Ahrons, in a prodigious work drawn mainly from the extensive written record, particularly copies of the periodical *The Engineer*, covered development in the century up to 1925, writing from the premise that all his readers were not just familiar with the steam locomotive, but that the world revolved around the iron horse (as, of course, it did). Ahrons however, did not cover the wider aspects of the steam locomotive, because at the time there was no need, they were part of everyday life. It is easy for the historian to forget the rule that today is tomorrow's yesterday.

When O. S. Nock contrived to tell the rest of the tale forty years later, his viewpoint, despite the obvious and sweeping changes then in train, tallied with that of his predecessor, and concentrated upon development and performance of individual locomotives. This too was a tale told from the background of the times he lived in, taking for granted the enfolding technologies, though the star of the steam engine in 1965 was rapidly setting, and not just in Britain. Today, the technology that gave birth to and sustained the locomotive, is, like the locomotive itself, history. The designers, metal bashers, foremen, firemen and drivers, their accumulated knowledge and traditions, are all vanishing in the mists of times past.

Of the pictorial histories, perhaps there are more dedicated to the steam locomotive than to any other man-made utilitarian object.

Society is now unused to the hard physical labour that running steam locomotives demanded; a new technology that required operatives to stand on a shaking and rolling plate in a howling gale within too easy reach of a roaring furnace, performing a precisely co-ordinated task in a bedlam of noise that precludes reasoned conversation, to avoid being blown to Kingdom Come, would receive short shrift from the company health and safety manager. A rail safety case? You jest. Most of the players are no more, and surviving locomotives, if not actually stuffed and mounted, are now maintained in a fashion that has little to do with the harsh realities of even fifty years ago. Of the rest: works, running sheds, design and drawing offices, the steam engine dependent communities such as Tebay or Crewe, only the memories and a few buildings remain.

The tale to be told here is a British one, and is told in Fahrenheit, foot-pounds and gallons just as it happened (converting the figures to metric merely demonstrates the unsuitability of a system with an arbitrary starting point). In this tale it is still possible to believe that Britain led the world almost from first to last, starting in South Wales, moving quickly to the North East, and concluding in the future, because the steam locomotive *invented* the future. Where credit is due to foreigners, it is duly, albeit grudgingly, given.

This is the story of the first technology where the objectives of speed and travel are, and seem set to remain, major world religions.

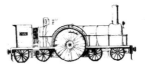

Chapter One:

Genesis

In the development of any technology, there are frequently threads that start in obscurity and end in oblivion. Dead ends, such as post coaches and turnpike roads in the eighteenth and nineteenth centuries, and airships in the twentieth, are common. This is due, not to the concepts being unworkable, but to the fact that competition from alternatives is not always, or even usually, upon a level playing field. Technology is only *one* component in the matrix, and when fashion throws its weight behind even a markedly inferior competitor, well, anything can happen. Interwoven with these false threads are strands that represent true and substantive lines of development. With the steam locomotive there are two elements in the mix; the iron road, without which there may have been travel, but there would have been no speed, and the locomotive itself, derived from the stationary pumping engine over a period of thirty years. Despite their common origin, history dictates that one came before the other, and in this case it is the iron road (which started life as a wooden road) that precedes the recognisable iron horse, as distinct from the steam pump, and by the clear margin of a hundred years and more.

Fortunately for the history of the steam locomotive, the thread of development that led to iron railways, and the steam pumps that led to the locomotive, can be summed up in a single phrase: London, and its insatiable demand for fuel.

Coals from Newcastle

As Feudalism decayed in the latter half of the sixteenth century, it was to the towns and cities of Britain that people flocked to give birth to the industrial age. London, by the time it was reduced to a smoking ruin in 1666, was by a factor of three the largest city in Britain, with a population of at least one hundred thousand souls. To reach this stage of development, London had abandoned the traditional fuel of the Middle Ages, coppice grown timber, and taken with a will to coal. Coal mining had commenced supplying large towns and cities, such as Bristol, in the early seventeenth century, but cartage from Coalpit Heath to the slave capital of the western world was only five downhill miles. London was different; nearly a hundred miles overland to the nearest known coalfield, three hundred by sea from Durham and Northumberland.

That northern coal, dominating the London market, was supplied by an established and efficient coastal shipping fleet; small sailing vessels carrying upwards of twenty or thirty tons of black gold. The North East was the only coalfield that had direct access to the sea at a reasonable distance from the capital. South Wales, while trading with London, struggled to compete owing to the longer and more dangerous sea passage around Lands End. The coal was not cheap; as a monopoly supplier to an utterly dependent market, it had no need to be, and the 'Grand Allies' of the Durham coal trade were merely indulging in the sort of monopoly market rigging that would be illegal today. The trade was long established in 1666, sufficiently robust (i.e. extremely profitable) to be a target for taxation, and supplying a demand that brooked no obstacle to its continuance and expansion. Coal from the Continent, nearer by a hundred miles, surprisingly seems not to have ever entered the equation.

The single factor that mitigated against the coal trade in 1720 was that which faces any exploiter of a non-renewable resource; you cannot mine the same lump of coal twice. Having started by picking up coal off the beach, and moved on to driving adits to follow the exposed coal seams into the cliffs, you ultimately face two problems; the coal needed to satisfy your market is now both a long way from navigable water, and worse, below the water table.

Enter steam pumps and the tramway.

Savery and Newcomen

The places of both Savery (credited with the concept of the steam pump) and Newcomen, who receives the plaudits for achieving a practical working engine, in the history of the steam locomotive are a little dubious, for neither theory or reality of the working steam locomotive had been remotely approached by their inventions. Their fame is due primarily to two related achievements; that the energy of coal could be converted to useful work by boiling water; and that the rudiments of pistons, cylinders, furnaces, boilers and valves, all of which would be ultimately required to serve the steam locomotive, were invented at a date that would allow considerable development before they would be needed in the real thing. The steam pump of 1730 was not a steam engine *per se*, but a coal fired vacuum pump, and even by the standards of the railway locomotive of 1830, amazingly inefficient.

Thomas Savery (1650-1715) and Thomas Newcomen (1663-1729) both conceived the idea that condensing steam could be used to generate a vacuum against which the pressure of the atmosphere could do useful work. Savery, who takes the credit for being first, used a pipe and steam vessel with an external condensing water spray to draw water from a well, and high pressure steam to expel the water up the delivery pipe. It was the high pressure element that caused the problem; without the technology to produce pipes and vessels to take the pressures involved, the concept is workable, but success is avoided by application of the silk purse/sow's ear syndrome, for 'you cannot design beyond the measure of your materials'.

Where Savery failed to command, Newcomen saw the dilemma and navigated the fine line of the available technology to produce a machine that delivered the goods, or rather the water. Newcomen's engine could do one task; pump water up from depth. The engine form that he designed, the beam engine, takes the credit for being the oldest steam engine, on the basis that an engine is defined as a machine capable of continuous sustained and useful work. At its simplest, this engine comprised three major components; a large open topped cylinder in which moved a piston connected by chains to the beam; a set of pump rods and a plunger piston which actually lifted the water up the pump shaft; and a primitive boiler and furnace which supplied the steam at, or slightly above, atmospheric pressure.

The cycle of operation, and it is relevant to consider the first useful engine's *modus operandi*, commences with the working piston being pulled up the cylinder by the weight of the descending pump

13

rods and piston in the pump cylinder. Into the space underneath the working piston is fed steam, supplied from the boiler via a manually (probably more correctly 'childually', as this was a job for the young, not infrequently the very young) operated steam valve, almost certainly at this early date a tapered plug cock, with a lever handle to turn it through ninety degrees. As the piston reached the top of its stroke, steam was turned off and condensate water turned on to produce a partial vacuum in the cylinder below the working piston. Atmospheric air pressure in the open top of the cylinder then drove the piston down, raising water in the pump cylinder, the cycle being repeated until water commenced to flow from the delivery pipe, at which point the engine was balanced against the load.

The reasons for success are simple; only the delivery pipe and pump cylinder were subject to pressures above atmospheric; the important bits at the cutting edge of technology, the steam boiler and the working piston and cylinder, all worked at a mean pressure that was atmospheric, or less.

Newcomen's engine, then, was the industrial revolution's first and most important object lesson; successful because it did not demand more of the materials than could be delivered. Wood and metal only performed duties that had been proved elsewhere. The working cylinder was a casting of bronze (later iron) not wildly dissimilar from products cast for munitions or water supply (Morice's tide-driven water pump had been at work supplying London with water of a sort for over a century prior to 1700) the piston a metal or wood reinforced disc sealed in its bore with junk (old tarred rope) held down with iron weights; the beam an iron bound tree trunk resting on a massive masonry wall. Manufacture and assembly was all of a piece with the construction, needing masons, founders, millwrights, plumbers and carpenters. There was no need for engineers and mechanics yet, but the future, when those people would emerge from the artisans to claim the steam engine as their own, was not too far away.

By 1730 the beam engine, working to Newcomen's principles, was an established technology, sufficiently practical and useful to be applied to the task of pumping water from the mines that supplied it with fuel. As the century advanced the numbers in use grew in line with the demand for the coal it consumed by the tens of tons. The technology of those stationary engines can be summed up as falling into two sections; boilers and motion, and even at this stage we need to examine these items, for while they were very far removed from the hardware of the railway locomotive in the century to come, they represented the first works of boilersmith and foundry, and the beginnings of skill acquisition and honing that culminated in the launch of the steam locomotive.

The first boilers

The task of the first boilers was simple; generate sufficient steam at atmospheric pressure to fill the working cylinder's swept volume half a dozen times a minute. On an engine of six foot stroke and three foot diameter, this represents an evaporative rate of 600lb/hour, heating water from say 50deg.F, to steam at 212deg.F, and needing 676,800BTU (British Thermal Units) to accomplish it, energy contained in about 50lb of good Durham coal. Practically, the combustion and boiler efficiencies of the middle of the eighteenth century were a little less than one (100%), nearer 25% in fact, which meant that in order to generate the steam necessary to keep a Newcomen engine nodding, 200lb coal/hour had to be burnt, and the size of the grate necessary dictated the boiler layout. With natural draught from a modest chimney it is possible to fire a grate at a rate of about 10lb/sq.ft/hour, so a boiler needing to burn 200lb/hour will need the grate to be about five feet square, allowing for uneven firing and the reduced rate of combustion at the edges.

By a bit of crafty empiricism then, we have deduced what Newcomen had to find out the hard way, namely that the boiler for his engine needed to be at least five feet square. Practically it was quickly realised that a circular plan and a hemispherical container were the best ways to accommodate the stresses and strains of an iron or copper boiler, and this was enclosed by a brick beehive, which supplied the necessary flueing and the all important thermal stability and insulation. Working continuously, this hungry monster would eat two tons of coal a day, a fact that mitigated against use anywhere except in, or very near, coal mines. This boiler form, the haystack, was still in common use in the nineteenth century, though it was quickly rendered obsolete by technological progress.

By using nineteenth century data, we have demonstrated just a few of the practical difficulties that faced designers and builders of beam engines in the eighteenth century; how much steam will the engine use? How much fuel will be needed? How big must the grate be? How big must the boiler be? How much chimney draught can be generated? What losses will occur? Can we use iron in the boiler? To these questions in 1730 there was only one answer; we will have to find out. A hundred years later that was still the answer to some of these questions, and to a great many more besides, which had cropped up in the intervening ten decades.

Just how many mines in the North East were using steam to pump their workings by 1800 is a moot point, for there were (and still are) significant coal deposits that remained above the water table. Adoption of James Watt's patent of separate condensation, transforming the operation of the beam engine; application of rotative motion, allowing engines to do work other than pumping; capping the cylinder to make the engine double acting, and realisation that a slight rise in steam boiler and delivery pressures would make the engine more effective, are just the most visible facets of technology's march in the eighteenth century. By that century's end we have, on the eve of invention of the steam locomotive proper, solid boilers, pipework, pistons, valves, connecting rods, and on the tramways, wheels and axles, all ready and waiting for the genius to step forward and say 'what if?' I hesitate at this juncture to call these products 'reliable', but without these items in the technology cupboard, that inventor would have been a forgotten Leonardo da Vinci.

The legacy of the eighteenth century, then, is the technology of the stationary engine and tramroad, needed, together with the men with hands-on experience, to turn fantasy into reality in the nineteenth. It is no accident that 'old Robert' Stephenson, George Stephenson's father, was a 'fireman' (stationary steam engine operator) at a variety of pits around Tyneside, but before we focus on George, we have to admit that one or two others arrived at practical working locomotives first, and that we have not as yet taken a look at the iron road all these inventors would need, to allow their steeds to gallop.

The Iron Road

As demand for coals from Newcastle grew in the early eighteenth century, colliery owners and mines lessees adopted two strategies to satisfy that demand; digging deeper with the aid of Newcomen's pump, and searching farther afield, inland to the edge of the coalfield proper, and north of the River Tyne at least, beyond in search of the limestone coals west of Ponteland. In both areas a move away from the coast and banks of the tidal and navigable rivers meant that land transport, the horse and cart, was adding substantially to the cost of coal delivered 'FOB' (Free On Board) to the shipping staithes. Far-sighted colliery owners realised that, in

County Durham at least, an evenly graded and smooth road from pit to shipping staithe would allow gravity to offer significant assistance to loaded coal waggons, in an area where the canal (in wide use on the continent by this time) could not hope to be of assistance. From the first decade of the eighteenth century then, colliery owners were building graded roads to ease their transport problems, and very quickly fitting them first with timber, and then iron, rails, to reduce friction to the point where gravity could reduce the horse's role on loaded runs to that of controller, rather than haulier.

From this period we have a survivor, the Tanfield Waggonway, and the world's first railway bridge, the Causey Arch, a large single span bridge attributed to the mason Ralph Wood, and dated to 1725, both now preserved and deservedly receiving world heritage status. So effective and dominant did tramways become in the North East coal business, that when canals were built elsewhere in Britain, after 1750, Durham and Northumberland were the only two coalfield counties in which not a single mile of canal proper was ever built. By 1800, large parts of the working coalfield were traversed by tramroads, and while the prize for being first slipped away elsewhere, here groundwork for the successful and economical steam locomotive was laid out, and regular steam traction proved the system, before speed generated its own economics and swept all before it.

While extensively developed in Durham and Northumberland in the eighteenth century, the tramway was not invented there (the actual origins are uncertain; the idea may have originated in Roman times). As industrial development spread across Britain's coalfields, so tramroads became the staple transport in areas where rivers or, later, canals could not be pressed into service. Virtually unique to the North East was a system of wayleaves, whereby tramways paid dues for crossing the land of others, without having to buy that land. Buying land in coal mining areas was very difficult and costly because of the mineral rights that went with the sale, and wayleaves were an effective way around this problem.

From construction of the Sankey Brook Navigation in 1757, Acts of Parliament for digging canals usually included provision for connecting tramroads under 'eight mile' clauses. This allowed the company owning the canal to build connecting roads, and in default, any prospective user could build a tramroad if the canal company declined to, without further recourse to Parliament. From 1790 to 1835, extensive networks of tramroads were built over the principal coalfields of Britain, many, when not converted to railways, surviving until the first decade of the twentieth century. Thus, while the Stockton and Darlington Railway was being built in 1822-5, a successful London indigo merchant turned country squire, John Christie, built the Brecon Forest Tramroad (twice!) out of his own pocket, to design parameters that, while over thirty years old, could not in any way be said to be outmoded, and whose alignments in far more demanding terrain were not markedly inferior to that of the would be steam railway.

The tramway continued to thrive until the middle of the nineteenth century, and if in the beginning there was much variety in the use of edge rails, cast iron, wrought iron, timber and the 'L' shaped tram plate, and gauges that varied from two to five feet or more, it was the cast iron 'L' tramplate and stone sleeper block, beloved of George Overton, pre-eminent among tramroad surveyors, that came and stayed longest, in spite of cast iron's general unsuitability for anything other than animal power. Tramroads were usually 'public'; anyone could use them on payment of the appropriate tolls and compliance with regulations in respect of types of vehicle and maximum loads. This system was an expensive disaster on the first railways with steam traction, and was quickly abandoned. Similarly, the building of hybrid railways, that were at least half tramroad in principle, but included long runs of rope haulage on inclines that were too steep to ever see steam traction, continued through the nineteenth century. Both the Stanhope and Tyne Railroad, and the Cromford and High Peak, were two that survived to the second half of the twentieth century, being spectacular both in concept and operation.

In conclusion then, we can look at the end of the eighteenth century, and see that transport networks in England, Scotland and Wales were expanding rapidly. Fifty years earlier there had been only dirt roads and uncontrolled rivers to move the goods of the infant industrial revolution, and the few people whom wealth or need drove to travel. Just how bad those roads and rivers were can only be imagined today. Tales of travellers drowning in potholes on the King's highway were probably just that; tales to impress the tavern idlers. Some roads were undoubtedly passable with large and fairly heavy loads. Sections of the Roman road network, such as the north Lincolnshire section of Ermine Street, were in good order at the start of the twentieth century, nineteen centuries after it was built, and where roads and tracks crossed well drained and stony ground they were certainly navigable in most weathers with the requisite amount of care. Such instances of 'good' roads did not however constitute an effective national network. Bridges over the larger rivers were few, and the first river crossings on all the major estuaries were a long way upstream from the mouth. Distances between towns were frequently much longer than their actual physical separation.

The road network was thus very much a curate's egg, good only in very small parts. Much of the maintenance of roads was in the hands of the parish, where the custom of labour service by the villagers (under the 1555 Highways Act) was a duty to be avoided completely if at all possible. The setting up of turnpike trusts (the 1663 Turnpike Act) was resented by the population in general; tolls were evaded if they could be, and the better transport facilities offered were not perceived as being 'pro bono publico', but very much 'pro' private profit. Only one hundred and sixty nine trusts were set up prior to 1750, a miserable rate of under two per year. Travel was an unknown quantity to most people. Where ground conditions were poor, such as in the river valleys and flood plains of the wetter western parts of Britain, there were often no roads at all. In these areas the packhorse remained the beast of burden, and carts and coaches played little or no part in life on the move. It is true to say that movement of goods and people in mid-eighteenth century Britain was more difficult and expensive than it had been seventeen centuries earlier; dictators in Rome had taken a greater interest in the highways than did the democratic government in Westminster.

If the roads were bad to the point of disbelief, rivers were little better, as transport arteries at any rate. The only river to offer reliable water levels and unbroken navigation for a distance was the Severn, and the upper tidal reaches of this highway were so hazardous that a canal was eventually built to by-pass it. Bow hauling was the alternative to sail when the wind was contrary. On all other rivers there were either shallows, rapids or mill dams, and usually a combination of all three. On tidal stretches the navigable channel changed frequently. The pound lock proved to be the means for dramatic improvements in river navigation, but low water and floods, meant navigation was irregular rather than assured.

It was onto this canvas that the tramroad had made its bow at the start of the eighteenth century, and after 1750 new tramroads, and turnpike trusts were being established at a comparatively brisk rate of between fifteen and twenty each per year. A century later there were perhaps 5000 miles of tramroad and 30,000 miles of turnpike road (under 15% of the current road network). The day of the tramroad though, was waning in 1850, and the turnpike a dead duck, run over and squashed beyond redemption by the steam locomotive. A transient answer to a continuing problem.

Canals were entirely privately funded. Westminster's contribution was to cream off substantial fees for parliamentary bills, but the fifteen hundred miles of canal that the years 1757 to 1800 produced were the first national transport network to supercede the roads of Rome. To those canal arteries were added the feeder tramroads, and on all of these; canals, rivers, roads and tramroads; horses, donkeys and men laboured at a pace set millennia earlier. Times were changing faster in 1800 than fifty years earlier, but the pace of life was still that of the hoof and the footstep.

Having looked then at the precursors of the railway and steam locomotive, glimpsed the transport landscape onto which the steam revolution will be pasted, and laid some rails, the stage is now set for the arrival of the first entrant in the hall of fame.

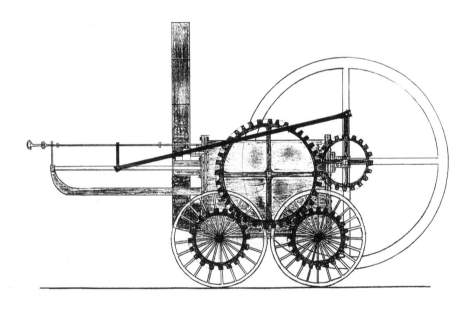

Figure 1: Penydarren, elevation

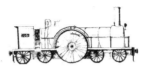

Chapter Two:

Slow and Dangerous: The First Steam Locomotives, 1804 -1828

The prize for being first goes to Richard Trevithick (1771-1833). His locomotive is now universally known as the *Penydarren Engine*, and first ran on the tramway of that name (between Merthyr Tydfil and the Navigation Inn, Abercynon, in the Taff Vale, Glamorganshire), on the 13th February 1804. Trevithick had to depart radically from stationary engine practice to produce both a power plant and a vehicle of sufficiently small size to run on the Penydarren tracks, yet with enough output to move itself and a useful load. Exactly how he achieved this may never be fully known, for while the engine worked, it could not be made light enough to operate on cast iron tramplates, and made only a few experimental runs, reaching perhaps five miles an hour top speed. The locomotive weighed about five tons, and for a pioneering locomotive appears to have possessed a sturdy simplicity, drive train apart, that was not to be universally replicated over the next twenty five years.

The locomotive that Trevithick designed, and which is conjecturally illustrated in Fig.1 opposite, was based upon a large cylindrical boiler, probably either a single iron casting, or built up out of wrought iron plates, flanged to receive the flat or slightly dished end plates, which were probably bolted into position. This structural tube carried the wheels and formed the vehicle structure, all other components being bolted onto or into the boiler. Inside the boiler was a 'U' shaped return flue, holding a small fire grate, accessed via a fire door and ash cover, and connected to a vertical flue that supplied some draught. Above this return flue the single, double-acting cylinder, was mounted in the boiler and fed with steam at a pressure of at least 10psi (pounds per square inch) and probably nearer 25 or 30psi. The valve was of the then conventional plug cock arrangement illustrated in Figure 2 below, actuated by a trip arm fixed to the piston rod, and running between two stops on the valve actuation rod, slamming the valve over as the piston approached the end of the stroke.

Drive to the wheels was indirect; the connecting rod drove a massive flywheel that had cast iron gearing to connect to the four running wheels. Starting could be effected by handling the valve actuation rod, but as with all single cylinder machines, care had to be exercised to avoid stopping the engine on back or fore centre, from which, if hauling on the flywheel was ineffective, the engine had to be eased forward with pinch bars until the crank could gain an effective turning moment. The locomotive 'regulator' was a simple plug valve operated by a long reach rod, running parallel and adjacent to the valve actuation rod and fitted with a similar 'D' handle.

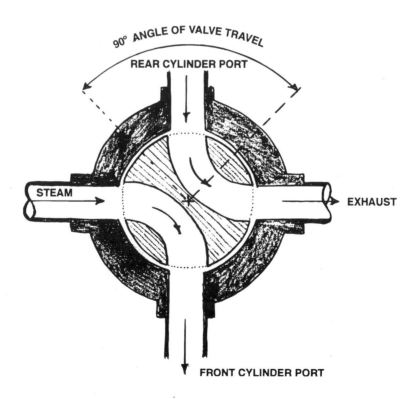

Figure 2: Tapered plug valve.

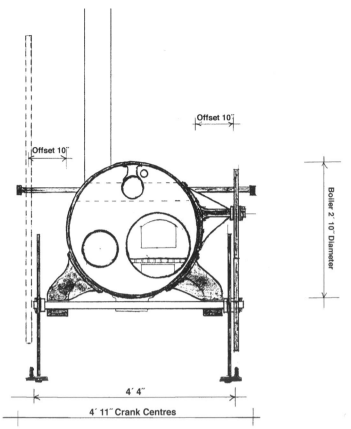

Figure 3: Penydarren, section.

Figure 3: Penydarren, section.

While Fig.1 is more or less a copy of existing ideas based on surviving drawings of locomotives credited to Trevithick for use elsewhere, when that elevation is resolved into a transverse section, a number of inconsistencies are revealed. The section, Fig. 3, admits only two certainties; the gauge of the track, and the profile of the tramplate. All of the rest is conjecture, yet the section raises issues that Trevithick must have addressed when he designed the original, and no attempt has been made here at a redesign. Both the two known facts have a crucial impact on the locomotive design, and with a modicum of knowledge of casting practices, these effects can be demonstrated. Firstly, there is the track gauge; at four feet four inches this dictated the wheel spacing on the axles, to four feet two inch centres. Tramplates were cast to reflect this, with a thickened section on the underside. With the illustrated boiler only three feet in diameter, large cantilever brackets are needed to bring the axle bearings close to the line of the wheel centre, and the drive train needs must be likewise supported.

Would Trevithick have accepted this? At the design stage almost certainly not. With the boiler forming the vehicle frame, the closer the boiler diameter comes to the track gauge the better, reducing the bending moments and the metal needed to resist them. The only problem with a larger boiler is more weight, and here a simple calculation tells us that a four foot diameter boiler will be about half a ton heavier than the three foot boiler shown, including twice as much water to keep the flue tubes covered. Most of that increase will be mitigated by smaller brackets to attach the wheels and drive train; indeed the larger engine might actually be lighter. The large boilered engine would also be mechanically more robust, though greater thermal mass would mean a longer period to get up steam.

The second item to consider is the relative placing of controls, firehole and the drive train. A four foot long boiler has room for a firegrate just over a foot wide and two and a half feet long. The fire cannot be more than five or six inches deep, as above that depth there would not be enough space over the top of the coal to insert a shovel. Such a fire could not be made up at the start of a run and left to provide steam for a distance; light and frequent firing would be needed. With the firehole below the slide bars, firing while in motion would have been a foolhardy contortionist act. The National Museum of Wales' 'replica' reverses the relative positions of cylinder and firedoor, and the controls, to enable the engine to be safely driven and fired. If Trevithick built what contemporary illustrations suggest, then the impracticality of the footplate arrangement may have been a crucial factor in the experiment not being repeated.

Thirdly, we have seen that the weight of the engine was to a degree dictated by the gauge of the track; at a track gauge of three feet or a little more, the engine could have been half a ton lighter. Success may have been avoided simply because the Penydarren track was too wide.

Much remains unanswered as to what Trevithick actually built, and why it did not take the world by storm.

Whatever the reasons, Trevithick did not persevere with his design, whose only critical fault appears to have been its excess weight. With this, and lack of success with the *Catch Me Who Can* engine in front of an unappreciative London audience, Trevithick ultimately left Britain to pursue a career in South America, where fame and fortune eluded him. Trevithick had, however, conceived the inconceivable and proved that the steam locomotive was not just a pipe dream, but was close to being reality. Just how much feedback was gained from this inspirational pioneer is not clear, as a number of fundamental weaknesses in the Penydarren Engine's design, such as the single cylinder and the gear train, would have emerged with long term use. The initial triumph of steam, though, is there; by burning coal and boiling water, energy was added to the steam by raising its pressure well above that of the atmosphere. That energy was then converted into motion and useful work, by pushing a piston back and forth in a cylinder, converting the motion to rotative, and driving wheels along a track. Use of high pressure steam, to replace the liquid/gas change of state and limited force of atmospheric pressure that had been the basis of stationary power plant in the eighteenth century, produced a compact machine that was immediately a vision of the future. From then on it was only a matter of cometh the hour, cometh the man.

Eight years elapsed before the world was to witness a second attempt at a working steam locomotive, and in moving from South Wales to Leeds we are heading in the right direction geographically, though perhaps into a bit of a technological siding. During those eight years, the proponents of steam traction on the road had made some progress, particularly John Gurney, but as George Stephenson was to cryptically remark at Rainhill, their products lacked the guts to perform useful work beyond moving their own weight, and on the coalfields at least, where there was substantive capital available to develop steam power, there was little place for such non-utilitarian frippery.

John Blenkinsop's locomotive, and the Middleton Railway of 1812 that he designed for it to run on, are clearly a result of learning from experience, no matter how limited that experience might be. To solve a number of perceived problems, Blenkinsop, in association with Matthew Murray, designed a complete system of both engine and track, and in doing so sought to avoid both the issue of excess weight, and that of the limiting value of friction between cast iron wheel and rail. Casting rails with a series of rack teeth, to mesh with the toothed traction wheel of the locomotive avoided the need (considered essential at the time) for all wheels to be driven and the full engine weight be available for adhesion. The locomotive could then have carrying wheels to distribute its weight, a frame to give it a reasonable wheelbase, and by avoiding the monocoque structure of the *Penydarren Engine*, allow more freedom for resolution of design problems posed by individual components.

The *Prince Royal*, again speculatively illustrated in Fig. 4, opposite, displays a number of points that clearly represent an advance over Trevithick's pioneer. First and foremost is the robust quality of the design; the engine looks as if it will work and be famous for more than fifteen minutes. Secondly, there is the practical application of eccentrics to drive two sets of valve gear; in order to maintain a straight line of action from eccentric to valve, the rodding and actuation levers pivot on brackets at either end of the boiler. Thirdly, though this is a retrograde step, there is no interest in drawing the fire with the exhaust steam, and the steam chimney is fitted with an attenuation chamber to dampen the bark of the exhaust. Finally, the engine can be fired and driven without the risk of it devouring the driver and fireman, in stark contrast to the *Penydarren Engine*.

As with the first pioneer, there is much that remains unknown. There are two test cocks to check on the boiler water level, and the arrangement of the rodding from the eccentric that drives the feed pump at the 'front' end by the chimney, appears to suggest that it may have been a pioneer 'gab' design, where the rod could be lifted out of engagement at will to turn the feed pump on and off. The chimney is designed to be dismantled to facilitate cleaning, and the location of the slide valves and steam chests suggests that the valve faces were vertical rather than the later popular horizontal layout. Fixing the cranks and gearing to the chassis means that the engine could have had springs, but there is no suggestion that it did.

The twin exhausts for fire and steam may well have not lasted long; eight feet of flue were scarce enough to make steam in quantity. With an operating lever extending along the boiler top from the plug valve regulator to both ends (not illustrated), the driver could be at the front whichever way the engine was running; the chassis being symmetrical meant no need for turntables. The driver doesn't actually have anything else by way of controls, though there is no reason why a simple block and lever brake could not be fitted and operated from the 'footplate'. Loads are distributed onto three rail sections, rather than two, but there is no intermediate support for the rail; castings thus supported would simply have broken their back in service. With mud holes to access the inside of the boiler, cladding to provide insulation, and a frame as robust as any built in the next twenty years, *Prince Royal* is all there, barring the little detail of safety valves.

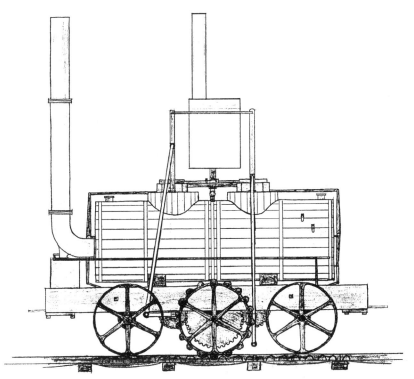

Provenance: The first commercially successful steam locomotive, many parts supplied by Murray, Fenton and Wood, Leeds.
Designer: John Blenkinsop.
Principal Features: Timber frame, vertical cylinders, slide valves, single fire tube boiler, separate steam and fire exhausts.

Figure 4: Prince Royal.

Blenkinsop, then, was on sound territory with his rack locomotive and railway, and the use of two cylinders with the cranks set at ninety degrees out of phase, avoided some (but by no means all) of the problems of persuading the engine to go forward. Turning the cylinders into the vertical plane (which with the *Prince Royal's* geared indirect drive was *not* a handicap) slowed development of the steam locomotive for fifteen years, but when first shown to the world on the 'glorious twelfth' of August 1812, it worked, and worked well. The engine proved sufficiently reliable to warrant construction of three further engines, enabled valuable experience to be gained in the running and maintenance of steam traction, and meant that a lot of other industrialists beat a path to the West Riding. While details of the engine are scant beyond the general layout, *Prince Royal* almost certainly was the first locomotive to sport Matthew Murray's slide valves, the critical component when it came to simple but efficient steam distribution.

At least two of those curious visitors were sufficiently convinced of the worth of what they saw to provide resources at their own collieries for construction of experimental machines in their workshops. Given the extent of tramroads in the North East, it will come as no surprise to discover that the collieries concerned were Wylam, on the banks of the Tyne, and Killingworth, north of Newcastle. The two pioneers charged with the task of constructing working steam locomotives were William Hedley and George Stephenson, and in the latter's case, backing came from the 'Grand Allies', perhaps the most powerful group of land and colliery owners engaged in supply of coal from Newcastle to London.

This rapid deployment of resources to develop steam traction can only have come about for one reason: Blenkinsop's engine shifted coal at less cost than a horse. It was almost certainly faster, took a payload average of about fifty tons a trip, and despite needing fuelling, watering and oiling almost continuously, needed less labour than the five horses it replaced. Critically also, the locomotive did not need hay and oats, and while the slow expansion of transport networks in the eighteenth and early years of the nineteenth century appear not to have run up against the limiting factor of equine reproduction, the inevitable result of a rapid expansion of horse-drawn transport would have been a rise in the cost of horse 'fuel', competing as it did with the use of the land for crops for human consumption, and timber. Estimates of the number of horses at work in Britain in the years prior to 1850 range from one million to nearly twice that number; a substantial proportion of agricultural land was devoted to fodder crops for the horse. Further industrial expansion without the steam locomotive would probably have proved very difficult.

The prospect of a form of traction fuelled from their own coal resources was an attractive one to mine owners throughout the land, freeing them from the vagaries of the price fluctuations caused by poor hay harvests, and from the prospect of a long term steep increase in the cost of horse haulage. The horse was a notoriously fickle animal to keep, seemingly being vulnerable to more illness than all other domesticated animals put together, and in an age when casual brutality to animals was part of their lot, the working life of the horse as a draught animal generally was neither long or particularly pleasant.

Small wonder then that the steam locomotive, now a profitable proposition, quickly found backers waving their blank cheques.

What Blenkinsop achieved, with the aid of the Leeds foundry of Murray, Fenton and Wood, was speedily copied. Both William Hedley at Wylam, and George Stephenson at Killingworth, strove to resolve the problem of putting on the existing cast iron rails of the North East, locomotives that would equal or surpass the work done by locomotives of the Middleton Railway on their specially designed track. History records that Hedley was first, for in as little as twelve months, Hedley and his team both tested the hypothesis that friction between smooth wheels and rails offered enough adhesion to move a useful load, and built a locomotive, *Wylam Dilly*. The problem that this presents the historian is that, as far as biographers of the nineteenth century were concerned, George Stephenson was first (as his title 'Father of the Locomotive' was meant to put beyond doubt), and all the rest were both some way to the rear, and fighting over the scraps left by the great man. The reason for this obfuscation is that all the pioneers' biographers were trying to sell their books, and were deliberately cooking events to suit their purpose, blurring the past as a consequence.

Unfortunately for us, biography is a major source of information for this period, and they are generally not contemporary, rely heavily on recollections of old men, and are perhaps more closely related to the gospels of the New Testament in that they record past events in story form rather than number-crunching facts. From this point on, the writer has every need to be extremely circumspect about information available in the written record.

Wylam Dilly, then, has a place in history, as does the designer William Hedley. Archer's biography, *William Hedley, the Inventor of Railway Locomotion*, is less well known than Sammy Smiles' instant glorification of George Stephenson, but you get the drift of 'History As It Was Invented' in the nineteenth century. The team that turned the design into reality included Timothy Hackworth, but his place in the history of the locomotive lies elsewhere, for at this juncture we must clearly identify the designer as receiving credit for the locomotive, and not the fitters or boilersmiths, irrespective as to whether or not those individuals have contributed to the design's ultimate success. On the roll of credits for a locomotive design, the designer takes all. This is his privilege (there were no lady contributors to locomotive design), even when, as we shall see later, the designer is head of a team rather than acting individually. This concept caused a lot of trouble in the nineteenth century, and resulted in not a little distortion of the history of the steam locomotive.

Wylam Dilly

Hedley's locomotive took the familiar four wheel layout, and true to form, proved too heavy for the track, where axle loads of $1^1/_2$ tons were the norm, and *Dilly* was comfortably a ton over this. Boiler and motion were mounted upon a timber frame, as in the Blenkinsop arrangement, and gearing and grasshopper motion transferred drive from a pair of cylinders mounted outside the boiler, which sported a return flue. In use of exhaust steam to draw the fire, Trevithick's ideas were adhered to, and unlike Blenkinsop, Hedley probably paid the thirty pound patent fee first, rather than later.

Provenance: Development of 'Wylam Dilly'.
Designer: William Hedley.
Principal Features: Return flue boiler,
Watt parallel motion, vertical cylinders.

Figure 5: Puffing Billy.

Where Hedley took the baton forward was in his refusal to throw in the towel over the weight problem, which he solved by adding two extra carrying wheels at the rear, to effect some load transfer. In this form the engine was a success, and gave many years' service, reverting to four wheel form when the tramway was relaid with wrought iron edge rails. At long last, a steam locomotive using adhesion only was at work earning its keep on an iron road, hauling goods in direct and effective competition with the horse. Hedley's later locomotive *Puffing Billy*, built on similar lines to *Dilly*, is now the world's oldest surviving steam locomotive, just three years younger than the world's oldest *working* steam engine. Just how much of this locomotive is original, either in design or in actual metal content, is open to debate.

When, in July 1814, George Stephenson first steamed *Blucher*, built in the West Moor, Killingworth, shops of the 'Grand Allies', George had no claim to be first. The locomotive was a copy of previous designs except that it had chain link drive between the two axles, and the connecting rods drove directly onto crank pins on the wheels. Cylinders were vertical (as with Blenkinsop's) and mounted inside the boiler, which had only a single boiler flue. This feature meant the locomotive was always going to be short of steam, even when the exhaust was used to draw the fire, as was the practice in Hedley's return flue designs.

George dispensed with the beam and lever and Watt parallel motion favoured by Hedley, the piston rod driving a guided crossbar, the outer ends of which carried the connecting rods. With the greater resources of the 'Allies' at his disposal, Stephenson could claim that over the next decade he was to design and manufacture numerous engines at Killingworth, and while there was to be virtually no technical innovation in the eleven years from 1814 to the opening of the Stockton and Darlington Railway in 1825, the experience of building, running and maintaining a fleet of locomotives at Killingworth was essential to the success of a railway designed with steam power in mind, if not initially as prime mover.

The Stockton and Darlington Railway

The Stockton and Darlington Railway was conceived as an alternative to a canal; even on the southern edge of the Durham coalfield, where the landscape could be described as 'gently rolling', a canal was the first thought of promoters with over twenty miles of haulage between pit and shipping staithe. The objective of the proposed railway was the exposed coalfield west of Bishop Auckland, where coal was to be had without difficulty in an area that had up to that point not been seriously exploited. The railway's title was a misnomer, as the real destination was a place called Hagger Leases; Darlington lay somewhat to the south, at about the midpoint of the line. The economic justification of a railway to exploit these coal reserves was the lower cost of raising coal from shallow workings, the saving being enough to offset the extra haulage. That said, but for the ridge that is now occupied by Shildon (the first 'railway town') with no water supply, and a long easterly dip slope to deter canal tunnelers, a canal would probably have been both preferred and built. This ridge meant that rope-hauled inclines were going to be needed, and the experience of the Lancaster Canal at Preston, where a tramway connected two canal sections, probably tipped the balance for a railway, if only by reducing coal degradation, an inevitable consequence of transhipment.

George Stephenson's experience with the 'Grand Allies' coal trains, and the slender but clear economic case thus made for steam traction, persuaded backers of the Stockton and Darlington Railway, particularly the influential Pease family, to amend that Railway's Act of Parliament to permit use of steam engines. In addition to the engines, it was also crucial that the promoters agreed to provide wrought iron rails, that made five ton two axle locomotives a practical reality. Obtaining that Act had a further benefit, unforeseen at the time, of preventing objectors from using the courts to keep engines off the tracks. With three years to design and manufacture locomotives for the opening day, George Stephenson had time to assemble a team, build a tailor-made erection and maintenance depot at Shildon, and with the benefit of ten years' experience, construct a locomotive of rugged reliability, even if the design was in its essentials the same as set out a decade previously.

Locomotion No1 had connecting rods where *Blucher* had chains, and exhaust steam was led into the chimney to draw the fire from the first, but weight was now up over 6 tons, well beyond the loads that could have been permitted on a cast iron track. The success of *Locomotion* and its fellows, while impressive by the standards of the time, was dimmed by two inherent weaknesses; the boiler was still poor at raising steam, and the weight was in excess of that which, when added to impacts from the track and hammer blow from the cylinders, could be carried by the cast iron wheels. This latter fact illustrates how the critical path of a new technology treads a fine line between success and failure. Cast iron wheels were employed on Britain's tramways because they were cheap; the alternative was the built-up cart-type wheel, a masterpiece of timber technology that selected various timbers, primarily oak and ash, and formed them in such a manner as to allow for flexibility and strength. The whole system was held together by a wrought iron tyre that provided the built in compression of the components, and the smooth running face. While such a wheel and tyre could have been employed on the tramway, there was no need; cast iron wheels were harder wearing, and if they broke, the remains could be recast at modest cost.

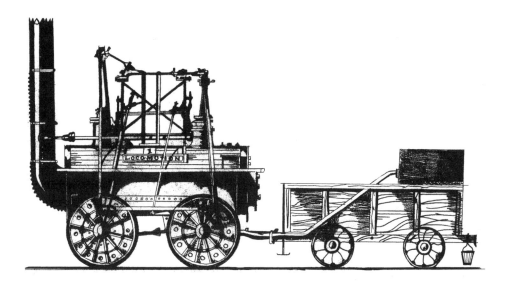

Provenance: Development of the Killingworth locomotives for the 'Grand Allies', reflecting ten years development of manufacturing improvement.
Designer: George Stephenson.
Principal Features: Single fire tube boiler, vertical cylinders with connecting rods and slide bars, cast iron wheels.

Figure 6: Locomotion No. 1.

The use of both cast-iron wheels and rails was fine, until the steam locomotive came along, and then it was realised just how limiting cast-iron was. That limit could have proved the death of the locomotive, but in appointing Timothy Hackworth to the running shop at Shildon, Stephenson had made an admirable choice, for Hackworth was equal to the task of day to day redesign of locomotives to overcome material weaknesses in the original concept. In respect of the wheels, he designed and had made a built up wheel that could be accurately trued and fitted with a shrunk on wrought iron tyre. It is clear that the inspiration for this built-up wheel, whose success ensured the triumph of both the locomotive and the steam powered railway, was borrowed from cart and carriage timber wheel design.

In the first years of operating steam-hauled coal trains between Shildon and Stockton (the lines beyond, to Auckland, Hagger Leases and Tow Law were horse and stationary engine worked), drivers of locomotives were paid by the tonnage delivered. There was thus every incentive for drivers to maximise both the speed and haulage capacity of their steeds. The company enforced a speed limit of eight miles an hour, but the way the railways' gradient profile was set out, as a series of almost level stretches interspersed with lengths that could be gravity-worked on the down grade, had important consequences for drivers and engines alike.

With a relatively low boiler pressure of 25psi, and a single straight flue, the locomotives were always short of steam. Coal, available at a very modest price of under four shillings a ton, meant the easy way to improve steam production was to sharpen the exhaust steam's effect on the fire. This turning of the exhaust steam pipe into a blastpipe is simply done by reducing the diameter of the orifice in the flue. In a locomotive with a real chimney, rather than the later smokebox, the air entrainment generated is in direct proportion to the speed of the steam ejected through the blast nozzle. With a single wide combined firegrate and smoke tube boiler, that entrainment can easily be made to pull burning coal off the firebars and eject it from the chimney. Hackworth already had experience of sharpening the draw on the fire, and pressure by the drivers to improve steam production led to locomotives throwing out burning coal to the extent that the company had to station fire beaters at the lineside to prevent the countryside being incinerated. Not perhaps a desperately serious business, but the next trick was one that Hackworth could not condone.

One of the ways in which a steam locomotive can be persuaded to surrender more power for short periods than it is capable of giving continuously, is to mortgage the boiler by allowing steam pressure to drop, drawing off more steam than is being generated. How much power you can obtain by this depends on the energy stored in the boiler. On the Stockton and Darlington Railway the locomotive had to supply power to provide the kinetic energy of the moving train, and to overcome the resistance to motion when the gradient was too low or adverse. On loaded downhill runs this meant that power was only needed in short bursts. Drivers realised that speed would be increased, wastage from jumping valves eliminated, and transit times reduced, if they raised steam when coasting to supply demand when motoring, and more steam could be stored if the safety valves were tied down. Two fatal boiler explosions resulted, and in response, Hackworth designed a spring-loaded safety valve in place of the more usual weighted lever arrangement, effectively preventing unauthorised tampering and over-pressing of the boiler.

Any locomotive engineer in Hackworth's position could only have viewed his motive power resources with a degree of pride, tempered by the realisation that, modern and impressive as they might be, complete masters of their task they were not. In 1827 Hackworth produced his own solution to this problem in the shape of *Royal George*, and it is a measure of the additional power this locomotive provided to six wheels, from a return flue boiler, that its driver headed the earnings table on the railway, and by a comfortable margin. Technically though, while better suited to the task of hauling coal than the smaller and lighter Stephenson design, Hackworth was little further on than his rival, and would not contribute further at the leading edge of steam technology. Six-coupled engines akin to the *Royal George* would continue to be built at Shildon for a further nineteen years, by which time they were as dated as dinosaurs.

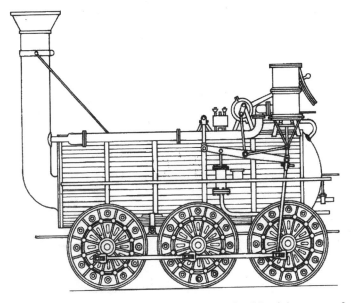

Provenance: Extended and simplified 'Locomotion No 1', in terms of maunufacture, sharing many of the components (wheels, boiler cladding) of its predecessor.
Designer: Timothy Hackworth.
Principal Features: return flue boiler, vertical cylinders, Watt parallel motion with direct drive to rear axle.

Figure 7: Royal George.

In December 1827 Robert Stephenson returned from a three year mining position in Central America to the works of Robert Stephenson and Company at Forth Street in Newcastle, a company set up at his father's behest to build steam locomotives. Within two years Robert was to turn the steam locomotive from a basic industrial tool into the driving force of a new age.

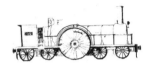

Chapter Three:

Getting There: A Review of Steam Technology to 1828

Locomotives being built and run in 1828 were doing useful work reliably and regularly, by the standards of the time at least, and had proved themselves both cheaper and less troublesome than animal power. Judged by criteria of our own age, steam engines designed by William Hedley and George Stephenson were unreliable, cumbersome and inefficient, and much of the engineering was crude in concept and execution. Materials technology could only offer the most basic materials in the form of wrought and cast iron, copper sheet, and various alloys of copper and tin, bronze. Steel was effectively a precious metal, unavailable in quantities that made its use an option.

Metal working taxed machine tools of the age to the utmost; lathes could not turn metal to dimensions that were accurate beyond a hundredth of an inch; hand files were prime metal shapers, and sledge hammers held an important position in the workshop toolkit. Casting of metals, while by far the most sophisticated metallurgical process in 1825, was inaccurate dimensionally and unreliable qualitatively. Inevitably this lack of command of materials was reflected in the end product; failures were numerous, 'wasters' an all too common fact of life. That even this relatively low technological proficiency could produce a working and profitable means of goods transport is a good indication of how desperate the age was to free itself from the shackles of the past. Casting was employed extensively to produce parts for the steam locomotive, including some, such as wheels, that would have been much better made by other means. There was much, though, that could only be made in thin sheet materials, materials with a high tensile strength, and these need must be forged and rolled.

Cast materials, with their essentially crystalline structures, were ideal for small components such as cylinders and valves, but rolled and forged plates, rods and bars were needed to perform the duties of boilers, axles, connecting rods, and later frames, springs, and tie bars. Producing these components challenged locomotive builders to the utmost; for the whole of the period under review metal bashing struggled to satiate the demands of locomotive engineer and designer, and most challenging of all these demands was construction of the locomotive boiler.

Boilers

Steam locomotives relied primarily on wrought iron to form the major components of both vehicle structure and boiler; the only alternative to iron when it came to boiler shells was copper, and iron was preferred despite its limited workability. This iron was supplied in the form of small sheets known as 'blackplate', laboriously produced from puddled iron by rolling ingots in a 'two high' or 'three high' mill. The rolls were power driven, but sheets were manipulated by hand, limiting sizes to weights that two men could handle. Once produced, these sheets had to be punched or drilled along their edges to take the riveting, curved to the boiler profile, and have holes for attachment of ancillaries formed either by punching, drilling, or in the case of larger orifices, cut out with a sledge hammer and cold chisel. The fire tube or flue was formed in the same way. When these preliminary operations were complete, the boiler shell was riveted, wrought iron rivets being heated to red heat and then beaten with hammers to expand them into their holes and form the second head. As the rivets cooled the contracting metal drew the overlapping plates together, and the seams were then caulked with a special chisel, beating down the metal edges so that the two sheets of iron were in complete contact. If the sheets were a distance apart, a flogging hammer was used first to close them up.

When the two tubes of iron were complete, specially formed curved angle sections were riveted to the tube ends to receive the end plates, which were fabricated from blackplate in the same way as the tubes. As riveting of the ends had to be done from both sides of the plate, there had to be an opening in the boiler large enough to admit the unlucky soul who was to perform the task of holding up the hot rivet while the closer worked the head on the outside. Return flues were easier, as they could be fabricated completely before the whole assembly was riveted up.

All locomotive boilers produced up to 1828 were made by hand, with little in the way of machinery to assist, and, while later boilers were undoubtedly better built than their predecessors, the intensive use of hand labour mitigated against their being either cheap, or able to take steam pressures that were, at 20psi to 30psi, too low to offer reasonable power/weight ratios. Without any effective quality control, blackplate supplied by ironworks was an extremely variable commodity, and 'best boiler plate' was to be the pride of all manufacturers' sales catalogues for much of the century to come.

The actual steam-raising ability of the resulting boiler was governed by a number of factors, principally but not exclusively, grate size, flue tube surface area, and firebed and flue gas temperatures. Fire grate size was limited by flue dimensions; a twenty inch tube would have a grate perhaps fifteen inches wide and two or three feet long. Under that grate would be a small space for air supply, and for receipt of ash and small coal that fell through the firebars. That ashpit airspace was inadequate for the twin needs of air feed and ash storage, and had to be regularly raked out whilst in transit, to prevent ash choking the fire. Even with assiduous attention, the bottom third of the flue tube would normally be covered in ash after running a few miles, reducing effective heat transfer in this area to nil.

The flue tube transferred heat from the combustion process by both radiation and convection; by radiation above the fire bed, and by convection elsewhere. The mechanics of fluid motion in a tube or pipe, however, mitigate against complete transfer of heat from moving gases; those gases in contact with the tube walls move relatively slowly due to friction between gas and metal, leaving the greater mass of gas to rush through the middle of the tube and not come into contact with the wrought iron at all. The larger the tube, the greater the heat loss by this action, effectively a conundrum. The theoretical heat transfer from gas to water is a function of the contact surface area and the temperature difference. With a single straight or return flue, enlarging the flue diameter increases the contact surface area, but at the same time permits the gases to travel with less surface contact.

The return flue's advantage over the straight flue thus stemmed not just from increased surface area, but from increased turbulence imparted upon the gases by the 180 degree bend, forcing the hot gas in the centre of the flue to come into contact with the flue walls.

It appears that these fundamental elements of the mechanics of fluids were not appreciated by the pioneers, and chronic steam shortages occurred, despite use of exhaust steam to draw the fire.

The great blastpipe controversy that erupted after 1830 was just the first of many storms in teacups generated by biographers looking for grist to mill. Samuel Smiles appears to have been chief stirrer in this instance, in his efforts to inflate the image of George Stephenson. The reality of the chain of events is simple; Trevithick thought of it, and used it first; locomotive engineers who subsequently used or failed to use the idea for their own reasons, were doing so from a standpoint of full knowledge of the effects of exhaust blast. That not all engineers in this period used this steam-raising aid is due to the blastpipe's effects, not universally beneficial. Scoring of boiler plates and setting fire to the surrounding countryside were just two problems Hackworth had to cope with in the early days at Shildon.

It is not clear if the steam blastpipe was the first application of generating a vacuum by entrainment of two fluids in a pipe; the laboratory vacuum pump, where a jet of water is used to evacuate air, is exactly the same principle using different fluids, and if Trevithick conceived the idea, rather than adapted the principle, then his genius, already of the first order, takes on a new dimension. The idea of flue draught had been developed to supply stationary engines in the eighteenth century, and chimneys a hundred feet high and more generated a few fractions of an inch of draught, as measured by a water gauge.

The relationship between flue gas temperature, flue height, diameter, and the resulting draught was appreciated, and flues successfully built to provide adequate draught for grates of twenty and thirty square feet. The locomotive chimney was but a new application of these established principles, and with eight or ten feet of hot flue, natural draught on the fire was certainly enough to sustain reasonably vigorous combustion, especially when the fire was new and clean (free of large amounts of ash and clinker). For reasons discussed above, not everyone was happy with reasonably vigorous combustion, because it did not on the whole result in enough steam.

Trevithick appreciated that exhaust steam ejected up the chimney would provide a strong and sure draught, a draught that would keep the fire bright, and reduce, if not completely eliminate, the risk of a poor fire. The single or twin exhaust pipe(s) from a locomotive that could not be worked expansively, and where exhaust steam pressure, expanding to atmosphere, would be as much as 5psi, or more at the orifice, was enough to provide two or three inches of draught (water gauge), ten times that available from a chimney a hundred feet high. Against that fierce draught, with a single straight or return flue twenty inches in diameter, there was almost no resistance, and engines with this exhaust arrangement could be run with the ashpit dampers almost closed, and firebox door shut. With *Wylam Dilly* and *Puffing Billy*, William Hedley was unconcerned about burning too much coal. To generate enough steam to do the job in hand, any means were considered, and if found suitable, put to the task. Upping the draught was the most obvious means to that end.

Hedley used constriction of the exhaust orifice to increase the pull on the fire, but it was left to Timothy Hackworth on the Stockton and Darlington Railway to take the tapered exhaust nozzle to its logical conclusion and demonstrate the true potential of the locomotive blastpipe; a blast so fierce that it would lift the fire off the grate and throw it out of the chimney. How exhaust steam achieved this was unclear at the time, a fact that was to cause endless trouble over the next century. Hackworth, though, proved the power of the blastpipe was everything the locomotive needed to make coal burn.

As we have suggested, the blastpipe was not universally beneficial in its effects; ejection of cinders caused scoring and high rates of wear on the boiler flue plates, and like all seemingly good things, while it made the fire burn, it revealed that coal was not just carbon, but a complex mixture of carbon, hydrocarbons and contaminants, and high temperatures made for some interesting reactions.

When coal is thrown on a hot fire, firebed temperature can be anything from 600degF to 1200degF or more. At these temperatures volatile elements distil off and are ejected with the flue gases, unless some means is devised to burn them. This represents a loss of efficiency in that some of the fuel's calorific value is lost, but this is not critical, at least not in the times under consideration. The carbon then commences to burn by oxidising to carbon monoxide; if enough oxygen is present the carbon monoxide then burns to carbon dioxide. It is with the contaminants however that the trouble really begins.

Sulphur will readily oxidise to sulphur dioxide, but the ash, up to 15% or more of the coal by weight, will fuse to a clinker if it is hot enough, and block the firebed, and any iron pyrites will be blown off, to condense in a mess known as 'swallows nests' on the boiler tube plates, where it will prevent effective heat transfer. Raising coals' combustion temperature quickly demonstrated that there are coals and there are coals, and that as far as raising steam is concerned, only the right coal will do a good job and the rest are more trouble than they are worth. Identifying the low ash, medium-caking, non-clinkering, medium-volatile, pyrite-free coals that came to be celebrated for their excellent steam-raising qualities took some time. This led to the renowned 'Admiralty Trials', and adding 'navigation' to many a colliery title. Coals to bunker both navy and merchant marine were a major market until displaced by oil during and after the First World War, hence the word association.

With blastpipes very much double-edged swords, it is perhaps not surprising that George Stephenson was not among enthusiasts for adoption; he saw drawbacks as well as appreciating the extra steam production. Others, though, took his engines and altered them to make them steam better. History records that they were more right than wrong.

If boilers were difficult to construct and steamed unreliably at a rate below that which allowed locomotives to operate continuously, then ancillary equipment and controls that driver and fireman relied on to tame this beast were crude to the point of being lethal. Footplatemen needed to ensure the boiler remained within narrow safety parameters at all times, and while tall chimneys minimised blowbacks through the firehole door, boiler water levels had to be kept within fairly close limits.

The reason for this is that the top of the flue tube above the firebed is exposed to the full heat of the fire and unless kept covered with water will rapidly overheat, causing the plates to lose strength and making collapse a near certainty. To monitor and maintain water levels there were feed pumps driven off either the piston crosshead, or eccentrics on the driving axle, and a hand-operated test cock. As steam use varied depending on load and gradient, the pump did not feed continuously, but was cut in and out as required, either by turning the feed water on and off, or by disengaging the pump drive.

The test cock was simply a pipe flanged to the boiler at a short distance above the fire flue tube, and fitted with a tapered plug valve operated by the enginemen. If steam issued from the cock when it was opened, then water levels needed topping up. While on the move though, boiler water would be sloshing back and forth. Test cocks were thus less than an absolute indicator of a safe water level. Low water has been a source of boiler failures and explosions from the very first, and as locomotives had little in the way of safety precautions, those who became complacent in the presence of danger stood a fair chance of losing their lives as a consequence. If this posed a threat to life and limb, then maintaining high boiler water levels posed a similar threat to the locomotive's health. Steam was taken from a pipe inside the boiler top, feeding the cylinders, and if water was carried over into the main steam pipe then it could, and would, land in the cylinders, where it was very definitely not wanted.

Cylinders, Pistons and Valves

Casting metal objects in prepared moulds was already two millennia old at the start of the nineteenth century; cylinders for pumps had been produced for two hundred years, for steam engines for seventy five years. Casting techniques, compared to other metal working skills, were sophisticated, with complex shapes being produced by impressing wooden patterns into split mould boxes of casting sand. Simple cylinder castings, with flanges for end covers, were not a challenge to industry in 1800; twenty years later a casting incorporating steam passages and ports, and slide valve faces, while more difficult, was comfortably within the technical repertoire. Of prime importance, an importance that cannot be overemphasised, to steam locomotives throughout the nineteenth century, was the slide valve, invented by Matthew Murray (of Murray, Fenton and Wood, Leeds) in 1802. This valve dictated locomotive development in the area of steam distribution and use, until the end of steam itself.

Whether or not Murray had any inkling that his invention would be **the** valve as far as steam railway locomotives were concerned is not an issue, for it was ideal for admitting steam to double acting cylinders of beam engines, increasingly being built to the more efficient designs of Mr James Watt. In essence the valve was simplicity itself; three slots set in line in a cast iron plate covered by a moving plate that was hollowed out into a 'D' section on the contact face. Enclosing the whole ensemble was a steam chest fed with steam from the boiler, the steam pressure holding the two valve faces together. The moving plate alternately exposed the outer slots, that led to the cylinder, to the steam chest, and linked the slots to the central port, which led to the exhaust. A single valve to perform four functions, that could be driven from one eccentric, that was in addition both self-sealing and self adjusting.

Trevithick's semi-rotary four-way plug valve, in contrast, was limited critically in both absence of a steam chest, and in cross-sectional area that could not allow large amounts of steam into the cylinder when piston speeds were anything other than very modest. The slam action of the piston rod actuating arm was also unsuitable

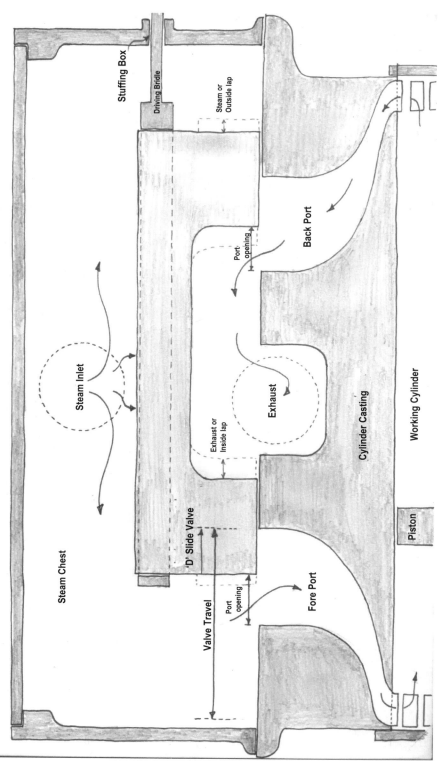

Figure 8: Slide Valve

for high speed engines. Murray's invention came before locomotives that would demand it, but without slide valves the age of steam on the railway would have been very different.

Slide valves, then, were a compact, and above all, simple, means of feeding steam to both ends of a cylinder, allowing a reasonably free exhaust on the return stroke, closing the port at the right point to allow some cushioning of the piston as it approached back or fore centre. To add to the valve's advantages, it also cut off steam supply when the torque of the crank was falling rapidly, preventing steam being wasted. At this early date, the disadvantages of this valve were a long, long way in the future; with low speeds and modest loads the limits of slide valves were not even a glimmer on the horizon. Even in 1840 there was no hint of operational limits of slide valves; the problems faced in 1825 were not those of efficiency, but of competent and reversible actuation.

As discussed briefly in Chapter Two, Trevithick's *Penydarren Engine*, with slam actuation, meant that the valve actuation rod was not fixed to the piston rod that moved it when the engine was running. Thus, when stationary, the valves could be operated by hand to admit steam as required to make the engine go forward or back at the driver's will. Slide valves run by a fixed link from piston rod or eccentric were not adjustable, and use of a floating slam action, even at low speed, was not an option if long term reliability was needed. The question of how to reverse had not applied to stationary beam engines, and those with rotary motion could be eased over to the correct starting position if they needed to be reversed.

Locomotives without ready means of reversing had to be pushed to the right starting position, not an option if there was fifty tons of coal coupled behind the tender. This problem was faced by both Blenkinsop and Hedley, and it appears that teams of horses were kept for starting trains, at Middleton, and on Tyneside, in the steam locomotive's first working decade. This difficulty restricted these engines to use on reasonably long hauls, where motion was in the same direction, and shunting and marshalling manoeuvres absent. This basic lack of flexibility was an annoyance rather than a real handicap; the horse as a shunter of wagons was a feature of the railway network both in the century before, and the century after Rainhill, and the practice may well not yet be extinct on rail networks of small private mines, even at the start of the twenty-first century.

This problem of reversibility was only partially solved by adoption of 'gab' gears, the solution tendered, but not apparently invented, by George Stephenson. With gab gears, the extension rod from the valve eccentric sits in a slot in the valve rod, from which it can be lifted by means of a handle. The slide valve can then move independently to the appropriate starting position, the 'gab' dropping back into its slot as the eccentric moves round with the motion of the engine. George was justifiably proud of this arrangement, and while satisfactory in principle, absence of brakes caused problems when it came to using the engine in reverse to slow or stop a train. At even five miles an hour, lifting valve rods as they moved required both strength to overcome system forces (which would prevent disengagement when the spindles were being driven), and skill to time the action on both cylinders to synchronise shifting into the reverse eccentric. Difficult enough on a fine day; a well-nigh Herculean task on a wet night.

The Birth of Machine Tools

In 1800, when Trevithick was contemplating the possibilities of high pressure steam, the number of manufacturers of steam engine components could be listed on the fingers of one hand: Boulton and Watt's Soho Foundry, The Carron Iron Company, Wilkinson's Berstham Ironworks, Neath Abbey and one or two of the other South Wales Ironworks, Harveys of Hayle, and not a lot else besides. For the most part, these works cast and forged components needed for purchasers to erect their own stationary engines, and usually only the larger pieces at that. Most smaller items would be made locally, and the best description for these would be "blacksmiths' work". Dimensions and tolerances were approximate, fitting up made each unit unique, to the extent that nuts and bolts had to be marked, as there were no common sizes or thread patterns. While casting a cylinder was not an extraordinary challenge, the problem of boring cylinder castings to be both circular and parallel had not been mastered. Working fits of pistons to cylinders were measured by trying various coins of the realm, and there was no immediate prospect of measuring tolerances beyond the nomenclature of the day, when terms such as a 'full sixteenth' (of an inch) meant smiths' or carpenters' work rather than engineering.

Watt's parallel motion, designed to guide piston rods through top stuffing boxes of his double acting cylinders, was in itself a recognition that, without means to form accurate flat surfaces, the later near-universal arrangement of crosshead and guides could not be made with the machinery and skills available. No means had been devised to measure the accuracy of a component closer than one hundredth of an inch, and that meant the process of 'running in' was quite as likely to equate to 'wearing out'. Large beam engine cylinders were finished by hand, a tacit admission that machine tools simply could not deliver an acceptably accurate product. When what is now the world's oldest working steam engine (the 1812 beam engine pumping water for the Kennet and Avon Canal at Crofton, Berks) was erected a decade after Trevithick's first trials, technology had already made enormous strides, measurement was being actively studied, and the first tentative steps taken to make machines with good working fits.

A quarter of a century later a revolution had taken place and foundations for the machine age had been laid, primarily and practically, by Henry Maudsley. In train with accurate measurement to one ten-thousandth of an inch came lathes and planing machines that could machine cylinders and pistons accurately enough to use high pressure steam; motion that had proper centering, and good working fits to bearings. Firms such as Murray, Fenton and Wood, who made most of the parts for Blenkinsop's engine, were setting new standards of accuracy, demonstrating that Maudsley's work in London was not just theoretical. When Robert Stephenson and Company was set up specifically to make steam locomotives, their workshop was part of this revolution, the end result of which was a fresh generation of much more robust and reliable steam power. The hour, 1829, then cometh the man, Robert Stephenson, the place Newcastle. Enough of the necessary technology is in place, the mind that is to conceive the plan has returned from the Central American mines of Santa Anna.

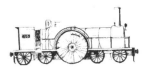

Chapter Four:

1829: Twelve Months that Shrank the World

Robert Stephenson's arrival back at Forth Street in December 1827 was to find the company that bore his name in poor shape. With George heavily embroiled in construction of the Liverpool and Manchester Railway, the firm lacked both direction and an intellectual driving force. Robert's return was the cue for the would-be Lancashire railway to order a locomotive to assist in the construction works. That order was somewhat premature, and may well have been a ploy by friends of George, at his request, in order that Robert could try out his ideas for improving the steam locomotive. Whatever the reason, when built, the locomotive was sent to the Bolton and Leigh Railway, where, unlike its more ambitious neighbour, there were rails upon which to run it, and where also it was named the *Lancashire Witch*.

Lancashire Witch saw the introduction of fresh ideas; use of two straight flue tubes and firegrates to improve steam raising, and direct inclined drive from cylinders to wheels. This latter development was aided by use of the modern type of crosshead and slide bar, reducing the number of moving components in the drive train to four: piston, piston rod, crosshead and connecting rod. Inclined drive meant that springs could be used instead of George's rather curious steam piston suspension. This reduced the unsprung mass of *Lancashire Witch* to that of wheels and axles only, making for a locomotive that was light on the track, travelled with a smooth if slightly rolling gait, and was insulated to a degree from shocks from the uneven road. To Robert's dismay, despite all his efforts, the *Witch* was still visibly and chronically short of steam.

While it might seem incongruous to the modern observer, that so large and expensive an undertaking as thirty six miles of railway, should be commenced without any clear idea as to what should run upon it, this, on the face of it, is what happened with the pioneer modern railway. That the Liverpool and Manchester was the prototype is beyond doubt: a deep rock cutting at Olive Mount, Liverpool, the first modern viaduct over the River Sankey and Sankey Brook Navigation, and an alignment that cuts straight across the landscape in defiance of obstacles. This was a railway designed for high speed, even if at its conception there was no sign of the motive power. It is clear that in 1828-29 a number of influential people had staked their reputations on Robert Stephenson producing a steam locomotive equal to the Liverpool and Manchester Railway's demands, and equally clear that, act of faith or desperation, have it as you will, there was no 'Plan B'.

A leading light among those optimistic railway promoters was Henry Booth, treasurer to the company, and acutely aware that the railway was in difficulties over raising capital (the line was only completed as a result of an Exchequer loan, hence George being embroiled in the construction). In 1828 no decision had been made as to the traction the new railway would use; the Stockton and Darlington Railway had shown that locomotives of the design employed thereon, hauling coal trains downhill and empty trucks back up, would scarce do for a railway where loads were going to be hauled, on average, against the grade.

To examine the issue of motive power on behalf of the company directors, a committee had been formed to inspect Timothy Hackworth's fire-throwing Shildon steeds. The committee had not been particularly impressed. Rope haulage by stationary engines, as on the Stockton and Darlington's Brussleton and Etherley inclines, was a serious contender, and the world's cranks were queuing up to offer all manner of impractical devices. Clearly something had to be done, if massive investment in the line of rails was to be fully utilised. Following a further inspection of the Stockton and Darlington Railway by engineers James Walker and J. U. Raistrick, Walker suggested that a premium (perhaps better described as a prize) be offered. The idea was to stimulate locomotive and other designers to construct prototype engines that would solve the directors' problem for them, but at this point we are left wondering if this was a calculated wheeze to let Robert Stephenson have a second bite at the cherry, or a severe attack of incipient despair.

At a meeting on 20th April 1829, Walker's suggestion was turned into the world's most famous board minute, in which the Liverpool and Manchester Railway directors

> 'Resolved that a premium of five hundred pounds be
> advertised for a locomotive engine which shall be
> a decided improvement on those now in use, as respects
> the consumption of smoke, increased speed, adequate
> power, and moderate weight, the particulars of which
> shall be specified in detail by the Preparation Committee.'

Unlike most competitions, and perhaps to the majority's surprise, this most famous event not only achieved its ends, but the right man won as well. Henry Booth and George Stephenson were each prepared to back their horse, and between them put up the money that enabled Robert to build *Rocket*. The date for delivery and trial was set as 1st October 1829; the conditions included a series of direct condemnations of the locomotive practices and performances of the Stockton and Darlington Railway.

Summary of the competition terms and conditions.

• No smoke permitted.

• Six tons of locomotive shall haul twenty tons on the level at ten miles an hour, steam pressure not to exceed 50psi.

• Two safety valves, one tamper-proof.

• The engine shall have springs and not exceed fifteen feet in height.

• Weight must not exceed six tons in working order carried on six wheels; lighter engines shall be required to draw proportionately less load; if weight is four and a half tons or less four wheels may be used; Boilers may be tested (hydraulically) to 150psi.

• A mercury pressure gauge shall be fitted.

• Engines for trial to be at Liverpool on 1.10.1829.

• Price of the winning engine not to exceed £550.

• The company to provide water and fuel for the test. Rail gauge four feet eight and a half inches.

The implications of these rules are clear; whatever the outcome, the directors were not going to run a railway throwing smoke and burning coal to the four winds. As the railway intended to carry passengers (it was to be over a decade before the Stockton and Darlington carried people officially), it had to do so at a speed that at least equalled the fastest road coaches, then averaging about 11mph. Goods to be carried included cotton, which would burn if showered with cinders, and engines needed to run up hill and down dale without laying waste to cargo or countryside. The directors had both an eye for safety and publicity, in limiting boiler pressure and saying, even if they did not intend to carry out, that a hydraulic test, to three times the maximum working pressure, would be made on elements of the engines that made and used steam.

Since his return from the New World, Robert Stephenson had constructed locomotives other than *Lancashire Witch*, but in January 1829 he had not solved the problem of adequate steam production. When analysed systematically this came down to two problems; how to produce a large enough grate on which to burn enough fuel at a rate that did not involve blasting the fire off the grate; and how to exchange that heat into the boiler water. In the combined fire tube and grate, the grate area was limited, and ash disposal and air admittance hindered by the necessity of a circular tube to resist boiler pressure. That steam pressure, acting on the outside, effectively limited flue tube diameter and with it grate size. The need to escape from these constrictions was paramount, and in contemplating a separate firebox, Robert was faced with practical design problems that had not been addressed before. The obvious fact that radiant heat from the fire contributed significantly to raising steam meant that some form of a water jacket to any separate grate was essential. How to make that jacket withstand a working pressure of 50psi was the essence of the problem.

Exactly how the first water jacket firebox was conceived and made is not clear. Robert Stephenson and Company did not make *Rocket's* firebox, and we have no information as to whether the firebox design was Robert's alone. The firebox appears to have been an outer sheet of iron and an inner of copper, folded to cover two sides and top, with the water space held together and apart by a series of closely spaced rivets. Only Raistrick's sketch of the engine at Rainhill survives, showing that the backplate was an iron sheet with a firebrick inner, and the water jacket connected to the boiler by top and bottom circulation pipes. That Robert waited for the firebox to arrive while the rest of *Rocket* was nearing completion, indicates that the manufacturer had some difficulty over the product (Robert commented that the box when delivered was not quite square). This is not surprising; that the first stayed firebox should work 'straight out of the box' is a remarkable achievement. The conceptual design, though, is faultless. The firebox enclosed a grate that was slightly over square and about five square feet in area. Above the grate was a high combustion chamber, below it an ashpan with dampers to control air supply. Conditions had been created in which a near perfect fire could be maintained, a critical point, as the fuel was to be coke, which will only burn well if kept under a strong draught.

As with the firebox, so too the boiler, though here we have a design that stems from a mathematical approach, and Forth Street made the end product, as recorded by Robert in letters to Henry Booth. The principle of the multi-tubular boiler is exactly the same as the conundrum of steam crossing the Atlantic Ocean, only reversed; it is the relationship between square and cube, neatly espoused by Brunel five years after *Rocket's* famous debut.

The key to the problem is that the volume of a vessel (not just the sea-going kind) increases (and decreases) as the cube of its dimensions, while surface area varies as the square. In a steamship that merely meant making a ship large enough to carry the coal needed to reach the destination; in the boiler it meant making the flue tubes small enough to ensure that the surface area was as large in proportion to their volume as was possible. While that tube or tubes carried the grate, there was inevitably a conflict between the two demands of grate area and heating surface. With a larger tube you obtained more grate and heating surface, but that surface was proportionately smaller when compared to the volume of the tube. With a separate firebox all the relationships could be idealised, and the tubes made small and numerous. The mathematics is simple once you have appreciated the principle.

Who thought of this first? Robert Stephenson attributed the idea to Henry Booth, but before going ahead and trying it out, Robert, as literate and numerate as his father was not, would have been able to prove the proposal by calculation, and must have done so before working out a practical design. There is also the possibility that Booth presented the mathematical proof along with the idea. Whichever way, there is no halfway house; from two fire tubes in *Lancashire Witch* to twenty-five in *Rocket*; a 'step change' of the first order, made possible only by invention of the separate firebox.

Having designed a theoretical engine, Robert was faced with the problem of turning dream into reality. On the basis that he cannot have had more than twelve months (probably nearer six or seven) in which to firm up the concept and put *Rocket* on the rails (the design of the 'premium engine' was almost certainly being considered before the competition was announced), limit of time is the most likely reason why the firebox was subcontracted. Manufacture of the firebox appeared marginally the easier of the two tasks, for when Forth Street came to build the world's first multi-tubular locomotive boiler, they were obliged to build from scratch two components that had never been made before; tubeplates and small diameter thin-walled fire tubes, and then join them together.

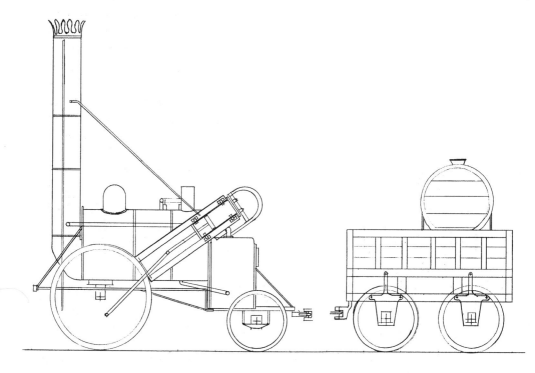

Provenance: Progenitor of the modern steam locomotive, building on twenty years design and manufacturing experience.
Designer: Robert Stephenson.
Principal Features: Inclined cylinders, multitubular boiler, separate firebox, partial bar frames.
Principal Dimensions: Cylinders 8in diameter, 17in stroke. Working Pressure 50psi. Tractive Effort, 818lb at 85% of boiler pressure. Driving wheels, 4ft 8in diameter Valves slide valves on top of the cylinders, direct action eccentrics and gab gear.
Weight in W. O: 4 tons 3cwt

Figure 9: Rocket.

Rocket's two tubeplates were made from wrought iron, and unlike previous dished ends of locomotive boilers, were made flat, to enable all fire tubes to be equal length. It is not clear if it was anticipated that they would stay flat when pressure tested, but they didn't, and extra iron stay rods were needed to keep the tubeplates in shape. In each tubeplate was punched or drilled, probably the former, twenty five three inch circular holes, the pattern being identical in each plate to keep the firetubes straight and parallel. While these made new demands on the accuracy of setting out and forming the holes, they were simple in comparison to the task of making and fitting the tubes.

As late as 1829 the only way of forming thin walled pipe was the method used by the Romans; folding sheet and forging or brazing the seam on a mandrel (an iron or bronze bar the same diameter as the inside of the tube being formed). Cast iron and bronze alloy pipe was available, but this was thick walled and not of sufficient strength for the task in hand. Each of *Rocket's* twenty five tubes was hand made from copper sheet in this time honoured fashion, and then a thread formed on the ends and backnuts added before being hand beaten to seal it into the tubeplate. When tested hydraulically the result was a failure at well below the threatened test pressure, and we are left to guess as to how the boiler was made steam tight for the trial runs. Later, the soft copper tubes were supported through the tubeplates by having iron ferrules driven into the ends. The demand for thin walled pipe resulting from this use was such as to provide the impetus for manufacturers to improve their production methods, and it was not long before solid drawn pipes in iron, brass and copper became available.

Robert Stephenson did not attempt to prove the boiler to 150psi, having been tipped off that such a test would not be made at Rainhill, and after a short trial in Northumberland, *Rocket* was dispatched by horse and cart to Carlisle. From there, the journey to Liverpool was made by water, first on the Carlisle Canal, then coaster, arriving at Crown Street, the railway's yard, on the 18th September 1829. Re-erection of the partially dismantled locomotive then commenced, and the engine connected to its locally made tender. At this stage it is probable that the locomotive was given its 'war paint' colours of yellow and black. On October 2nd 1829 the complete locomotive was taken by wagon to Rainhill and put on the rails.

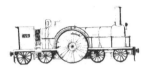

Chapter Five:

The Future Arrives: Rainhill

The choice of Rainhill for the Liverpool and Manchester Railway locomotive trials in October 1829 was due to the fact that this flat section of country, unlike the also flat Chat Moss further east, had needed little in the way of civil engineering work. The railway here was complete, including the rails, a state of affairs that George Stephenson would dearly have wished to be able to say extended to the rest of the line. That it was some way out of town did nothing to deter large crowds from coming to watch, and the railway company is believed to have employed up to three hundred 'constables' to give some measure of crowd control. As many as fifteen thousand people turned up to view proceedings, much in the way of a free day's entertainment. On the serious side of events, Walker and Raistrick were joined by John Kennedy, a Manchester textile engineer, and after the first day's preliminary running on October 6th, these three officials drew up a detailed pro forma of the tests each competitor would undertake.

The railway company had installed a weighing machine ('measure everything' was a sound nineteenth century dictum), and the trials started by each engine being weighed and allocated a load equal to three times its weight, a weight that included a boiler full of water, but no fire or tender. The tender was deemed to be part of the trailing load. The fire was then lit and time and fuel taken to bring boiler pressure up to blow off at the safety valves noted. Fuel and water were provided to the tender, the engine with its load then proceeding to make ten return trips along a course one and three-quarter miles long, with an eighth of a mile at each end for slowing and getting up to speed, which was to be ten miles per hour pass to pass on the test section, thirty miles at this speed, thirty five miles in total.

Rocket was not the only contender; both *Sans Pareil* and *Novelty* were strongly fancied, deriving their technology from the Stockton and Darlington Railway and steam road carriages respectively. A horse-driven machine, *Cycloped*, also entered, but was withdrawn without offering serious competition. Hackworth's *Sans Pareil* was unable to complete the required number of trips, and its phenomenal coal consumption led to its designer being denied further opportunity to show its mettle. *Novelty* lacked both boiler output and general robustness to survive the course, and failed to complete even half the stipulated mileage. The trials increasingly became a one-horse race; on the first unofficial day *Rocket* had hauled its load of twelve and a half tons for an hour at an average speed of ten miles an hour, cruising at twelve to fifteen miles per hour, and touching eighteen miles per hour when running light. Clearly *Rocket* was good enough to win the prize, but George and Robert, with the assistance of Joseph Locke, were putting in some sharp ice axe and piton work on the learning curve, and appreciated that, while the engine was good to the point of disbelief, it was still not achieving its full potential.

On the first 'official' day, October 8th, the course was completed in three hours ten minutes at an average of 11mph. After watering and refuelling, the distance was re-run in two hours fifty-two minutes, 12.2mph on average. In just over six hours *Rocket* had travelled seventy miles, and burnt scarcely half a ton of coke. The last eastbound run was taken at an average of 24mph. *Rocket* had performed without fault, covered twice the prescribed distance and roundly beaten the required average speed. These were feats unparalleled, but it was clear to the father and son partnership that *Rocket* was not steaming as well as it might, and attention rapidly focused on combustion and in particular, flue draught.

When the locomotive was erected and tested in Newcastle, the exhaust was turned into the chimney and the resultant induced draught measured by a crude water vacuum gauge. This was found to give a three-inch vacuum, plenty to draw the fire of a single fire tube locomotive. What was *not* realised, was that the multitubular boiler offered considerable resistance to passage of flue gases, and vacuum generated at the chimney base was not a reliable indicator of draw on the fire, but to a significant degree a reflection of the resistance offered by long, narrow fire tubes.

As first tried at Rainhill, *Rocket* steamed without ejecting any part of the fire out of the chimney, and the temptation to increase the draught by contracting the exhaust pipe orifices, and determine the maximum steaming capacity of this wonderful machine, could not be resisted. That capacity was essentially the 'grate limit', maximising the amount of coke that could be burnt without ejecting burning fuel out of the chimney. *Rocket* could not be worked expansively; any steam the boiler could make, the cylinders could use. What was also realised was that power output varied with speed; up to a certain limit, the faster the engine went, the more steam was produced. The rate of combustion varied with draught, which increased in direct proportion to the amount of exhaust steam passing up the chimney. With some adjustments to the draughting, *Rocket* hauled forty tons at 14mph, three times the effort sustained on 8th October, and could top 35mph when running light.

Scarcely two years after stepping off the packet that had brought him back from the New World, Robert Stephenson had by November 1829 led the assault on the established order of steam traction and made all previous speed achievements pale to insignificance. History records however that the energy of the race to build the modern steam locomotive was not expended in a single push to build a competition winner, but was the beginning of a sustained drive to a brave new world, untarnished as yet by any doubts as to the wisdom of the destination.

Speed had captured the imagination; mankind was hooked.

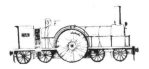

Chapter Six:

From Magic to Science:
Development of the *Rocket*

Such was the pace of steam locomotive development, that when the Liverpool and Manchester Railway opened on 15th September 1830, *Rocket* was already outdated. As a machine to prove the promise of steam power, Rocket was without equal, rightly holding the title of most famous engine ever built. As a reliable daily workhorse, the locomotive's weaknesses quickly became apparent. Prime among those shortcomings were the tendency of the chimney base to fill with ash and cinders and block the fire tubes; for water to be carried over into the cylinders (priming), and an uneasy rolling gait as a result of the steeply inclined cylinders. Success at Rainhill had led to the immediate placing of an order for four further locomotives of similar pattern, and these four, named *Arrow, Comet, Dart* and *Meteor*, incorporated experience gathered from the pioneer engine, insofar as cylinder inclination was concerned at least.

Robert Stephenson had gained a crucial commercial advantage in the shape of feedback from *Rocket's* running experience, feedback that gave his company a clear lead in steam locomotive technology. Robert had guessed at the minimum diameter needed for boiler fire tubes to have adequate gas flow to perform their task. Having experimented with blast and chimney vacuum, and finding that resistance in *Rocket's* boiler was not enough to prevent fuel being pulled off the grate, he determined to alter the design parameters in what he rightly identified as a crucial area for steam generation. In the first 'production batch' of locomotives, boiler length between tubeplates remained at six feet, but the tubes were reduced to two inches diameter, and their number increased from twenty-five to eighty-eight.

This change fundamentally altered the boiler proportions; free gas area (the total cross-sectional area of the fire tubes) increased from 1.2 square feet to 1.9, with heating surface more than trebling, from 90 to 328 square feet. The effect of these figures was to enable cylinder diameter to increase from eight to ten inches, the stroke remaining at seventeen inches. The reward was a batch of locomotives that were more free steaming and could haul heavier loads faster than their famous predecessor. Further engines added to the railway's stock before the line opened had tube numbers increased again, to one hundred and thirty two, and their diameter reduced to one and five eighth inches, maintaining the free gas area at 1.9 square feet, but raising the heating surface slightly to 337 square feet.

The implications of this series of changes to the boiler layout are fundamental to appreciating the development of the steam locomotive. Robert Stephenson was the monopoly supplier of steam power to British railways, and in the absence of performance data from any modern locomotives but his own, was determined to discover, by practical experiment, the limits of steam-raising capacity of the 'Rocket type' of boiler. Having sharpened the blast progressively on *Rocket*, to the point at which it became obvious that, while the rate of combustion increased, there was no corresponding increased production of steam. The conclusion was that the blast could draw against an increase in resistance beyond that offered by the twenty five fire tubes. It was then a simple calculation to show that both free gas area and heating surface could be increased, along with the increased resistance of larger numbers of smaller tubes, and the exhaust blast would still draw the fire satisfactorily.

This is the lesson of the 'Arrow' batch of engines; the relationship between blast, resistance of the fire tubes, and surface area of those tubes was critical to the boiler thermal efficiency. If the tubes were too large, gases would pass to the chimney without exchanging the maximum amount of heat. At speed, large tubes would allow the blast to lift the fire and throw it out of the chimney. The tubes were thus reduced in diameter, but without the mathematics to calculate the resistance, or instrumentation to measure gas flow, Robert was once again only guessing that two inch tubes six feet long would offer sufficient resistance to maintain boiler efficiency at full output. While avoidance of throwing the fire out of the chimney also meant not contravening the first rule of the railway, enshrined in the Rainhill Rules, and in the company's act of incorporation, it was also a measure of maintenance of the revised boiler design's efficiency. Not throwing the fire meant no loss of efficiency at speed, a much more important criterion than a rule drafted upon another railways' experiences.

The third batch of locomotives represented the maximum number of tubes (132) that could be fitted to a three foot diameter boiler without weakening tube plates or reducing water and steam spaces. The critical dimensions of the boiler, free gas area and heating surface, were effectively unchanged, but boiler resistance to hot gas flow is dramatically greater, as the sectional area of individual tubes is reduced by over a third. This was as far as Robert Stephenson could go with these boiler dimensions. While Robert had transformed the steaming characteristics, he had not reached the limit at which blast at full output was balanced by boiler resistance, for with a sharply contracted blastpipe, it was still possible to lift the fire off the grate. The lesson learned, to be exploited later, was that a boiler much longer than six feet between tubeplates, and much fatter than three feet in diameter, could be made to steam successfully, and be more efficient into the bargain. These last 'Rocket type' locomotives were more economical than their predecessors, but could not produce more steam than those with two inch fire tubes.

The first two of the third batch of locomotives, *Phoenix* and *North Star*, were delivered in the summer of 1830. Having developed the boiler steaming capacity to a very acceptable optimum, and improved running by lowering the cylinders, Robert Stephenson made a further series of alterations, all of them based either on sound experimental principles or on running experience. The second batch of locomotives had been built with enlarged cylinders, because it was realised that a train's starting resistance was larger than its running resistance. Likewise the power needed to accelerate fifty or sixty tons to thirty miles an hour was of an order greater than that required to maintain that speed. Similarly, gradients on the Liverpool and Manchester Railway might be adverse, but they were not long. Lessons learned on the Stockton and Darlington about mortgaging the boiler, were now applied to give the engines the necessary starting tractive effort, and capacity to keep up a good speed on a steep but not over-long gradient.

Phoenix and *North Star's* cylinders had an extra inch tacked on to their diameters to increase tractive effort (tractive effort being a function of the piston surface area). That surface area had nearly doubled over that of *Rocket*, from 50 to 95 square inches, for while boiler heating surface had more than tripled, firebox surface area was unaltered. Relative proportions of cylinder to heating surface were thus approximately the same for first as last engines in the 'Rocket' series, but the most dramatic alteration was removal of the flared chimney base and fitting of the first smokebox.

Smokeboxes were a logical solution to ash collecting in the chimney base, and it is perhaps surprising that the second batch were not fitted with this item of such obvious utility. The smokebox however proved to be a double-edged sword, though not fortunately with the 'Rocket type', where exhaust steam was led directly into the chimney. Smokebox design, or more usually lack of it, was to prove the ruin of many locomotives and designers over the next century. Robert Stephenson's smokebox was essentially that fitted to all subsequent steam locomotive fire tube boilers; a plain forward extension of the boiler barrel beyond the front tubeplate, with a front door for tube cleaning and shovelling out accumulated ash.

This latter factor was very important, for with a good induced draught, a lot of ash was pulled through the fire tubes but not ejected from the chimney. This ash, and the accumulated ash and clinker in firebed and ashpan, limited the distance a locomotive could travel without servicing, dictating provision of motive power depots for the whole of the steam locomotive's dominance of Britain's railways. The final engine in the 'Rocket' series, delivered in October 1830, was named *Northumbrian*, and introduced the integral fire tube boiler and water jacket firebox.

Once again, the concept of a single unit to hold the fire and perform exchange of both radiant and convected heat was only that of the original single fire tube locomotives. The brilliance of the single unit fitted to *Northumbrian* stems from mastery of materials and excellence of design. *Rocket's* water jacket firebox challenged Forth Street's technical ability sufficiently for manufacture to be contracted out (possibly to the ship builder Lairds). In less than a year, Robert Stephenson and Co. made seven further locomotives, yet the company also mastered production of the first modern locomotive boiler. The enormity of this feat cannot be underestimated, as it is an entirely different proposition from the cylinder and fire tube arrangement, and separate firebox.

The difficulty of manufacture centres on the rear tubeplate and its connection to the inner firebox, of which the tubeplate then becomes a part. For reasons of workability and heat exchange, inner fireboxes were made in copper, but the strength of iron was needed to support the fire tubes, which had to be riveted into position by flaring and bossing up the ends. All surfaces that were not strong enough to hold their shape by being circular in section, had to be supported by copper stays at close centres, again riveted over at both ends. Even at the modest pressure of 50psi, this was a challenge, one that must have absorbed a large slice of the profit being yielded on production locomotives in 1830.

Finally in this hectic period, we have development of the steam dome, an addition at once quaint, and applied more often in the rest of the nineteenth century as a work of subtly proportioned art than a functional addendum, functional though it is. Britain in this respect generally managed to remain aloof from the uncivilised excesses of foreigners, who opted for two or more and made a mess of their locomotive aesthetics as a consequence.

The dome is one of those enigmatic items of the steam age. Domes exist to solve the problem of water carry over from boiler to cylinders, by raising the level of the steam take-off pipe to well above the highest level of the boiler water. When cylinders were sited on top of the boiler, water carry-over was not a serious problem, but priming (water getting into the cylinder when it shouldn't) troubled Rocket and it was soon given a dome. Domes proved necessary on all locomotives where the cylinders were at or near axle level.

Domes too were symptomatic of what quickly became the hidden essential of the locomotive, the regulator. The best place for the main steam valve, that controlled steam admission to the cylinders, was immediately below the steam take off. The working dome, a heavy cast section bolted onto the boiler top or firebox, quickly gained an attractive thin copper, bronze or painted iron cover, which, when copper or brass, was polished until it glowed. Necessity and decoration hand in hand; access was needed at this point on a regular basis, and there was no reason why the dome should not be a statement in itself.

If the regulator was little more than an on/off valve in the days when boilers could not supply enough steam for continuous operation, it assumed a new importance when safety valves began to lift with regularity and locomotives had to be reined in to prevent excess speed. Design of regulator valves posed special difficulties, and these problems increased with larger engines and higher boiler pressures. Tapered plug valves sufficed for the early days, but that state of affairs did not last long. By no means every designer could produce a successful regulator valve, and access for maintenance, via the dome, was needed more on some railways than on others. Not all engineers and railways saw the necessity for a dome, notably the Great Western after Churchward, who designed a safety valve cover as a replacement therapy for obsessive polishers. The dome shrank, but did not disappear, as boiler tops rose to meet the loading gauge after World War I.

At the end of 1830, then, Robert Stephenson and Company bestrode the narrow world that was the railway network of Britain; in technical development they were in a league of their own, but that did not mean that there was no competition. Competitors there were, and they amounted to opposition that was vociferous to the point of professional envy.

Chapter Seven:

An Explosion of Talent:
Locomotive Building 1829-1838

Even allowing for the primitive engineering facilities which locomotive and general engineering works had at their disposal, the ability to build a locomotive to compete in the 1829 Rainhill Trials was not possessed by more than a handful of establishments in Britain. In all those premises, technical expertise in high pressure steam engines was minimal to the point of absence. That the Liverpool and Manchester Railway managed to attract five entries was in itself remarkable. Had fortune favoured more than the winner, there might well have been a variety of locomotives in use in 1830. As it was there was no entry from the Leeds works of Murray, Fenton and Wood, who had built Blenkinsop's engines nearly twenty years earlier. There was no Cornish participant, from the likes of Harveys of Hayle. Absent too was interest from the Soho Foundry in Birmingham, the Carron Works in Scotland, and Neath Abbey Ironworks in Wales, in 1829 perhaps Britain's (and thus the world's) three premier foundries.

The engineers who were to initiate the nineteenth century's accuracy revolution were equally inconspicuous; from the machine tool industry only Richard Roberts ever designed a steam vehicle, and that was a road carriage. While railways grew and provided a market for the tools of Maudsley, Nasmyth and Clement, it was left to the minnows to provide the Stephensons with any competition, and ultimately create a heavy engineering industry from scratch.

Perhaps the most unfortunate competitors at Rainhill were Braithwaite and Ericsson, for their adapted steam road carriage was popular, and had the advantage of modest weight. Their engine relied on a forced draught, and a blowback into the bellows caused *Novelty* to drop out of contention. Failure of a lightweight machine to stay the course, as predicted by George Stephenson, was a reflection of the limited strength of available materials. The need to tread a fine line between limits placed on axle loads by available track designs, and the high risk strategy of using thinner plates and castings than was advisable, was one recognised by the 'heavyweights' at Rainhill. Braithwaite and Ericsson took the risk, made a vehicle as light as was possible, and paid the price. Robert Stephenson built up to the weight limit for two axles, and his strategy won the day.

Timothy Hackworth competed at Rainhill, and was to continue to manufacture locomotives for the Stockton and Darlington Railway after 1830. At Rainhill, Hackworth was regarded as a quality heavyweight, but was unable to offer a product that departed sufficiently from the fire-throwing plodders for which his works and railway had become just a little notorious. The world needed to move on; his engine was overweight, underprepared and lacked the steam raising ability, springs, and simple motion that the judges had set out or implied in the premium conditions. Hackworth's locomotive was purchased by the Liverpool and Manchester Railway, but appears to have been little used until sold a year later. Hackworth himself appears not to have had the technical innovation to change his designs, or the commercial expertise to sell them, even though the world was virtually beating a path to his door. We are left to conclude that as a technician, Hackworth was an able man, but as a designer, lacked ability to conceive the unconceived and turn it into the future.

If competition at Rainhill was a little thin on the ground, then the shock waves *Rocket's* success sent through the country had wannabees and copycats putting in some good spade work immediately afterwards. A few people spent their energies crying 'foul', but others sat up and noted that the Stephensons had not patented the multi-tubular boiler, and that most of the winning locomotive was not patentable anyway. Foster and Raistrick, and Burstals of Leigh had built engines before Rainhill. Burstal's entry, *Perseverance*, travelled hopefully but did not arrive. Edward Bury made up a lot of ground with the locomotive *Liverpool* in 1830, and

Laird the shipbuilder eventually took the plunge, after being the most likely source of *Rocket's* firebox. These pioneers were not to be on their own for long.

Enthusiasm generated by the whirlwind development of steam power, and successful launch of the steam passenger railway, had no immediate impact upon development of the locomotive, for the simple reason that there were only a small number of relatively short railways being built in Britain at the time, and most of them were either being built by the Stephensons, or were, even as late as 1836, proposed with horse power as prime traction. George, being set upon dominating the civil engineering side of rail transport, had constructed the first two steam railways, and was determined to ensure continuance of his monopoly. Thus both the Canterbury and Whitstable, and Leicester and Swannington Railways fell to the father and son partnership, and while Robert was eventually to take over on the 'civils' from his father, he had not finished with steam locomotive development by a long chalk.

Robert Stephenson and Co. led the field by a margin in 1830 with construction of *Northumbrian*. That lead was stretched again by *Planet*, completed shortly after *Rocket* had run down and fatally wounded William Huskisson MP, on the Liverpool and Manchester's opening day. In under three years Robert effectively completed the transformation of the steam locomotive into the form it was to take for the next thirteen decades.

Provenance: Development of 'Rocket'.
Designer: Robert Stephenson.
Principal Features: Partial double frame, inside cylinders, smokebox.
Principal Dimensions: Cylinders 11in diameter, 16in stroke, inside frames.
Working Pressure: 50psi.
Tractive Effort, 1,371lb at 85% of boiler pressure.
Driving wheels 5ft 0in diameter.
Valves: slide valves between frames, gab gear with direct action eccentrics.
Weight in W. O: 8 tons

Figure 10: Planet.

Planet in lineage terms was an adventurous design in that it discarded the engineering simplicity of outside cylinders driving directly onto crankpins set in the wheels. Reversing the cylinder position from the back of the engine driving forward, to the front driving backward, made operation of the valve gear both remote and complicated. The problems these innovations generated were overshadowed by the challenge of designing a competent crank axle. The benefits were that cylinders were now located under the smokebox, and piston thrust acted close to the locomotive centre line. A timber and iron 'sandwich' frame now supported the wheel bearings and took boiler and buffing loads. Inside the frame were further plates and bearings to support the crank axle, which was to remain the weakest point of locomotive design for the next fifteen years.

The locomotive had now reached the point where behaviour of the engine as a vehicle was becoming important, and *Planet*, with four wheels and a firebox that completely overhung the rear axle, was not ideal for the long runs at high speeds (30mph) that were now envisaged. That both smokebox and cylinders overhung at the front as well did nothing to assist smooth running. In commercial terms though, the 'Planet type' was a runaway success, dominating the market at home and abroad to the extent that Forth Street could not cope with demand.

Why *Planet* had inside cylinders

The decision to bring the cylinders inboard on *Planet* can only have been as part of the quest for smoother running. The complexity this arrangement generated, with multiple bearings and support plates, did nothing to simplify engine construction. Extra bearings were needed to prevent a crank axle breakage resulting in derailment and a potentially fatal accident. The wheelbase of the two-axle locomotive design was too short to accommodate both smokebox and firebox. Without a radical redesign of the vehicle frame, piston thrust, acting outside the rail gauge, generated a substantial turning moment about the centre line of the engine. With cranks set at ninety degrees to each other, the left crank was being pushed by its piston with a force of nearly four thousand pounds at a distance of two and a half feet from the locomotive centre line, a total turning moment of ten thousand foot-pounds. At the same time the right hand crank was pulling with the same force, making the total turning moment approximately twenty thousand foot-pounds. As the right crank rotated to lead, this turning moment was reversed.

So long as the steam port is open, and without the ability to 'cut off' steam admission in these early engines, that meant for about 75% of the stroke, steam pressure in the cylinders, as well as turning the wheels forward or back, was also attempting to obey Newton's third law of motion in the horizontal plane. Action and reaction being equal and opposite, the limited stiffness of the locomotive frame on a short wheelbase had no great ability to resist these forces. The result was a tendency for *Rocket* and all her immediate successors to move crabwise down the track, alternately twisting to left and then right. To make matters worse, the turning moment varied only with cylinder steam pressure, and was unaffected by the position of either pistons or cranks. This produced a 'hammer blow' effect from side to side, as the valves opened to let steam into and out of the cylinders.

With low speed and modest loads, these forces in the horizontal plane were of no consequence, but the problem became severe when the natural frequency of locomotive and thrust of pistons came into harmony. *Rocket* and sister locomotives down to *Northumbrian*, with short wheelbases and front and rear overhangs, when running at a speed that synchronised with their natural frequency, were clearly in danger of derailment. *Rocket* certainly derailed while on the Liverpool and Manchester Railway, and locomotives continued to 'dance off the track' owing to this phenomenon, for the century to come. Adoption of inside cylinders for *Planet* must have had resolution of this problem in mind.

Robert Stephenson's dominance of development of the steam locomotive was now reaching a plateau, from which he would eventually stand aside to let others take up the torch of progress. Two further offerings would add to his hall of fame: the 'Patentee' and 'Long Boiler' locomotives, and from these two designs was to stem a whole family of locomotives, some of which would still be running a hundred years later.

Patentee, emerging in 1833, addressed the overhanging firebox problem by adding a third carrying axle, allowing for a modest increase in weight, essential to cope with increasing demands for more haulage capacity. In other respects, use of double framing, inside and outside the wheels, was a copy of *Planet*, but the new steam counter pressure brake and flangeless driving wheels were inventions that could be patented, and duly were, hence the name. *Patentee's* longer wheelbase as a result of the third axle made the locomotive much more stable in running, and eliminated the rear overhanging firebox. The lesson seems to have fallen on deaf ears though, for the 'long boiler' design that was, with one small but vital exception, the last Stephenson contribution to locomotive development, had a firebox with a rear overhang, this time behind the third axle, and again proved unstable as a consequence. The 'long boiler' was suitable for low speed heavy haulage, but was never a serious high speed locomotive. In the 1830's though, high speed was what everyone was trying to produce.

Provenance: Development of 'Planet'.
Designer: Robert Stephenson.
Principal Features: Partial double frame, inside cylinders, deep firebox between the driving and rear axles.
Principal Dimensions:
Cylinders: 12in diameter, 18in stroke, inside frames.
Working Pressure: 50psi Tractive Effort: 1,836lb at 85% of boiler pressure
Driving wheels: 5ft 0in diameter. Valves: slide valves between frames, direct action eccentrics.
Weight in W. O: 10 tons.

Figure 11: Patentee.

Forth Street, having had the inestimable benefit of being first, found that demand at home and abroad rapidly expanded to the point at which it was no longer possible to keep that monopoly. Edward Bury had proved that other engineers could make a successful contribution, and the need to supply numbers of engines at short notice led to the Stephensons sub-contracting work, allowing their designs to be made under licence. Experience of designing, building and running locomotives thus quickly spread across the north of England, and as the rail network expanded after 1840, to the rest of Britain also.

Convenience and necessity made the first locomotive builders crowd near the railways they were supplying; around the Liverpool and Manchester and other railways of the Lancashire coalfield were Rothwell, Hick and Rothwell of Bolton; Jones, Turner and Evans at Newton Le Willows; George Forrester at Liverpool; Tayleur and Co. and Bury and Kennedy. Similar concentrations of manufacturers were setting up centres of engineering excellence on Tyneside, around Leeds and at Glasgow. While the southern companies were smaller and less thickly sown, Birmingham, London and Bristol all had their own firms as soon as rails arrived in town.

This dilution of the Stephenson's monopoly was inevitable; much development was needed to turn the engines of 1830 into the reliable express and freight hauliers of fifteen years later, running tens of thousands of miles between overhauls and relentlessly squeezing more work out of the same amount of fuel. That flowering of talent led to many curiosities that briefly held the limelight; oval boilers, indirect motion with large right angled cranks, intermediate combustion chambers; all departing to a hasty oblivion as they offered no advantage or only solved imaginary problems. The intended market for this talent was any and every railway that needed power, and while trunk route companies could afford to buy and learn from their mistakes, or build their own misfits for some hands-on experience, equipping the main lines loomed large in the minds of everyone after 1838, the learning curve sweeping vertiginously upwards.

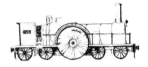

Chapter Eight:

More Power, More Speed:
Equipping the Trunk Routes, 1838-1848

While the Liverpool and Manchester Railway connected two rapidly expanding northern towns, it could not be construed as a long distance trunk route. The idea that you could travel at an average speed of over twenty five miles an hour between the major cities of Britain fired the imagination of a nation overnight. Turning that dream into reality took just a little longer, not least because an Act of Parliament was needed to purchase land necessary for these new passenger railways. Many landowners sat in either Lords or Commons and adopted the 'OMDB' - over my dead body - attitude. Long delays to the first main lines from London to Birmingham, Bristol and Southampton resulted. Less controversial schemes, such as the Leeds and Selby Railway were up and running quite quickly, but the first 'main line' to open was the Grand Junction, connecting Liverpool and Manchester to Birmingham in 1837, and its motive power from the start was of the 'Patentee' variety.

The speed at which trunk routes followed this pioneer railway, built entirely by hand and animal power, suffices to highlight the shambles that was twentieth century project planning and management. By 1848 London was linked to Southampton, Exeter, Bristol, Birmingham, Manchester, Liverpool, Glasgow, Newcastle, York, Leeds and Hull, and was only a viaduct or two short of a picnic on the route to Edinburgh. After forty years of motorway building, both Edinburgh and Hull are still lucky enough to lack a motorway to London, and of the rest, only Birmingham had a complete link in under a decade. The spur this *blitzkrieg* construction programme gave to locomotive development (large numbers of Irish, Scots and itinerant English labourers employed as navvies often justified the battlefield allusion) fuelled by an insatiable demand for faster travel, was to change fundamentally the way in which steam locomotives were designed and built.

The Grand Junction Railway was not a spectacular line; it opened first, not least because it had little by way of major engineering works, but at eighty two miles in length it demanded a new order of sustained output and reliability from its traction. The alignment, as it climbed off the Cheshire plain to cross the Trent/Mersey watershed, included nine uphill miles commencing at 1 in 330, steepening to 1 in 177, southbound from Crewe to Whitmore Summit. While modest by the standards of some lines that were to follow, these gradients, combined with both the distance and sharp connecting curves between the Grand Junction and Liverpool and Manchester Railways, quickly showed up just how fragile locomotives were in day to day running. The railway company had bought no fewer than twenty five 'Patentee' locomotives, and by August 1838, all appear to have broken their crank axles in just thirteen months of operation, leaving the company with both a hefty bill and little left by way of motive power to shift traffic.

This was the sort of feedback a fledgeling company would wish *not* to have on its new engines; it prompted though, not a long and bitter court battle over liability, as we might expect today, but appointment of a 'Locomotive Engineer', charged with resolution of the problem. That man was William Barber Buddicom (1816-1887), then a young man of twenty four.

When the Stockton and Darlington Railway had commenced operations fifteen years earlier, it had quickly organised a maintenance regime under the auspices of Timothy Hackworth at its Shildon Works. It was clear though, that a man of even greater talent was needed on a railway that had every prospect of being one of the most successful and profitable in the land. Joseph Locke, then engineer in chief of the Grand Junction, realised that what he needed, to organise and run the railway's motive power resources, was a man with imagination and breadth of vision, to plan and make the strategic decisions necessary to pull the railway out of crisis and make sure the rosy future happened. Buddicom fitted the bill admirably, and in setting out to address both the immediate problem, and the long-term one of adequate and reliable traction, set a theme which was essentially copied by all major railway companies in Britain, and led to the eclipse of private engine builders, who had hitherto held a monopoly of both designs and supply.

Buddicom, in his analysis of 'Patentee' crank axle failures, realised that while the axles ran in inside and outside bearings, it was the outside bearings that were sprung and took the load. The inside bearings had little part to play except to prevent derailment in the event of a fractured axle. A redesign of axle bearings led to removal of the ineffectual inside plates and substitution with what amounted to a partial double frame, complete with a sprung bearing inside each driving wheel. With the axle fully supported at four points, it was no longer subject to large bending moments. Likewise the tendency of the axle to flex under piston thrust, due to axle bearings being remote from the plane of the cylinders, was much reduced. The redesigned locomotives were an immediate success, and it is clear that the solution, involving both knowledge of, and ability to calculate, bending moments, was one that was the province of the engineer, as distinct from the mechanic.

When rebuilding the 'Patentees', the Grand Junction Railway had at its disposal the Liverpool and Manchester Railway's workshops at Edge Hill, Liverpool. As a base for operation of its own railway, Edge Hill, sixteen miles from the nearest Grand Junction metals, was somewhat less than ideal. It is probable also that facilities for construction of new locomotives, rather than just repair of current stock, were limited. Buddicom's arrival did no more than throw this unsatisfactory state of affairs into sharp relief, and when he put pen to paper to turn out the first 'in house' locomotive design, it was clear that the railway needed somewhere of its own to build engines. How much of the plan to build a new works complex at Crewe was Buddicom's is unclear, for after a brief stay of eighteen months, he resigned to pursue a lucrative career on the opposite side of the Channel.

Buddicom's replacement was Francis Trevithick, son of Richard, and to him fell the credit of presiding over development of what was to become the largest locomotive works in Britain. Buddicom's revised 'Patentees' had eased the motive power crisis by mid 1841, and construction of Crewe Works could proceed without the pressing necessity of providing instant traction. As an interim measure, four locomotives were purchased from Jones and Potts to supplement existing stock; they were not to be the last outside purchases by the company by any means, but the outside 'design and build' concept would henceforth take an increasingly back of house role. Buddicom had not departed before he had laid out the design of what was to become standard locomotive practice on the 'Premier Line' for the next decade and a half, the 'Crewe Type'.

The first 'Crewe Type' locomotive to emerge from the new works did not do so until 1843, and is remarkable for being the first locomotive (the actual identity is unknown) to be designed and built in-house by a railway company for its own express passenger use, manufactured in a locomotive works erected for that purpose. In one other respect was this series of engines important, for with the use of an ingenious arrangement of double plate framing and inclined cylinders, the drive from the connecting rods was once again placed upon outside crankpins.

Provenance: Development of the 'Patentee', three axle fixed wheelbase locomotive with single driving wheelset and higher boiler pressure.
Designer: W B Buddicom/Francis Trevithick.
Principal Features: Partial double frame, outside cylinders, deep firebox between the driving and rear axle.
Principal Dimensions: Cylinders 15in diameter, 20in stroke, outside frames.
Working Pressure: 75psi (later engines had increased boiler pressure).
Tractive Effort: 3,984lb at 85% of boiler pressure.
Driving wheels: 6ft 0in diameter.
Valves: slide valves between frames, inside Stephenson Link Motion (early engines fitted with gab gear).
Weight in W. O: 16 tons

Figure 12: Crewe Type.

Where Crewe led, others followed; the fiasco that had been Brunel's contribution to motive power on the Great Western (a discreet 'atmospheric' veil is needed for what the South Devon Railway received in this respect from the same source), led to Daniel Gooch following the Grand Junction's lead to produce Swindon's first locomotive in 1846. Matthew Kirtley took the Midland Railway down the same path once the latter company had divested its affairs of the attentions of George Hudson. As other main line railways emerged from the railway mania, they too set up works to design and manufacture their own motive power. This individualism contributed to some startling regional variations, and gave the top fifteen railway companies their own striking identities, right down to the 'Grouping' over seventy five years later, and beyond, into the era of nationalisation.

The reason behind this rapid challenge and eventual eclipse of the private locomotive builder as exclusive designer and supplier, was the feedback loop. In day to day running, locomotive departments were at the 'sharp end' of any untoward events, in a way that private works could not be. Experience, thus accumulated, rapidly meant that those companies with a lot of rolling stock, could not only justify plant, machinery and buildings to build their own, but could also put into their new stock improvements learned the hard way. The implication of this was that the railway companies, the larger ones at least, would lead the field technologically in a relatively short time, and so it proved. Crewe Works may have been first, but by the end of the period under review, the Great Western and its cohorts on the broad gauge had reached Exeter; the West Coast route was complete to Glasgow; the Midland a continuous line of rails from Gloucester to Leeds and York; all meaning that these companies could justify their own locomotive workshops. Long distance running quickly became commonplace, and a premium placed upon both speed and reliability, a premium the railway companies believed they could keep in their own coffers if they built their own engines.

To meet this demand, in design terms there were really only 'Patentees' and 'Crewe' locomotives, but honours for both speed and reliability went to the broad gauge, where the youngest of the new profession of Locomotive Engineer, Daniel Gooch, was demonstrating that the broad gauge was best, in a way his standard gauge competitors could only envy. Gooch was only twenty one when he was appointed to resolve the Great Western Railway's motive power crisis while it opened in stages during 1838-40. The solution Gooch had arrived at was the purchase of two modified export

'Patentees', originally made for the broadish gauge of five feet six inches, but with new axles to suit the Great Western's seven foot. Unlike standard gauge locomotives, the distance of nearly seven feet between the driving wheel inside faces, was ample for provision of a strong inside frame (to supplement the outside framing) and allow for bearings on cranks and axles to be the right size to do the job, rather than thinned down to fit the four feet eight and a half inches of the 'standard' gauge. The same criteria also applied to the firebox, where a wide firebox was easily fitted between the wheels; on the standard gauge, wide fireboxes of the time had to overhang at the rear, and engines were then unstable at even a modest speed.

Accordingly, the Great Western romped away with the speed honours, and in 1846 a modified 'Patentee' came within a whisker of the first 60mph start to stop average speed, on a run over the seventy seven miles from Paddington to Swindon. Gooch's analysis of defects in the 'Patentee' was the same as Buddicom's, his solution made easy by the space the broad gauge allowed between the wheels. Henceforward, the broad gauge was to use the double frame derivative of the 'Patentee' until the end in 1892. The records set proved embarrassingly hard to beat, for locomotive design on the standard gauge had to compromise again and again, and while frames were eventually designed to mitigate the restrictions of inner space, firebox design was always compromised, sometimes critically.

By 1848, locomotive works at Crewe and Swindon were setting the pace for development of the steam locomotive, fuelled by feedback generated by running trains. In 1838, the steam engine relied upon a complex arrangement of the 'Gab' gear, with slip eccentrics laboriously engaged and disengaged to make engines go forward or back. In 1848, reversible and variable admission valve gears were in use, and first in the field was Robert Stephenson and Co., though this time it was not Robert's idea.

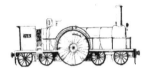

Chapter Nine:

The Metal Heart: Slide Valves and the Link Motions

The claim for invention of the first reversible link valve motion is disputed between two employees of Robert Stephenson and Company. This is hardly surprising; virtually everything about the steam engine that was not patented in the nineteenth century was subject to dispute. Patents were no guarantee of their owners being credited with the invention. Be that as it may, development of a valve motion that allowed for easy reversing of locomotives was obviously going to take the railway world by storm. Near universal adoption of the link motion followed its arrival in 1841, and having demonstrated the principle of adjustable link valve actuation, there was no shortage of inventors to design and market alternatives.

When we consider valves and valve motions, it should be remembered that these are two different items. On the steam engine, the principle of Matthew Murray's slide valve, managing and manipulating the hot life blood of the locomotive, suffered no serious challenge for a century; how it was moved was an entirely different matter. Where complex and sophisticated valve actuation gears were developed for both stationary and marine engines, the rigours of the working environment and restrictions of space inherent aboard the steam locomotive meant that only the rugged and simple were destined for survival. The age of sealed bearings,

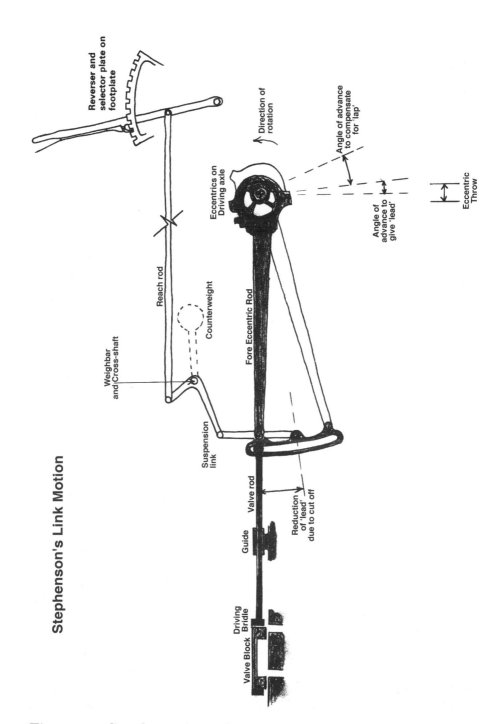

Stephenson's Link Motion

Reverser and selector plate on footplate

Reach rod

Weighbar and Cross-shaft

Counterweight

Suspension link

Eccentrics on Driving axle

Direction of rotation

Angle of advance to compensate for 'lap'

Angle of advance to give 'lead'

Eccentric Throw

Fore Eccentric Rod

Valve rod

Guide

Reduction of 'lead' due to cut off

Driving Bridle

Valve Block

Figure 13: Stephenson Link Motion.

pressure lubrication and geared transmission barely touched the locomotive and had no influence upon design of valve motions until almost the very end. Motion transmitted by rods from either eccentrics or piston/connecting rod served the locomotive from first to last.

Two valve motions were ultimately developed, whose actions, more or less, were a copy of Stephenson's arrangement, and are known as the Gooch and Allan link motions. A third, on different principles, was developed by David Joy, and the fourth, and best, was invented by a Belgian, Egide Walschaerts. The problems that ultimately arose from these valve actuation arrangements were not at all obvious in the 1840s, but realisation that valve timing and port openings were the root of limits to locomotive performance dawned slowly over the next five decades. This realisation led to all manner of interesting and cunning devices (notably the 'trick' port and the 'long D' valves) which attempted to a greater or lesser degree to mitigate the defective operation of link motion actuated slide valves.

The problem was this; Murray's slide valve was simply a machined and slotted block that slid back and fore over a valve face, alternately connecting engine steam and exhaust passages to the valve ports at either end of the cylinder. Put another way, one slide valve performed the function of two inlet and two exhaust valves for a cylinder, enabling it to be double acting (the steam pushes both on the out and return stroke). To achieve this the valve had to compromise, and the compromises the valve made affected the efficient use of steam. Prime among these compromises was the point at which the valve opened to steam, and the cross-sectional area of the cylinder ports. Likewise opening and closing of the exhaust port on the return stroke. It is a reflection of the difficulty that the solution of these problems posed, and the lack of simple and robust alternatives, that the slide valve, and its similar successor the piston valve, continued to dominate steam locomotive design to the end.

At this point too, it is critical to realise that Murray's slide valve, operated by Stephenson's link motion, is not an expansion gear; there is no facility to 'cut off' the steam in the cylinder and permit work to be done by expansion. The reverser on the footplate is just that; it allows the locomotive to be driven in either direction at will. Adjusting the position of the eccentrics on the driving axle allows valve ports to open to steam before back or fore centre is reached (known as 'lead'). To expand steam in the cylinder needs a little extra, and that is where the fun began.

Murray's valve, while a masterpiece of simplicity, is also a masterpiece of complexity, because it can be so constructed to provide for expansion of steam in the working cylinder, and the way this is done is by widening the 'D' valve so that the valve faces are larger than the ports they cover. The additional width is known as 'lap', and valve lap alters the valve port openings by providing a period between closing the inlet to steam, and opening the exhaust to the chimney. Lap was provided at an early date, because it had the benefit of preventing a worn valve blowing directly from boiler to chimney, but that lap could be either on the inlet or exhaust side of the valve, and how much lap, and where, were much debated. The effect of providing 'lap' on a typical engine of 1830 is illustrated in Fig. 14, opposite.

The first point to note is that the total travel of the valve is only 1in. Allowing $\frac{1}{8}$in. lap on each side of the valve (to prevent the valves blowing), and not adjusting the eccentrics to provide any lead, means that the valves do not open until well after back and fore centre are passed, and close before the end of the stroke. While this arrangement worked, it was far from ideal. Over the next two decades, link-motion-operated slide valves had these two design variables adjusted: 'lap', as originally applied in the illustration, and 'lead', to make the steam or inlet valve open just before the piston passed the engine centre. To make the designer's task just a mite more difficult, there were other variables, as we shall see.

As Fig. 14 demonstrates, adding $\frac{1}{8}$in. inside and outside lap means that the total lap of $\frac{1}{4}$in. is equal to one-sixth of the total travel of the valve, resulting in periods when the ports are closed both to steam and exhaust. Some work was done by expansion, but that was mitigated by compression in the other end of the cylinder. The solution evolved by 1850, and applied to the 'Crewe' type locomotives is shown in Fig. 15, overleaf. The most obvious changes were the increase both in the total travel of the valve (more than doubled to 4in), and in the width of the valve ports, enlarging from $\frac{5}{8}$in. to 2in. More subtle were the alterations to the lap and lead. Gone is the exhaust lap, and the steam lap is increased to $\frac{3}{4}$in. To ensure the steam port opens just before the engine centre, the eccentrics have been advanced on the driving axle, providing $\frac{1}{8}$in. lead in full gear (locomotives had moved from direct eccentric drive to Stephenson's Link motion by this time). The 'Crewe' type engines could now be adjusted to run out of full gear, but the dashed and dotted lines graphically demonstrate the negative effect of attempting to increase the work done by steam expansion, by reducing the cut-off.

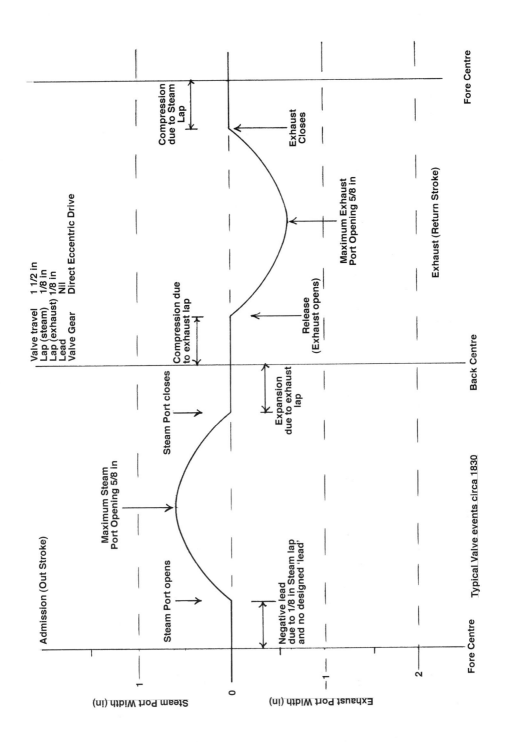

Figure 14: Valve Events, 1830.

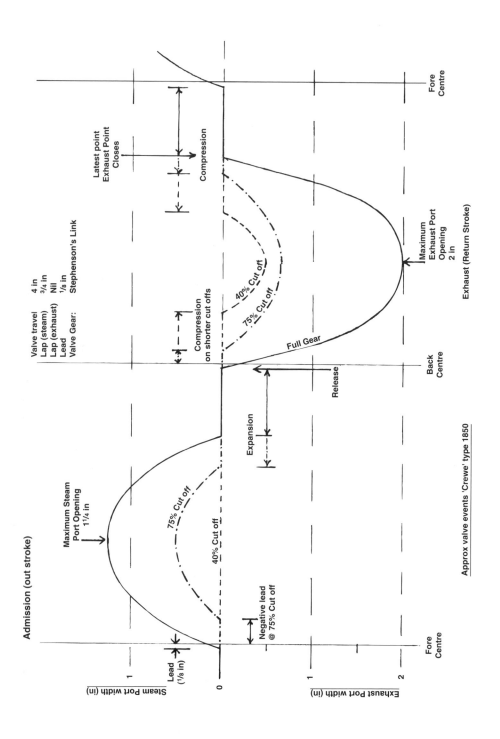

Figure 15: Valve Events, "Crewe" Type, 1850.

The first effect of reducing cut-off to a mere 75% is to give the engine a huge negative lead; steam admission does not start until the piston is a long way past its fore centre. This is not quite as bad as it seems, because the crank here has only a very small moment, and cannot do a great deal of work. The positive lead, though, designed to make the engine free-running and powerful, has been completely wiped out, and worse, the valve now opens less than half as wide as it did when the engine was in full gear, so disproportionately less steam can enter the cylinder. The only real 'plus' is that some work is done by expansion. On the exhaust side, a near ideal valve diagram in full gear also disappears at 75% cut off; this time the port opening is only a third of what is was, down from 2in. to under $^3/_4$in. Likewise compression periods increase and the point of release becomes negative.

If taking a 'Crewe' out of full gear pulled the plug on decent valve events, then the effect of reducing cut off to 40% was simply to prevent the inlet valve opening at all; engines with this valve set up could not be run at much less than 50% cut off because the inlet valve was not opening either early or wide enough. The analysis is simple; all of the steam lap has to clear the valve port before the valve can open, so at 50% cut off the valve travel is only 1in either side of its mid point, and $^3/_4$ of that inch is lap, meaning the valve only opens $^1/_4$in at its widest. A narrow opening late in the piston stroke was not enough to permit high piston speeds, and the reduced exhaust openings made for overheating and rough riding. Narrow ports also meant ' wire drawing' of steam (a serious problem where the steam actually cuts away the metal) leading to heavy wear on valve faces. Little wonder, then, that in 1850 engines were driven in full gear, with adjustment for speed being made on the regulator; this sort of valve setting scarcely permitted anything else.

Having arrived, then, at an acceptable, and above all seemingly simple and reliable, solution, by the middle of the nineteenth century, the onset of technological inertia made it very difficult for alternatives to gain a toehold. To take on, and replace, a simple piece of gear that does its job quite well, any alternative has to be radically better, and the margin by which it outperforms the old is also the margin by which new can exceed old, in cost and complexity. Trip gears and cut- off plates, developed for use elsewhere, could not meet these criteria, and the cam, now almost universal as valve actuator in the 'infernal' combustion engine, saw little application to steam. The parameter that *really* threw the spanner in the valve gear, a side effect of the link motion, was this variable 'lead', and it was fifty years before one man thought his way around the problem as a whole, rather than just considering one component.

Stephenson link motion, as illustrated in Fig. 13, uses an eccentric to provide valve motion (a second eccentric connected to the other end of the curved link provides for reverse motion), and the valve rod is given fore and aft motion by rotation of the crank axle. The valve throw is equal to twice the distance of the eccentric's centre from the axle centre. The motion is thus the same as a piston connected to a crank; speed is zero at the extreme ends of the stroke, and at a maximum at the mid point. This effect has a major benefit in that the valve motion slows and stops only at maximum port openings; at the critical opening phase to both steam and exhaust the valve is travelling at its fastest. "Ah but," those of you who are still following the argument now say, "adding 'lap' to the valve slows the port opening velocity", which is exactly the case. That slowing of the valve opening, accompanied with moderate steam lap and a shift of the point of admission to well beyond the desirable zone in anything other than full gear, was a disaster for the express locomotive. In their efforts to provide for expansive working, the engineers of the nineteenth century were throttling steam flow into the cylinders.

Unfortunately for the engineers, variable 'lead' was needed almost as much as work done by expansion of steam. 'Lead' was necessary in an engine to accommodate inertia of the gas flow; to put enough steam in the cylinder to do the maximum amount of work, admission had to start well before the piston reached the end of its stroke. The faster an engine ran, the earlier admission needed to start, and it would have been nice if adjusting the link motion to allow expansive working at speed also increased the lead. Alas it was not to be; the reverse was the case. Reducing the 'cut off' with Stephenson's gear reduced the lead in two ways; by shifting the admission as demonstrated above, and by the relative rotation of the point of actuation on the eccentric. Making the valve rods long marginally reduced the effect on the 'lead', but engines still had a negative lead when working on short cut-offs. If only *that* were the end of the issue.

Stephenson's motion has the ability to vary the point at which the live steam is cut-off and expansion begins. As we have shown with the 'Crewe' type, moving the curved expansion link out of full gear reduces valve movement or 'throw'. At low speeds with full gear and full regulator, this link motion provided maximum power but miserable economy. Alterations to this set-up risked making the engine sluggish when starting or running hard up a steep grade. As loads were calculated on the basis of what could be hauled up the steepest grade on any particular route, an engine that underperformed on this key task was an unwelcome liability.

The effect on the locomotive of 1850 was that it was difficult, or impossible, to run with the reverser set to less than 50% cut off. For many years cut offs of 60% plus were the norm rather than the exception, leading to the flirtation with compounding, of which more anon. This led to the technique of engines being driven on narrow regulator openings, reducing steam pressure in the valve chest, and none of these factors led to the steam locomotive heading the field in thermal efficiency. While this lack of economy was not of prime concern when actually making trains run remained the base line of performance, as the century progressed it became clear that with increasing loads also came the need to secure maximum efficiency. Increasing power outputs from a machine that had definite limits to its critical dimensions then became a serious issue.

With Stephenson's link motion, if the engine is stopped at or close to one of the engine's mid points, it is pot luck which way the locomotive will move when the link is lifted and the regulator opened. This is a feature of *all* link motions. As we shall see, there were locomotives that made going in the right direction seem a sort of miracle. Failure to put the engine into full gear, common when running light, and particularly with the later screw reversing gear, led to many a false start.

In 1850, then, the link motions of the time allowed for safe, if a little erratic, reversing, and much improved control of the steam locomotive, an essential ingredient in a recipe that included quantum leaps in the power department. The concept of short cut off expansive working remained a pipe dream. A lot of work on the design of the 'D' slide valve was needed, and true to the mechanical ingenuity of the age, spade work of a sort was done, and over the next fifty years applied, with very modest amounts of success, to both slide and piston valves. As was eventually proved, it was possible to maximise the positive aspects of the slide valve operated by Stephenson's link motion, and minimise the negative items, but that is a tale for the twentieth century, and having cracked the nut as far as was possible, Walschaerts' gear then stole the show, in the top link at any rate.

The prevalence of large numbers of locomotives, in service but not performing the duties planned for them, was a feature of the nineteenth and early twentieth centuries; having built something not up to the job, most railway companies were usually compelled to use them, if only for a few years. Only as steam pressures rose to cope with the traffic did the slide valve give way to the piston valve, owing to increased wear on the valve faces which the high pressures generated. On small engines engaged in light duties, slide valves were never completely displaced.

If Stephenson's link motion was both popular and widely used after 1841, and the Gooch and Allan copies likewise, then so too was David Joy's single rod jack link, if only because it was simple and cheap. Joy realised that the motion of the connecting rod varied at all points, and that motion could be utilised to drive the valve spindle. Joy's gear thus took its drive from the middle of the connecting rod, which would have been fine had the connection been properly designed. As produced, the connection was forged to form a pivot in the connecting rod, severely weakening it. The gear thus fell out of favour due to broken connecting rods, an illustration of how a poor detail can spoil a whole concept. Egide Walschaerts' link motion gained in influence more slowly, and for much more complex reasons.

Walschaerts was one of those inventors or designers whose grasp of the issues affecting steam admission to locomotive cylinders was well in advance of the thinking of his times. He realised that there were four components involved in getting the best out of every ounce of steam: when admission commenced; how much steam was admitted; and how much expansion could be achieved. The fourth factor, clearing of the exhaust steam, was dependent on the first three. Using single eccentrics to move the valve spindle meant that all four factors were dictated by one item. Deriving motion from two sources enabled greater control to be gained over the events of valve and cylinder.

The real problem was that if single derived motion was difficult to understand, then the compound motion of Walschaerts' gear was well nigh unfathomable. Engineering textbooks of the times dealt with valve motions; most failed to explain compound motion adequately, and the critical importance of valves being open at the right time *and* fully open as soon as possible after admission starts rarely received the emphasis it demanded. As with the motion, design of the slide valve itself placed a premium on simplicity and reliability, and if efficiency got in the way of other essentials, then that was just efficiency's bad luck.

The reasons why Walschaerts' gear found little favour in the nineteenth century are complex; with total valve travels of four inches or thereabouts, locomotives with this gear would be more economical but less powerful than the same engine fitted with

Stephenson's link motion. The risk of rough running on short cut offs remained, and with most express types having inside cylinders, installing the gear between the frames, and then maintaining it, was quite a challenge. The advantages of Walschaerts' gear were thus not immediately obvious, though the disadvantages, a less brisk start and less power up hills, were.

Matthew Murray's slide valve as originally proposed was a masterpiece of simplicity; one moving part, of simple construction, held together by the pressure of the steam it was distributing. Until wear reduced the inside dimensions of the 'D' to below the point at which it could do its job, the valve was self adjusting and self sealing, and if back pressure caused by condensation exceeded the live steam pressure, then the valve lifted off its seat to relieve itself, as it were, avoiding damage to the cylinder. While steam pressures remained low, slide valves reigned supreme. The last steam shunters built by British Railways, further copies of Worsdell's 1899 North Eastern Railway 0-6-0 tank engine, later LNER class 'J72', turned out in 1950, had slide valves little different from those being produced in 1850.

The slide valve, having demonstrated its near universal suitability, was quickly improved by adoption of cunning arrangements primarily aimed at reduction in numbers of moving parts. With the 'Patentee', siting of the engine cylinders underneath the smokebox and between the frames placed a premium on space. Where the valves and their enclosing steam chests had been sited on top of previous outside cylinder designs, such an arrangement lost the advantage of accessibility when placed under the smokebox. Turning the valves on their sides allowed both valves to operate in a single steam chest, and it was not long before someone (who, it is not clear) realised that crossing the front and back ports of adjacent cylinders enabled one valve to serve both cylinders. The disadvantages this produced in terms of steam admission were considerable, and crossed steam ports fell out of favour for general purpose use, though they were used to advantage on 'Big Bertha', the Lickey Incline banker, where four cylinders were thus served by two valves and eccentrics, in a specialist low speed machine.

Piston valves, in contrast to the early arrival and non-departure of slide valves, only usurped Murray's masterpiece when steam pressures rose to the point where wear on valve faces became unacceptable. The reasons are straightforward; the slide valve has only two machined faces, one on the cylinder and the other on the valve 'D', and they can be ground in to a steam-tight fit with simple hand tools. Piston valves are like pistons, only worse, in that they not only need a second cylinder alongside the working cylinder, but have to be made steam-tight while the piston runs back and forth across the circumferential steam ports. Leakage of steam past the single broad piston ring that did duty in 1850 and for many years afterwards was always a problem, and piston valves did not gain the upper hand until after the First World War. By the 1920s, multiple narrow rings were in use, reducing the dramatic loss of efficieny caused by steam leakage past pistons and piston valves that had run only modest mileages, loss that ruined the long-term performance of many express locomotives. Confidence in multiple narrow rings was marred by the risk of rings catching on the edges of the steam and exhaust ports, and breaking - a risk that, in piston valves, never entirely vanished.

Returning finally to the field of efficiency, this aspect of steam power was dominated for the whole of the nineteenth century, and beyond, by the marine steam engine, serving as an ever-present reminder to the locomotive engineer of his steed's abysmal performances. As a consequence, there was a constant pressure by the directors of the railway companies to reduce expenditure on fuel. Demanding improved efficiency from a steam locomotive is one thing; realising it is quite another, and it was to be many years before improved thermal efficiency could be delivered. When that delivery was eventually made, it was by the adoption of ideas that were completely beyond the engineer in 1850.

Chapter Ten:

Railway Mania - Hosts of Steam 1840-1860

With main lines opening to the four corners of the kingdom in the years either side of 1840, and defeat (buying off might be a more appropriate term) of the landed gentry's opposition to the steam railway, the way lay open for the start of a golden age in which all the major towns of Britain were linked into the rail network. By 1860 that process was nearly complete; lines were still being built in the more remote uncharted territories, and that filling in, together with a number of railways built solely for the purpose of competition, would continue for a further fifty years. Unlike the main lines, smaller companies were financially obliged to purchase their locomotives from private builders. This, combined with the railway company's products, and numerous privately sponsored efforts to design the ultimate in steam power, resulted in a flowering of talent (varying wildly in ability) and engines of every shape, colour, size and mechanical ingenuity. Everybody who was anybody wanted to design steam locomotives, and while there was no shortage of money, the value that was achieved from that money, in terms of useful motive power, was strictly limited.

Standing clear of the field, and showing the standard gauge up for the severe problems it posed for the locomotive designer, was Daniel Gooch and the Great Western Railway. In 1846 Gooch had designed a locomotive for the broad gauge, *Great Western*, in anticipation of Parliament taking action to resolve conflict between the gauges that threatened to prevent creation of a national railway network (fourteen decades later Parliament had second thoughts on the concept of a network!) *Great Western* was simply an enlarged 'Patentee', with a gothic top firebox, eight foot driving wheels and weighing in at about thirty five tons. Boiler pressure at 100psi and a grate area of just over twenty-two square feet were typical of the period. Teething troubles led to replacement of the front pair of wheels by a four wheel bogie, and some tinkering with the size of the driving wheels, but the revised design, after a short preproduction run, became the 'Iron Duke' class. These locomotives ran all broad gauge express passenger services until 1875, and as engines wore out they were replaced by virtually identical locomotives carrying 140psi boilers. These engines, albeit outdated in their later years, ran until the end of the broad gauge in 1892. In express passenger service this record was unequalled on any other main line in nineteenth century Britain.

Provenance: Development of the 'Patentee', three axle fixed wheelbase locomotive with single driving wheelset and higher boiler pressure.
Designer: Daniel Gooch.
Principal Features: Double frame, inside cylinders, deep firebox between the driving axle and rear axle.
Principal Dimensions:Cylinders: 18in diameter, 24in stroke, inside frames.
Working Pressure:100psi.
Tractive Effort: 6,885lb at 85% of boiler pressure.
Driving wheels: 8ft 0in diameter.
Valves: slide valves between frames, inside Gooch Link Motion.
Weight in W. O: 26 tons 2cwt.

Figure 16: Iron Duke.

Having set such an exacting standard the broad gauge rested permanently on its laurels, watching designers on the standard gauge struggle to reach standards of performance, reliability and durability exemplified by Swindon design, manufacture and operation. Perhaps fortunately for the history of the steam locomotive, life away from Brunel's racetrack proved full of successes and failures. The parameters for the steam locomotive had been set, with some minor exceptions, in the period 1840-45, by development of 'Patentees' and 'Long Boiler' engines. Problems with the first 'Patentees' had led to the 'Crewe' outside cylinder design. In 1850 there were basically these three types of locomotives; 'Long Boilers' with six coupled wheels, as freight locomotives; classic 'single driver' express passenger locomotives, and mixed passenger/freight types with four coupled wheels, either leading, with a trailing axle under the firebox, or with a leading pair of undriven wheels. That said, there were an almost bewildering variety of individual designs, and to these were added locomotives, such as the 'Crampton', where large driving wheels were set behind the firebox, that made a brief bow and then departed to a well deserved oblivion.

Designing these locomotives were the established private builders; Robert Stephenson and Co., R and W Hawthorn, Kitsons, Edward Bury, Vulcan Foundry, Jones and Potts, Nasmyth and Co., to name but a few of the famous many. Designing their own, a substantial host of railway company Locomotive Superintendents: Matthew Kirtley for the Midland, J. V. Gooch on the London and South Western, Robert Sinclair for the Caledonian. Not to be outdone, the 'Premier Line' had two; Francis Trevithick at Crewe, and J. E. McConnell at Wolverton, and an assistant, Alexander Allan, who subsequently laid claim to virtually every significant development made at both Edge Hill and Crewe during this period. To these were added freelance designers, people like Thomas Crampton and David Joy, who patented various aspects of locomotive design, and whose engines were built by both private builders and the railway companies .

Over the twenty years under review, the design of locomotives is characterised by a number of significant developments, and these can briefly be listed:

• Increase in overall weight from five tons to in excess of thirty tons.

• Increase in boiler pressures from 50psi to 100psi or more.

- Universal adoption of the reversible link valve motion.

- Emergence of distinct 'express', mixed traffic, and freight designs.

- Increase in boiler lengths from six feet to ten feet or more between tubeplates.

- Increase in axle loads from two or three tons to fifteen tons.

- The appearance of purely decorative items on locomotives, and the development of locomotive aesthetics.

- General increase in dimensions of cylinders, and in the length of piston stroke.

- Completion of the locomotive frame as a structural entity stretching from buffer beam to drawbar.

- A slow but inexorable rise in locomotive centres of gravity.

Not all of these evolutions were to be found in direct lineal progression, but as the rail network thrived after 1850, steam locomotives began to push against the physical limits imposed by the track gauge and, more importantly, the strength of materials used for both track and locomotive, particularly wrought iron. By 1860, the six wheel locomotive had reached a plateau of development, and curiously enough it was the perceived restriction of the fixed wheelbase, dictated by the small turntables in use (the reluctance to provide larger turntables was to prove a recurring theme nationwide) that was to cause as much trouble as anything, though the standard gauge of four feet eight and a half inches ran a close second. This period then, is characterised by restrictions, both real and imaginary, that were faced by locomotive designers, and it is useful to examine the problems these restrictions caused.

Perhaps the most challenging hurdle was a combination of maximum wheelbase and restricted gauge. In essence, this meant that, on the standard gauge until beyond 1850, fixed wheelbases were generally under 12 feet, and boiler diameters less than the track gauge, at four feet or slightly larger. If a locomotive was not to overhang its wheels, after two feet has been deducted for a smokebox, and three for firebox (often more), then the boiler length was limited to about six feet, and every inch added on the firebox meant less boiler space. In practice the idea of containing locomotives within this wheelbase proved impossible, leading to an obsession with keeping the centre of gravity as low as possible, to ensure stability. While the mathematics that enabled calculation of dynamic forces acting on a locomotive at speed were available, at this point the development of a free running, fast and stable locomotive was the subject of fierce debate.

Typical of passenger locomotives in the 1850s, in general format, if not in terms of its success as a reliable engine, was a 'single driver' similar to the 'Jenny Lind' class, produced from 1847 by E. B. Wilson of Leeds to the design of David Joy, and illustrated overleaf. The 'Jennys' as they came to be known were successful, both as fast and reliable engines, and were stable at speed. Weighing twenty four tons, divided between three axles, meant ten tons was available for adhesion on the driving axle, enough for loads of the time, but without a margin for the future. To fit a boiler on a wheelbase of 13ft 6in, both smokebox and front portion of the boiler overhung the front axle. The firebox, however, fitted between the driving and rear axles, necessitating termination of the inside frame plates at the firebox front, but still restricting firebox width to the distance between the inside faces of the wheels. Boiler pressure though was exceptionally high for the period at 120psi. That fact, combined with the modest driving wheel diameter of six feet, meant a substantial tractive effort, if, owing to low piston speeds and unsophisticated slide valve and steam port design, it meant a concomitant reduction in maximum speed. Inside cylinders of fifteen inch diameter and twenty inch stroke were also unexceptional.

The 'Jennys' stood out from their contemporaries because they did not challenge the physical limits of gauge or structure, and were modest in their dimensions, except where it mattered most: boiler pressure a clear twenty pounds higher than its rivals, and going on for twice the average of the time. While steam pressures were rising steadily, there was a reluctance to invest in stronger and heavier boilers and fireboxes that much higher pressures demanded. That reluctance was compounded by a general failure to appreciate the fact that as steam pressures rose, so the proportion of energy needed to turn water at 212deg.F to steam diminished. Higher pressures meant more work from each pound of coal burnt, less water used per useful horsepower produced, and more power per ton of locomotive, exactly as Trevithick had demonstrated fifty years earlier.

Provenance: Development of the 'Patentee', three axle fixed wheelbase locomotive with single driving wheelset and higher boiler pressure. Built by E B Wilson, Leeds 1847.

Designer: David Joy.

Principal Features: Partial double frame, inside cylinders, deep firebox between the driving axle and the rear axle.

Principal Dimensions: Overall wheelbase: 13ft 6in. (This fixed wheelbase was generally the norm for conventional locomotives until the 1950's, and was only a couple of feet longer than the first three axle locomotive, 'Patentee').

Cylinders: 15in diameter, 20in stroke, inside frames.

Working Pressure: 120psi.

Tractive Effort: 6,375lb at 85% of boiler pressure.

Driving wheels: 6ft 0in diameter Axle load 10t 0cwt (driving axle) Boiler 10ft 0in between tubeplates, pitch line 5ft 9in above rail level. Valves slide valves between frames, inside Stephenson Link Motion.

Weight in W. O: 24 tons 2cwt.

Figure 17: Jenny Lind.

David Joy's design was a success when success eluded many designers because the limits propounded by Robert Stephenson in the 'Patentee' and 'Long Boiler' types were being reached. Likewise wrought iron, the material for both rails and wheels, was too soft to accept, without plastic deformation, the point loads of twelve tons per axle, and more, that were being imposed on driving wheels. In 1860 steel was only being toyed with as a replacement material. Under high pressures the wheel/rail interface was deforming, and rails sagging between chairs, offering considerable resistance to motion (the baulk road of the broad gauge was superior in this respect as it offered the rail continuous support.) Short wheelbases and vehicle overhangs meant preference for inside cylinders in the interests of stability. That preference severely limited space for both axle and crank bearings, and valve gear, all of which had to be cut down to fit. Stability equalled low centres of gravity, or so most designers thought, restricting boiler diameter to less than the rail gauge, likewise the firebox width.

A stream of inventions improved the steam locomotive: new safety valves; gauge glasses; regulator valves; brick firebox arches (allowing coal to be burnt 'smokelessly'); feed water heaters, quickly replaced by Giffard's injector, making the force feed pump redundant by acting as both boiler feed and preheater. A further stream of inventions *didn't* improve the steam locomotive: wondrous variations on the locomotive blastpipe, designed to draw the fire more evenly/better/more economically, but ultimately achieving none of these; alterations to valves and their operating linkages to avoid patents or address real or imaginary operating inefficiencies. The cranks that plagued the Liverpool and Manchester Railway in 1829 found the railway age an ideal environment, and thrived.

Within this flowering of the imagination, not in any way restricted to this sceptered isle, were the ideas that were to push design forward over the next twenty five years, just keeping pace with the travelling public's demand for more speed, comfort and on board facilities. Those demands included little that we would now recognise as other than absolute basics (heating, beyond the private warming pan, was not on the list, for example) but they still placed demands upon the locomotive that were not readily met. This discrepancy between expectation on the part of the public and delivery from the locomotive designer, was still a broad gulf at the century's end, just as it was in the middle.

Having whetted the public's appetite, maximum speeds stalled after the flourish of the 1840s and 1850s, with no obvious cause. Train weights were increasing, and locomotives grew larger and more powerful to handle the traffic, but they were not faster. Given that some companies had still to be persuaded that trains needed brakes, perhaps this was no bad thing. The problem, though, with the phrase 'go faster' is that it is a treadmill; once hitched there is no way off, and anyway nobody wanted off in the nineteenth century. Locomotive engineers simply had to keep plugging away at raising top and average speeds, even though returns were meagre to the point of absence. One factor that eventually promised relief was the material to supersede iron: steel. Bessemer's converter had shown the way, and imported steel from Krupp's in Germany had demonstrated the benefits. Over the decade to 1879 steel came to the fore in the steam locomotive, and the iron road became a steel road, but the most important development of the 1860s was the realisation of the railway companies, enlarged and fortified by a round of mergers and take-overs, that in locomotive design and procurement, the payer of the piper not only called the tune but wrote the music as well; the age of the chief mechanical engineer had arrived, even if for the time being he had to accept the title of Locomotive Superintendent.

Chapter Eleven:

The Emergence of the Chief Mechanical Engineer

In 1860 there was work for every locomotive builder in the country. Railways at home and overseas were being built at a rate that today seems scarcely credible; North America alone built over three thousand miles of new railway, on average, *every* year from 1830 to 1900. Europe and the Indian sub-continent were only marginally less active. Britain's locomotive builders supplied much of that demand, with both India and Argentina being dominated by products from the 'Workshop of the World'. In the supply of motive power for the railways of this island, the resources and skills of private engine builders supplied locomotives railway companies could not build themselves, but the designs, on the whole, were not theirs, not as far as the main line companies were concerned.

The 'Premier Line', the London and North Western Railway (the product of amalgamation between the London and Birmingham, Grand Junction and other west coast companies) had locomotive engineers for its southern and northern divisions, and works at Wolverton, Crewe and Longsight in Manchester. The Great Western had facilities the equal of anything at both Swindon and Wolverhampton. Two companies formed from the fall-out of the Hudson empire, the Midland and the North Eastern Railways, had their respective works at Derby and Gateshead, with further works at Shildon and Darlington on the Stockton and Darlington section.

The London and South Western Railway built engines at Nine Elms, London (the site of the present Covent Garden wholesale fruit and vegetable market), and there were similar facilities at Brighton, Stratford (London), St Rollox (Glasgow), and Gorton in Manchester, to name but a few of the principal players. Whatever the state of the railway companies' works, come large or small, any company with aspirations to be a runner of trains and owner of stock had a locomotive superintendent or a chief engineer, and to that individual fell responsibility for providing locomotives to shift the traffic.

The attention focused on steam locomotive design in the second half of the nineteenth century is, at this distance, a little difficult to appreciate. Magazines such as 'The Artizan', 'The Railway Magazine', and 'The Engineer' followed development in almost microscopic detail, explaining to a rapt audience the intricacies of the innermost workings of every new offering at the altar of speed. The position of designers was thus one of eminence, certainly with as high a profile as today's most successful entrepreneurs (who don't seem either able or willing to make the trains run on time). The temptation laid out in front of every chief engineer to become one of this select breed was irresistible; from setting out broad specifications for tenders from private builders, to running a large design office and building their own in the company works, every shade of involvement was there. Once the 'chief' had found his feet, and persuaded the board that what he proposed would do the job, the chief mechanical engineer was king, and private builders danced to his tune, whatever their opinions or experience. A small number of men thus became responsible for directing development of the British steam locomotive, and from 1860 their designs held sway on the railways of Britain, with very mixed fortunes, as we shall see.

Here we need draw distinction between 'British' locomotives, and those engines built by British companies for export, mostly to the British Empire. Empire policy, as it extended to railways in the colonies, was in no way comparable with the state of play in England, Scotland and Wales. Only a few people made a fortune in the colonies, and those fortunes were generally made by exploitation rather than development. Railways built under colonial directive serviced that exploitation, and military necessity, and locomotives were supplied to run services that generally amounted to 'slow and sparse'. Accordingly, robust workhorses rather than sprightly thoroughbreds were the order of the day, built down to a price to compete with German or American suppliers. Where there is evidence of an export machine affecting design on a British railway, such as David Jones' 'Big Goods' on the Highland Railway (the first 4-6-0 to run on British rails) being markedly similar to the Indian 'L' class turned out by Dubs and Co. of Glasgow, their effect on the mainstream of British design was minimal.

In the forty years from 1860 to the century's end, then, there are two distinct threads of development in steam locomotive design: that of express engines, represented by a multitude of different designs dominated by the 'Battle of the Coupling Rods' (shall we have them, or not; more or less on the 'two wheels good, four wheels bad' level), and that of the goods engine, where a small number of basically similar designs were evolved independently around the six coupled inside cylinder layout, and built in large numbers. Locomotives in the 'mixed traffic' category were mostly supplied from the numerous ranks of failed express types, while shunting and branch line work fell to smaller tank designs. There were exceptions to this last statement; the Taff Vale Railway relied exclusively on tank engines, and was far from being alone in this within the confines of the South Wales coalfield. Likewise the Great Western ran its coal trains from Aberdare to Swindon with tank engines as prime movers. Tank engines are however considered elsewhere, for they are a branch of the principal theme.

The freight locomotive quickly came to be defined by the six coupled tender engine, a type that persisted to the end of steam on British Railways (in 1962, just prior to the mass slaughter of steam, out of eighty-three classes of tender locomotive in service, twenty four were 0-6-0's). First in the field with a successful design built in large numbers was John Ramsbottom, who laid down his first 'DX Goods' at Longsight in Manchester in 1858. Ramsbottom was locomotive superintendent of the London and North Western Railway, having being head of that company's North Eastern Division under Francis Trevithick, taking over the role of engineer for the whole of the Premier Line in 1857.

True to form, the 'DX' was ground-breaking only in the fact that it was a competent projection of best current practice, doing everything well and not making a stab in the dark after some imaginary quantum leap of power or efficiency. The design was 'modern' in many respects; inside straight plate frames, from front buffer beam to rear drawbar, were braced by cylinder and valve chest castings, and cross stays forward of the driving axle and firebox. Slide valves for both cylinders shared a common steam chest, on the engine's centre line, a feature designed nearly twenty years earlier by Robert Stephenson and Co., but an example of simplicity and economy that kept slide valves in favour until after the Second World War. Boiler and firebox proportions were adequate; boiler pressure, at 120psi a good average for the period. Ramsbottom added his own design of screw reverser, to make control of cut-off more precise, and an effective double-beat regulator valve that went a long way to mitigate the difficulty of opening and shutting the throttle against boiler steam pressure; but there was no protection for the crew, not even a spectacle plate.

Over eight hundred and fifty of these engines were built for the Premier Line over the next fourteen years, and apart from insertion of a brick arch and deflector plate in the firebox, to allow

Provenance: 1858 development of McConnell large wheeled goods for the LNWR.
Designer: John Ramsbottom.
Principal Features: Six coupled goods engine with rear axle behind the firebox.
Inclined inside cylinders and valves driving the centre axle.
Principal Dimensions: Coupled wheelbase: 15ft 6in.
Cylinders 17in diameter, 24in stroke, inside frames.
Working Pressure 120psi.
Tractive Effort: 11,410lb at 85% of boiler pressure.
Driving wheels: 5ft 2in diameter.
Axle load: 10t 0cwt (driving axle).
Valves: Slide valves between frames.
Weight in W. O: 27 tons.

Figure 18: DX Goods.

burning of coal in place of coke, the locomotives were effectively standardised, in design at least. Standardisation at this date did not mean interchangeability of parts: engines continued to be 'fitted' together, rather than assembled from a heap of identical components. Along with engines for its own use, Crewe built eighty six 'DX's' for the Lancashire and Yorkshire Railway, and the engine was still a standard type fifty years later, on the eve of the First World War.

John Ramsbottom has a good claim to be first to produce a standard mass produced product, long lived and robustly reliable. He was followed over the next twenty years by Matthew Kirtley on the Midland Railway, William Dean on the Great Western, Charles Sacre on the Manchester, Sheffield and Lincolnshire, and Edward Fletcher on the North Eastern. Francis Webb, who succeeded Ramsbottom at Crewe, built a further five hundred goods engines similar to the 'DX' during his tenure, the formula was simply too good to ignore.

If heavy freight haulage was solved simply and effectively by mass production, then it could be argued that the same approach would be a success on the express passenger side. Unfortunately for the main line companies, factors that made the freight locomotive successful, and led to a long period (it was not until the twentieth century that a substantially more powerful goods locomotive was designed and mass produced) in which freight was handled by the same engines at more or less the same speeds, were not applicable to the passenger railway. Once again, limits imposed by inadequate valve gears prevented production of a definitive 'express'. Designers for the most part spent their efforts in bypassing the problem rather than solving it. The frustrations encountered by chief mechanical engineers during the last quarter of the nineteenth century can be summed up in the career of Francis William Webb, and while his efforts to design a fast and powerful express locomotive were less successful and more amusing than most, his failures and semi-successes serve to hold a mirror to the general lot of the locomotive engineer in this period.

Webb's tenure as chief mechanical engineer at Crewe spanned thirty two years, from 1871 to 1903. When he took over from Ramsbottom, Premier Line locomotive stock was the equal of its competitors; that happy state of affairs did not, alas, last long. At Webb's retirement in 1903, George Whale, who succeeded him from the running department, took an axe to his predecessor's products in an unceremonious fashion. That the directors of the London and North Western Railway tolerated the fiascos of their chief engineer's tenure for so long is surprising to the point of amazement, but serves to underline the high public profile (God-like might be an appropriate description) held by the locomotive designer in the late nineteenth century.

In 1866, Ramsbottom had introduced a well-proportioned four coupled express locomotive with a leading axle (a '2-4-0'), tipping the scales at just over twenty eight tons, of which rather more than half was on the four driving wheels. Crewe Works continued to build these engines until 1873, when two new designs were put in hand to build top link motive power for the West Coast. First of these, named *Precursor*, from which the class took its name, were a slightly larger and heavier (by three tons) version of their immediate predecessors, fitted with five foot six inch wheels for working over the steep and long gradients of the Lancaster and Carlisle Railway's Grayrigg and Shap summits.

In performance terms the use of 'small' driving wheels (anything under six foot six at the time was regarded as small for a passenger engine) was one of those ill-judged mistakes that everyone can make. In power terms the locomotive was just a mite small to be master of the job. Crucially, the valve gear prevented free running at anything much over fifty miles an hour, whether on the flat or downhill, and the running department's view of these new locomotives cannot have been tinted with a great deal of enthusiasm.

The fact that Patrick Stirling on the Great Northern had just produced his famous single (No.1, now in the National Railway Museum, York) that was more master of tasks set it than the 'Precursors', should have set alarm bells ringing in the boardroom. Whatever bells did ring, they were not heeded, and it was all downhill from that point.

The next class, the 'Precedent', was essentially the same as 'Precursor', but with express size wheels. This last factor at least allowed for some reasonably fast downhill running, but short radius coupling rod swings were just one factor that added to the engine's resistance to motion, and use of Webb's own regulator was a disaster that even he acknowledged, by reverting to Ramsbottom's double-beat valve. So far, so bad, we might be tempted to say; already the Premier line lagged behind the East Coast competition, just as a third contender for Anglo-Scottish traffic was entering the lists. The Midland Railway, having ticked off acquiring its own access to London and Manchester in 1868 (between which cities Crewe had until then enjoyed a near complete monopoly) entered the London and Glasgow/ Edinburgh market in 1876, with completion of the Settle and Carlisle Railway and running agreements with both North British and Glasgow and South Western Railways.

The pressure on Francis Webb to come up with some real muscle on the 'Scotch' expresses was intense, the result almost nothing. We can say almost nothing, because Francis Webb was developing a circular slide valve, that was free to revolve in the driving bridle, a fact that should have prevented seizure (the risk of seizure in slide valves increases with higher boiler pressures, which were heading for 160psi at this time). The valve was a failure in that it had a tendency to seize. The fact that there was little in the way of success, and already a goodly amount in the debit column of Mr. Webb's account book, was not going to stand in his way of going right ahead and making a really big howler.

There are some people fated in life to hitch their postern to the most unsuitable horse, and Francis Webb attached his to the application of compound expansion of steam to the railway locomotive. Once hitched, he showed no desire to escape the fate laid out for him, and having failed to make compound locomotives that worked, he *continued* to design new classes of compound locomotives that didn't work, despite the fact that other people

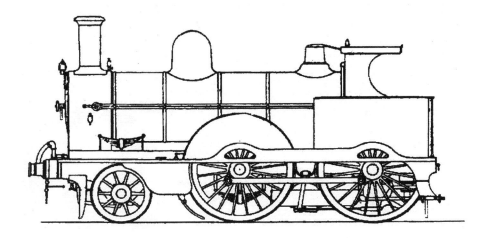

Provenance: Development of the 'Precursor' class with larger wheels, intended as the definitive West Coast express locomotive.
Designer: F. W. Webb.
Principal Features: Typical 1870's six wheel express, short fixed wheelbase, short boiler and smokebox.
Principal Dimensions: Cylinders: 17in diameter, 24in stroke, inside frames.
Working Pressure: 140psi.
Tractive Effort: 10,382lb. Driving wheels: 6ft 7 1/2 in diameter.
Boiler: Short boiler and smokebox, deep firebox between coupled axles.
Valves: Slide valves between frames, inside Allan 'Straight Link' Motion.
Weight in W. O: 32 tons 15cwt.

Figure 19: Precedent.

were at least making presentable prototypes, if not equipping railways with whole classes of top link racehorses. The West Coast came to rely on Ramsbottom's and McConnell's engines, despite instructions to use Webb's curiosities, with 'Bloomers' and 'Lady of the Lake' engines, over twenty years old, still in front line service in the 1880's.

Webb's first venture onto the slippery slopes of compound engine design came about as a result of developments on the Continent, where the principle of expanding steam twice betwixt boiler and blastpipe had finally produced a workable engine (courtesy of Anatole Mallett, who showed off his locomotive at the Paris Exhibition in 1878). Triple expansion in marine and stationary engines was by now in use, and the resulting economy made all locomotive engineers think twice about putting the same ideas onto the iron road. Fortunately for their shareholders, most chief engineers *did* think twice, and had nothing further to do with the concept. Francis, true to his nature, glimpsed the abyss yawning and rushed to throw himself in from the brink.

Conversion of a Trevithick locomotive produced an experimental compound, one cylinder being lined to reduce its diameter to a size that would allow expansion of steam in the second cylinder without generating excessive back pressure. The effect was to reduce tractive effort, and the engine was only suited to light branch line work, which it duly performed for four years. On the basis of this one trial, Webb designed an express locomotive, as a three cylinder compound. Readers will appreciate that with three cylinders, you can have one high pressure and two low pressure cylinders, or vice versa, and that the only successful compounds to run in this country were of the one high/two low format. There is then a certain inevitability in the fact that Webb chose the wrong arrangement. Having two high pressure cylinders and one low pressure creates an imbalance of volumes; there is more exhaust steam from the high pressure cylinders than can be used in the low pressure one. Webb addressed this by reducing the high pressure cylinder dimensions to the point where the engine, *Experiment,* was unable to start its train. *Experiment* emerged from Crewe Works in 1882, and was not repeated.

In 1884, Webb's next compound, first of the 'Compound' class, addressed the poor starting by increasing the size of the high pressure cylinders. The effect of this alteration was to reduce the locomotive's ability to expand the steam, mitigating the benefit of compounding to the point where it was pointless. To add to this sorry tale, Webb tried to remove the resistance of the coupling rods, by removing the coupling rods. The drive was divided, with high and low pressure cylinders driving separate axles. This proved spectacularly useless, because the first exhaust from the high pressure cylinder at starting entered the low pressure cylinder, and depending on the position of the crank, could drive it in either direction. The engines thus had the ability to stand still while the two sets of driving wheels rotated in opposite directions. Despite being as large as the 'Precedent' class in dimensions other than the motion, 'Compounds' could not do the same work, primarily because back pressure in the high pressure cylinders subtracted as much, if not more, work from the total performed by the engine as that performed in the low pressure cylinder.

If Webb was dismayed by this failure, and the 'Compounds' were four tons heavier than the 'Precedents' to which they were inferior, then he obeyed the first law of failure to the letter; if what you have doesn't work, then making it *larger* will make for a *greater* failure. The 'Dreadnoughts' that followed later in 1884 were true to their destiny, and at forty two tons in working order, over ten tons heavier than the 'Precedents'. This time boiler pressure was raised to 175psi, and both high and low pressure cylinders enlarged. As the 'Dreadnoughts' used the same steam distribution as their predecessors, they were just as inefficient, only more so. The following 'Teutonic' class were no improvement, though possibly not worse; in coal consumption they were no better than simple expansion engines of the 1860's, and in the critical area of maximum speed, they had no more success in cracking the sixty miles an hour speed barrier than the 'Precedents'. It was little consolation that later compound locomotives were on a par with simple engines built twenty years previously; other railway companies had moved on, and at the turn of the century the Premier Line was very much in the second division of express locomotive performance.

Provenance: Development of 'Experiment' locomotive with larger high pressure cylinders, intended as the definitive West Coast express locomotive.
Designer: F. W. Webb.
Principal Features: Typical 1870's six wheel express, rigid three axle 'Patentee' derivative with short boiler and smokebox.
Principal Dimensions:Cylinders: Three, two 13in diameter (high pressure), one 26in (low pressure), 24in stroke.
Working Pressure: 150psi.
Tractive Effort: 16,224lb (theoretical, nil back pressure).
Driving wheels: 6ft 3in diameter.
Boiler: Short boiler, deep firebox.
Valves: Slide valves, Joy valve gear.
Weight in W. O: 37 tons 15cwt.

Figure 20: Webb Compound.

On the rails of the other main line companies, no wonders were being wrought; the physical limitations of valves and valve gears, limiting efficient use of steam, had not been addressed. A degree of side-stepping had made for some progress, notably towards the use of higher boiler pressures, and a leading bogie, breaking away from the rigid three axle layout that had persisted since the days of

Robert Stephenson's 'Patentee'. Contemporary with Francis Webb at Crewe, Samuel Waite Johnson was locomotive engineer to the Midland Railway from 1873 to 1903, laying down principles of design and construction that were to outlast the Midland Railway, and live on to become a millstone to the biggest of the 'Big Four' at the grouping, the London Midland and Scottish Railway.

Provenance: last Midland railway express locomotive derived from the three axle fixed wheelbase of the 'Patentee'.
Designer: Matthew Kirtley.
Principal Features: Typical 1870s six wheel express.
Principal Dimensions: Cylinders Two, 18in diameter, 24in stroke, inside frames.
Working Pressure: 140psi.
Tractive Effort: 11,578lb.
Driving wheels 6ft 8in diameter.
Boiler: Short parallel boiler, short smokebox, firebox between coupled axles
Valves: Slide valves between frames, inside Stephenson Link Motion.
Weight in W. O: 40 tons.

Figure 21: Kirtley 2-4-0.

Matthew Kirtley's legacy to the Midland was similar to Ramsbottom's at Crewe; a stock of locomotives that were as good as any on the standard gauge, and in certain respects, better. Topping the list was the '800' class of six wheeled, four coupled express engines, with six foot eight inch drivers and boilers pressed to 140psi. Derby Works and the contractor, Neilsons, had built forty eight of these engines between them in 1870-71, an expression of faith in their capacity to haul the premier expresses that was not in any way unfounded. With outside frames, and inside cylinders and valve gear, these locomotives were typical of their age in appearance, and with their large wheels, fast enough on the flat and downhill to keep time in an era when maximum average speeds were in the 40-45 mph range.

Johnson's cautious approach to design is typified by his decision, three years after taking office, to rebuild Kirtley's engines with larger cylinders to cope with the newly opened main line from Settle Junction to Petteril Bridge, Carlisle, with its long 1 in 100 gradients. It was a wise decision, and to increase experience, his rebuilds featured engines with longer piston stroke or larger pistons, but not both. Boiler and firebox heating surface increased by about 20%, and weight went up from thirty-six to forty tons. While this sort of incremental increase in general dimensions of locomotives could not go on *ad infinitum*, Johnson was lucky with the '800' rebuilds in that the steam chest between the cylinders was large enough to handle increased quantities of steam for the larger stroke volumes. As more power, rather than higher speed was the essence of the rebuild, he did not quite reach the limit of the valve design.

As with all designers who wish to leave their mark on the world (without exception, we can safely say at this juncture, all designers have this wish), Samuel Johnson was not prepared to tinker with another's ideas for long. Having proved his proposals to his and the Midland directors' satisfaction, he proceeded in 1876, to build his first engines for express passenger work with inside cylinders, four coupled wheels and a leading four wheel bogie. The last engines of this design would emerge onto the London Midland and Scottish Railway in 1928, and British Railways would still have nine examples in service thirty five years later, whose duties in the 1950's included piloting expresses on the west coast over Grayrigg and Shap. Eighty seven years of continuous work from a single design concept may not be unique, but no other express engine could claim such a pedigree, despite the last engines being obsolete in design terms well before they were built. Johnson, then, had struck gold: a machine well up to the standards of the time, stable, owing to the leading wheels being forward of the smokebox and cylinders; a performance brisk enough, with seven foot driving wheels, to haul the heavy Pullman coaches the Midland had imported from the United States, and in the eyes of the aesthetes, very much the model of a modern locomotive.

In developing the 4-4-0 as the definitive express type, Johnson cannot be described as leading the field, for not even in Britain was he first; both the North British and Glasgow and South Western had put similar locomotives on the rails in the previous five years.

111

Provenance: Midland Railway definitive express 1875 -1923.
Designer: S. W. Johnson.
Principal Features: Typical 1870's express, with inside cylinders and valve gear,
leading bogie and large driving/coupled wheels.
Principal Dimensions: Cylinders: Two, 20 $^1/_2$in diameter, 26in stroke, inside frames.
Working Pressure: 160psi.
Tractive Effort: 17,585lb.
Driving wheels: 7ft 0$^1/_2$ in diameter.
Valves: slide valves between frames, inside Stephenson Link Motion.
Weight in W. O: 53 tons 7cwt.

Figure 22: Midland 4-4-0.

On the world stage, the outside cylinder version had been
defined by American railroads and produced in large numbers, both
by the railroads themselves, and by the Baldwin works (in 1870
well on the way to being the world's number one builder of steam
traction). Nonetheless, the essence of the British inside cylinder 4-
4-0 was epitomised in products turned out by Derby Works in the
three decades prior to 1900; in performance, proportions and livery,
the best all round locomotives of the last quarter of the nineteenth
century. When outside cylinder versions were needed, as with the
Midland 'Compounds', all the detail work was in place, and the
familial resemblance exact.

In designing a successful locomotive with a leading bogie,
Johnson had set a theme, repeated on all the other main lines
(Francis Webb at Crewe, of course excepted), of a design concept
that left behind the three axle rigid wheelbase locomotive, which
had been the norm since introduction of the 'Patentee'. Locomotives
of the old pattern continued to be built as goods and express types
for many years to come, and as goods and shunting tank engines
until after nationalisation. Neither was the bogie new, as Daniel
Gooch had used it in 1846. Johnson's design though, of a short boiler

and deep firebox set between the coupled wheels, was enlarged upon for thirty years without being superseded, and it was a locomotive of this form, *City of Truro*, that was the first to reach one hundred miles an hour. The last design with the 4-4-0 wheel arrangement, Southern Railway's 'Schools' class, would be introduced in 1930, built out to the limits of the loading gauge as a secondary express machine incorporating the best of twentieth century technical innovation. To the end of the nineteenth century though, the design was to have plenty of competition as the premier express type.

Patrick Stirling had been locomotive superintendent to the Glasgow and South Western Railway for thirteen years, when he moved to the Great Northern Railway in 1866. Patrick was a fan of the 'single', locomotives with only one pair of driving wheels, and proceeded to equip his new charge with singles for express work, exemplified by his preserved No.1. None of the gradients on the main line from Kings Cross to Doncaster are steep, compared with the climbs in South West Scotland, and over the twenty-nine years to his retirement in 1895, Stirling held true to this concept, helped by development of steam sanding gear. This latter invention tempted both Great Western and Midland railways to build singles

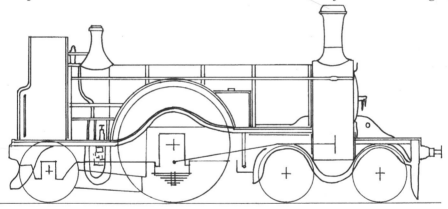

Provenance: Development for the Great Northern Railway of Stirling designs on the Glasgow and South Western Railway.
Designer: Patrick Stirling.
Principal Features: Classic large wheeled 'single driver' of the last quarter of the nineteenth century, outside cylinders of long stroke, inside valve gear.
Principal Dimensions:.Cylinders: 18in diameter, 28in stroke, outside frames.
Working Pressure: 140psi.
Tractive Effort: 11,129lb.
Driving wheels: 8ft 1in diameter.
Valves: Slide valves between frames, inside Stephenson Link Motion.
Weight in W. O: 38 tons 9cwt.

Figure 23: Stirling Single.

run alongside their coupled express engines, while the North Eastern and Great Eastern, and companies running south from London, built both types and the rigid three axle 'Patentee' derivatives, without any particular preference for one or the other.

Increasing use of steel rails and tyres after 1870 meant that locomotives had less work to do; steel is much harder than iron, and wheels could now be cast in steel instead of built up in cast and wrought iron. Steel forged, and built up, cranks, boiler plate, frames and motion parts were ultimately to replace wrought iron. That they did not do so immediately was due in part to conservatism within the industry, and time was needed to cure steel of some of its less attractive properties. Likewise, better manufacturing techniques enabled locomotives to be built to higher standards, lowering resistance to motion. The same applied to hauled stock, and, as a result, train speeds rose in the 1870s and 1880s, even though the same locomotives remained in use. This trend continued in the ultimate decade of the century, but as the Victorian age gave way to Edwardian, a revolution in design occurred at the very heart of the locomotive. The place was Swindon, the man, George Jackson Churchward.

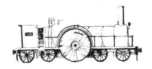

Chapter Twelve:

Leading but not Followed:
Swindon 1900-1925

The last express passenger locomotives of William Dean's tenancy at Swindon were not that dissimilar from the 4-4-0's Samuel Waite Johnson had introduced twenty seven years earlier. If they were a mite larger, then they looked dated by adherence to the outside frames the Great Western had fallen in love with and refused to divorce. Like Johnson, George Jackson Churchward did not rush to put his own designs on the rails, but developed his ideas by trying them out on new versions of Dean's engines. Churchward, in his research into the steam locomotive, reviewed and adopted ideas from both France and the United States, forging them into a completely new concept that went almost unnoticed among the rest of Britain's designers. The first indication that something was afoot was the record run by one of the new 'City' class, *City of Truro*, which approached and possibly exceeded 100mph, while running down Wellington Bank in Somerset on the 9th May 1904. While top train speeds had reached eighty miles an hour in the 1890s, due to the use of steel, better manufacturing techniques and large driving wheels, a locomotive that was free running to the extent that it could top a 'ton' with gravity assistance was something new. The 'new' item was the use of longer valve travel, giving better steam and exhaust port openings, and this was truly a new beginning.

115

Provenance: Development of William Dean standard gauge express locomotives for the GWR.

Designer: G. J. Churchward.

Principal Features: Double-framed (inside and outside frames), inside cylinders and valves, with long travel.

Principal Dimensions: Cylinders: Two, 18 in diameter, 26in stroke, inside frames.
Working Pressure: 195psi.
Tractive Effort: 17,345lb.
Driving wheels: 6ft 8 $^{1}/_{2}$in diameter.
Valves: Piston valves between frames, inside Stephenson Link Motion.
Weight in W. O: 55 tons 6cwt.

Figure 24: GWR 'City' 4-4-0.

Long travel valves

The idea that valves only need be moved just enough to give reasonable port openings in full gear was one that took firm root in the nineteenth century, and was not going to give way without a battle. Why this was the case is curious in itself. Murray's slide valve, first used in Blenkinsop's *Prince Royal*, probably had a travel similar to that of *Rocket* seventeen years later; the *Prince Royal* worked, and at a speed that can have given no clue as to the potential limits of slide valves moved by eccentrics. Ten years after adoption of Stephenson's Link Motion, in 1850, locomotives had an arrangement that gave four inches of travel to the valve, some expansive working, and, in full gear at least, a near ideal exhaust diagram. The problems of applying trip gears or cut-off plates to the railway locomotive, that gave the marine steam engine its advantage of economy, could not be solved satisfactorily.

In 1890, the combination of link motion and four inch valve travel still held sway after forty years; attempts to do something different had led in short order to disaster, and you have to ask the question 'Why?' Graphical analysis of Walschaerts' gear demonstrates, on little more than a sheet of 'A4', that more travel on the valve means more opening of the steam port. A handful of graphs will demonstrate both the effect of various valve travels derived from crosshead or eccentric, and the effect of taking the engine out of full gear. So why didn't the Victorians subject their locomotive valve gear to such a basic mathematical analysis? A century and more after the non-event, any answer to that question can only be speculative, and top of the list of speculations must be the effect the hierarchical structure of locomotive works management had on the adoption of new ideas.

It is little use pretending that the mechanics of human organisation are based primarily on the concept of a meritocracy, because they are not. Organisations are based on power, and any dictator will tell you that the way to remain at the top is to a) only employ 'yes men' and, b) get rid of anyone who dares disagree. Appointing, as happened after 1850, locomotive superintendents or chief mechanical engineers who were both good at organising and managing a workforce, and had the drive and ambition to get to the top, meant that the railway companies were not very likely to appoint young brains to solve, as Buddicom and Gooch had done fifteen years earlier, the fundamental problems that stopped the steam locomotive going faster. The locomotive superintendent needed to be able to manage a staff of thousands; it was asking a lot to expect that person to possess a spark of genius, or allow that spark to flourish under him. The long periods of tenure of Webb, Johnson and Stirling in the late nineteenth century, were paralleled by a period in which technical innovation effectively stalled on British railways.

The second question this poses is that if the railway companies were not a very fertile ground for innovation, then why weren't the private builders? The answer there is that for the most part in the nineteenth century, what the private builders made were low speed machines, and when they received orders from British main line companies, they were just that, orders. 'Thou shalt do this and nothing else.' As we have seen Stephenson's Link Motion was better at low speeds and short valve travels, and there was quite simply no demand for a more sophisticated set-up.

This still leaves unanswered the point that theoretically the problem is solvable on paper, and in a manner that leaves no room for doubt. Any professor of engineering or mathematics could have proposed the solution without having to go near a train. The Institute of Mechanical Engineers was formed in 1847; a goodly proportion of its members hailed from the rail industry. The inventor of a locomotive valve gear in 1860, that did what

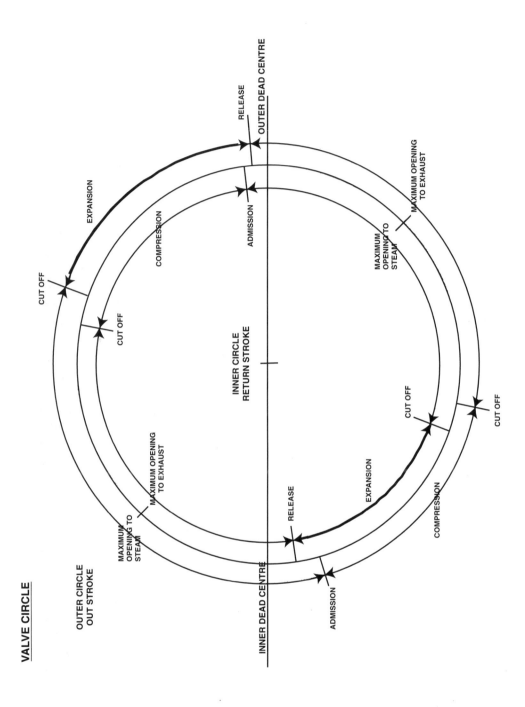

Figure 25: The Valve Circle.

Churchward ultimately made Walschaerts' gear do, could have booked his plinth in Trafalgar Square without further ado (or having to slaughter any foreigners). That no one achieved, between 1860 and 1900, what the master did in 1904-7 reflects strangely upon the backcloth of the age of inventors.

When it came to setting out the valve events of the steam locomotive on paper, the best that textbooks could come up with was the 'valve circle', and this is illustrated in Fig. 25, opposite. The valve circle is adequate in only one aspect; it shows when valves open and close relative to the position of the piston. This diagram does not display port opening velocities, port opening dimensions, the effect of 'cut-off', or variable 'lead'. In short, it does not tell the user anything useful about most of the matters that critically affect locomotive performance. Worse, it fails to explain the difference between the simple (sine wave) motion of Stephenson's gear and the compound motion of Walschaerts'. These were not the only link motions, but apart from shifting the event locations, the valve circle diagrams are the same for all valve gears. The superiority of graphical representation is that the effect of two derived motions is immediately obvious, that calculus can be applied to determine valve speed at any point (which is given by the gradient of the line of motion) and that areas under the curves give true representation of port openings.

In attributing George Jackson Churchward's solution to George Jackson Churchward, we are acknowledging the 'designer is king' rule. There are good grounds however to suggest that Churchward was the opposite of a dictator, employing young staff *and* encouraging them to think the unthinkable. The idea for long travel valves probably originated elsewhere, but Churchward gave it the light to thrive. The first 'Star' of 1907 had a valve travel in full gear of 6 7/8in, an increase of over 60% on the average for the time. This was a step change as fundamental as Robert Stephenson's multi-tubular boiler. By 1914 that travel had been increased to 7 1/4in. The travel was derived with 3 1/4in from the piston crosshead, equating to twice the 'lap'. The remainder of the travel came from the eccentric sheave, providing the valve opening and being controlled by the reverser in the cab. This was greater than was subsequently proved necessary, but as the 'Stars' had tortuous exhausts from the outside cylinders, having hit upon a solution to freer running and proper expansion of steam, adding a bit more travel to the valves when it was clear that the original design was not quite right, was an easy 'quick fix'.

Churchward's vision of the future of express locomotives was thus the result both of inspiration and careful and systematic experiment, experiments that produced, in addition to the valve settings, the intricately curved Belpaire type firebox and sharply coned boiler. This combination, when allied with steam pressures of first 200 and then 225psi and more efficient use of steam, resulted in locomotives of haulage capacity that were not far short of twice

the average of the rest of Britain's railways, when measured in pounds of coal per drawbar horsepower hour (dbhp/hr). Nor was this a five minute fantasy; these boilers could go up to 400,000 miles without a broken stay, and with top feed using the steam space as a water pre-heater, and trays to catch the resulting boiler sludge, set new standards of locomotive performance and reliability.

The first of the 'Saint' class of two cylinder 4-6-0's emerged from Swindon Works in 1904, and looked a complete break from all that had gone before, with a large, high-pitched boiler, outside cylinders and inside frames, on a railway that had shown a distinct preference for inside cylinders and outside frames. What was hidden from view was the magic that had been wrought on the valves and their operation. Churchward's arrangement of Stephenson's link motion addressed, as far as the gear allowed, issues of port openings and point of admission (lead), allowing the 'Saints' to run at cut offs of under 25%, giving a four- or five-fold expansion of steam. Steam pressure, set at 225psi, was forty to fifty pounds higher than the average on other railway's express locomotives

As with other Stephenson Link Motion fitted engines, the 'Saints' were markedly more powerful at low speed, when accelerating or climbing steep banks on long cut offs, when the valve travel was at a maximum. With piston valves inside the frames, the exhaust was explosively direct, leading to adoption of the adjustable blastpipe, with a 'jumper' top that lifted above a certain point of cut off. Whilst expensive, the 'Saints' justified their first cost by dramatically reduced running repairs and fuel bills, and for two decades were, by a margin, the best two cylinder express locomotives in the land. That they were not the best bar none was owing to the second Churchward design, the four cylinder 'Star' class.

The 'Stars' broke with Great Western tradition and used Walschaerts' valve gear in a form only adopted by that company on its four cylinder engines, deriving the valve motion from an internal eccentric, and operating the outside piston valves via rocker shafts. Dividing the drive between the front two driving axles allowed the valves to be driven without suffering from expansion problems caused by heating of valve spindles, at the expense of a tortuous exhaust from the outside cylinders. Apart from making the engines larger (and the belated fitting of high temperature superheaters and redesign of steam supply and exhaust) no further changes in Great Western express locomotive design took place after 1907, when the first 'Star' appeared, and this design of 4-6-0 was ultimately displaced only by diesels, after 1960. As front line motive power the 'Saints' and 'Stars' were for twenty years in a league of their own; other railway companies were unable to even remotely match Great Western express locomotive performance *and* economy. Just to rub salt in the wound, Churchward went one better and produced the definitive twentieth century British freight locomotive, the '2800' class of 2-8-0. Whilst this revolution will be discussed further in the chapter on twentieth century goods, so competent was this freight locomotive that it was only superseded by the very last of the standard designs for British Railways, the '9F' of 1954.

Churchward thus romped away almost unnoticed with the honours of the Edwardian age, while those in the master's shadow were having fun at their shareholders' expense. Leading the field in expenditure was George Whale at Crewe, where over thirty years, the quest for economy of production and running of locomotives had produced an express engine stock that was probably the most expensive to run and the least reliable in the land. Turning Webb's two, three and four cylinder compounds into scrap was doing no more than putting them out of their misery. To replace these machines, Whale had to design and build something new (it appears to have been inconceivable for a 'Chief' to contract out his design problems in 1904; contractors had to be told what to do, just as Fowler and Gresley told North British what was wanted for the 'Royal Scot' and 'B17' classes between the wars). The fact that George Whale went for a large 4-4-0, to be named somewhat confusingly 'Precursors', rather than an 'Atlantic' or a 4-6-0, then being actively built to replace the 4-4-0 on all the other main lines (Midland excepted) is virtual confirmation of both timidity and conservatism on his part.

Almost anything was better than the Webb 'Compounds', but the 'Precursor' class was barely competent by early twentieth century standards, and in the slack times of the 1880s and 1890s, standards of finish and quality at Crewe had fallen well behind the 'gold standard' of Swindon, and behind most of the rest of the railway workshops in the British Isles also. George Whale's successor from 1909, Charles John Bowen-Cooke, was also faced with the need to push the Premier Line kicking and screaming into the decade of the First War, and to that end built the four cylinder 'Claughton' 4-6-0 as the definitive West Coast motive power. The 'Claughtons' were more powerful than the 'Precursors', but the standards of their performance, particularly in coal consumption and reliability, left so much to be desired. When set against the much smaller Midland 4-4-0 'Compounds', in the comparative trials of the 1920's, the performances of the 'Claughtons' could only be described as woefully inadequate, though that epithet should have been be applied to numerous other 'express' locomotives of the times as well. In the Edwardian age rose tinted spectacles seemed to have been widely issued to observers of the railway scene; it was to be over a decade before reality began to bite hard on issues of locomotive design.

The Midland Railway, having done very nicely with its stock of handsome, inside cylindered 4-4-0's, met the challenge of the new century with a dabble in the muddy pond of compounding. A workable arrangement of three cylinders for compound operation had been proposed by W. M. Smith, chief draughtsman of the North Eastern Railway, and Johnson put the scheme into effect with an experimental batch of five locomotives built between 1901-3. Carrying boilers pressed to 195psi, the engines were both powerful and economical, and Johnson's successor, Richard Mountford Deeley, in his six years' tenure to 1909, raised the working pressure to 220psi, gave the driving wheels an extra six inches to make them seven feet in diameter, and produced the best British express compound ever. Midland Railway No. 1000 is a rare survivor from the era of compound propulsion, and was a good way in advance of the rest of what can only be described as a motley assortment of experiments. Deeley's departure in 1909 marked the end of locomotive development on the Midland Railway. The tracks of this company would not see another new design of express locomotive until 1934.

The problem of the 'Compounds' low starting tractive effort, that had plagued Webb, was addressed by Johnson allowing the three cylinders to use high pressure steam on starting, moving to compound operation when at speed. There was really only one problem with these engines; as not-too-large 4-4-0's they were just about adequate for the first decade of the twentieth century, but by the middle of the third, were too small for front line service.

The large numbers built as a result of the London Midland and Scottish Railway not having anything else worthy of the name 'express', were outmoded, outclassed and faintly ridiculous when set against their contemporaries of 1925. The cut-away 'Compound' illustrated in Fig. 26 gives an idea of the limits of this modest design. All of the steam the engine used after starting in 'simple' mode had to pass the pitifully small centre cylinder piston valve. Slide valves served the low pressure cylinders and a common steam chest acted as a receiver. While such an arrangement could have used Walschaerts' gear, this and other compound engines of the time were firmly wedded to Stepenson's Link Motion, with all the implied limits of rough running on short cut-offs and miserable economy in full gear. The Midland's 'Compounds' were only good when compared with locomotives of similar ilk, but it was the need for greater haulage capacity (most engineers had given up on better thermal efficiency, believing that the superheater had done all that could be done in that direction) that was driving the railway companies to the 'Atlantic' and the 4-6-0 in 1914.

The problem of greater haulage capacity was one that had four principal components: axle load, adhesion, thermal efficiency and steaming capacity. Steaming capacity, the ability to boil water, depends on the size of the grate and the surface area of the heat exchangers, and while the modest dimensions of the grate caused problems, the weight of the firebox that landed on the coupled wheels proved critical. Enlarging the grate threatened to overload the coupled axles. Two axles loaded up to eighteen tons each, accommodated perhaps three tons potential drawbar pull, plenty for even the heaviest expresses. Thermal efficiency, as Churchward demonstrated, made all your other problems little ones, and as no one else cracked this, they were landed with a host of potential and actual insuperables when seeking more power and speed.

It is perhaps symptomatic of attitudes to locomotive design in Edwardian Britain that superheating was more often used as a way of reducing boiler pressures (and thus maintenance costs) than it was to improve thermal efficiency and power outputs. Making a locomotive larger, in theory makes it more powerful; with the 'Atlantic' layout you gain a wide firebox but lose weight on the coupled wheels. The big 'plus' of the 'Atlantic' was that the rest of the locomotive was unchanged from the 4-4-0; pistons still drove the leading axle, there was space between the frames, and the locomotive was more stable and rode smoothly as a result of the trailing axle. That loss of adhesion though meant that train loads could not be dramatically increased, which is precisely what was happening in the decade of the First War.

4-6-0s proved to be dynamically very different animals from the 4-4-0. Driving the leading coupled axle only proved impractical; Churchward divided the drive between front and centre axles on the four cylinder 'Stars', and most other subsequent designs of 4-6-0 drove the middle axle. Outside cylinder versions of this type proved to be some of the roughest riding of twentieth century locomotives, meaning that the engines received a very mixed reception from their crews. The lesson of the 'Planet' on Newton's law on action and reaction held true in 1914 just as it had done eighty years earlier; a quantum

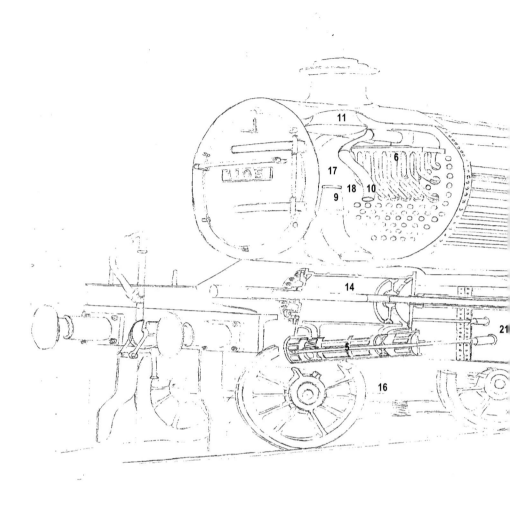

Provenance: Development of the Midland inside cylindered 4-4-0 with W M Smith's three cylinder layout for compound operation.
Designer: S. W. Johnson.

Principal Features: Three cylinder compound with one high pressure inside cylinder and two low pressure outside cylinders. Inside Stephenson valve gear with one high pressure piston valve and one low pressure slide valve. Reducing valve for 'simple' starting.

Figure 26: Section 'Compound'.

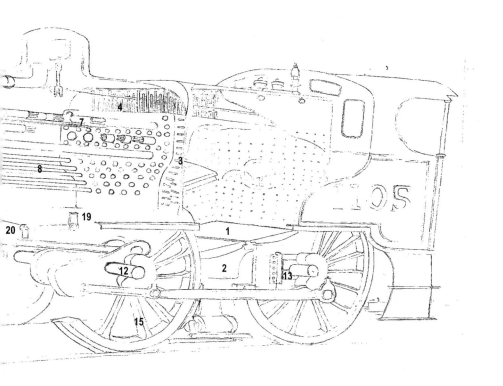

Principal Dimensions:Cylinders: Three, one high pressure 19in diameter, two low pressure 21in diameter, 26in stroke.
Working Pressure: 195psi.
Tractive Effort: 21,840lb (when starting)
Driving wheels: 6ft 6in diameter.
Valves: One piston valve (high pressure), one slide valve (low pressure) .
between frames, inside Stephenson Link Motion.
Weight in W O: 61 tons 14cwt.

1 Firegrate. 2 Ashpan. 3 side stays. 4 crown stays. 5 piston valve. 6 superheater header. 7 superheater flue and element. 8 smoke tube. 9 blastpipe. 10 steam pipes. 11 petticoat pipe. 12 crank axle (eccentrics omitted for clarity). 13 wheel bearing. 14 inside piston and cylinder. 15 driving wheel. 16 bogie. 17 smokebox. 18 blower. 19 reversing reach rod. 20 weighbar. 21 motion plate.

leap in power on a limited wheelbase meant substantial lateral forces, a bumpy ride, and the risk of derailment in the wrong circumstances. Keeping the coupled wheelbase as short as possible reduced the forces on the track on tight curves, but meant that the length of the firebox, carried over the third axle, was constrained by the closeness of the middle axle. That middle axle included a crank on three cylinder engines, two on inside cylinder locomotives. Adding an extra driving axle thus meant a complete redesign of the locomotive, chassis and boiler, and as locomotive engineers had spent many decades simply enlarging previous designs, starting again from scratch proved difficult for most of them.

The two East Coast companies, the Great Northern, and North Eastern railways (the third 'partner' on the east coast, the North British, spent most of its existence in the third division of locomotive design) had always displayed a certain independence of thought in locomotive design. After Patrick Stirling's retirement in 1895, H. A. Ivatt supplanted the single driver engines of his predecessor with a series of locomotives with the 'Atlantic' 4-4-2 wheel arrangement, characterised by a wide firebox on the rear carrying axle. Ivatt first tried four cylinders, and a brief flirtation with compounds, before settling for two cylinder propulsion. Both Wilson Worsdell and Vincent Raven used the 'Atlantic' wheel arrangement for express traction, but the North Eastern was not wedded to this or the 4-4-0, for it too built the larger 4-6-0, though with conspicuously less success than the Great Western.

The North Eastern, like so many other companies, found the transition to the 4-6-0 a difficult one, when the need for increased haulage capacity arrived in the run-up to the First World War. Free-running and low maintenance small locomotives (the North Eastern had classes of express locomotive that could run 200,000 miles between works overhauls) even if heavy coal burners were acceptable only so long as train loads remained modest. The same was true in Scotland, where the Caledonian Railway, long dependent on the 4-4-0 for its top link traction, built an impressive batch of large inside cylindered 4-6-0's for express passenger work, of which the famous *Cardean* was a member. Impressive or no, *Cardean* and her sisters were outclassed by Swindon products of Churchward's era, and were unable even to measure up to the best of contemporary 4-4-0's.

Perhaps the most significant event of this period, apart from the distance between best and rest, was the appointment of Nigel Gresley as chief mechanical engineer of the Great Northern in 1911. Gresley's most significant contribution to the age was the concept of the 'express goods' in the shape of a three cylinder mogul (2-6-0) with the Gresley-Holcroft version of Walschaerts' valve gear, using derived motion for the inside piston valve. Gresley's fame however rests on a later age, and while his first express 'Pacific' (4-6-2) emerged in 1922, it was construction by Charles Collet in 1923 of the first 'Castle' class of Great Western four cylinder 4-6-0, and publication of test results on that locomotive, that made the rest of the locomotive engineering establishment sit up and take notice. The differences between them, when it came to the nitty gritty, were boiler pressure and valve gear, and if raising boiler pressures on their own would have achieved little without the valve gear being altered, then it can be surmised that the issue of valve events in 1925, was still one that locomotive engineers did not study assiduously enough.

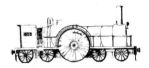

Chapter Thirteen:

Exchange is no Robbery:
An Outbreak of Co-operation, 1925-30

Little in the way of locomotive development took place during the First World War, but the railway companies' experience during the war was that of enormous demand set against minimal resources. The ability of main line companies' works to adapt their manufacturing plant to almost every form of munitions production surprised military and Parliament alike (it shouldn't have done; both sides in the Boer War used the railway workshops, at Mafeking and Bloemfontein, to produce munitions). The ability of the railways to survive on very short materials and manpower commons surprised the railways themselves.

What the railways could *not* do was resist asset stripping of their systems to fund the war effort. The inevitable result was that the whole system was close to bankruptcy in 1920. Few companies were able to invest in renewal of their infrastructure, reduced almost to rubble by over-use and less than minimal maintenance. All were feeling the cold wind of competition from truck, bus and, in places, the tram; these fifth-columnists would only too shortly be joined by the private car. The Westminster government's solution (it had no intention of paying reparations, despite demanding them) was to force the railway companies into marriages of convenience, forming from the multitude the 'Big Four', of which the only recognisable surviving company was the Great Western.

In the other three groups of railways, there were a few large mainline companies and a greater or lesser host of small ones. The London and North Eastern Railway found the North Eastern, Great

Northern, Great Eastern and North British Railways perhaps the most harmonious of partners. The London Midland and Scottish, with Midland and Premier Line performing a cat and dog act, was the scene of a struggle for power that was to leave the largest of the big four without an express passenger locomotive worthy of the name. The Great Western's survival almost intact was to lead to an engineering inertia that would last to the end of steam.

That inertia appears to have been underpinned by no small measure of arrogance; the Great Western lost no time in laying waste to the locomotives of 'conquered' companies. By 1960, the Great Western locomotive stock contained just three pre-1923 non-GW engines. The only 'non-GW' classes to last well into the 1950s were the small batch of ex Railway Operating Department (War Office) Great Central designed 2-8-0 '8Ks', purchased and 'Great Westernised' in the 1920s and a handful of tank engine designs, such as the Taff Vale 'A' class. Not a single locomotive, designed by any 'chief', for the Cambrian, Taff Vale, Rhymney or Barry railways escaped ultimate slaughter (though one or two were sold out of service rather than cut up) and neither did any 'bought in' design, handed over by nine of the ten smaller South Wales companies. Those 1960 exceptions were one engine from the Cardiff Railway, the prototype Davies and Metcalfe 'Vale of Rheidol' locomotive, and a shunter acquired from a contractor.

The single winner, if 'winner' is defined, as in war, as 'he who loses least', from the grouping, was the new Southern Railway. As bit-part players on the nineteenth century canvas of locomotive development, the Southern's principal constituent companies were the South Eastern and Chatham, London Brighton and South Coast, and London and South Western railways. Individually these companies had no part to play in the prime coal- and iron-shifting task that reaped in profits for the northern and Welsh-based concerns; the industrial revolution had nearly passed them by. In the 1920s that situation could be seen to be changing, and as a single company, the Southern Railway found itself in a position to contribute to the core history of the steam locomotive, albeit not always in the manner that it would have wished. Illustrating this point is the 'King Arthur' class locomotive of Fig. 27. As a none-too-big 4-6-0, with six foot seven inch driving wheels, such a locomotive would have found little place outside the gentle rolling countryside of southern England, and as a design it really only advanced Urie's concept of seven years earlier by modernising the valve gear. The boiler was too small for shifting heavy loads at high speed over long and arduous gradients, and the rating ('5P') by British Railways, showed that it really was only a 'Black Five' with bigger wheels.

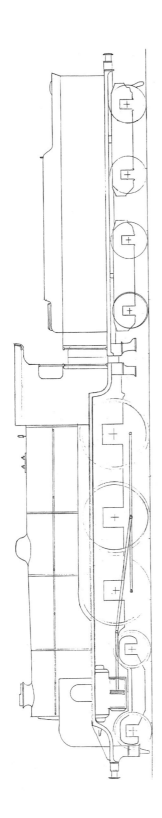

Provenance: Development of R W Urie Express 4-6-0 for the London and South Western Railway.
Designer: R. E. L. Maunsell.

Principal Features: Small express locomotive, parallel boiler, round top firebox, smoke deflectors.

Principal Dimension:

Cylinders: Two, 20 ¹/₂in diameter, 28in stroke, outside frames.
Working Pressure: 200psi.
Tractive Effort: 25,320lb.
Driving wheels: 6ft 7in diameter
Valves: Piston valves, Walschaerts gear.
Weight in W. O: 80 tons 19cwt.

**Figure 27:
King Arthur**

To consider the Southern fully at this point though, is inappropriate, for the single most significant event of 1925 was the decision of the 'Big Four' to co-operate and swap engines with each other. In this way the Great Western's secret was given an airing that no one could ignore, with the truth of Collet's claims on both performance and economy laid bare for all to see, and more pertinently, copy.

The locomotive tests and exchanges of 1925 and 1926 were as avidly watched and debated by the public as the Rainhill trials of ninety five years earlier. The origin of the exchanges though, are slightly mysterious. That they occurred at all was due to company rivalries and competition for every last passenger and ton of freight having abated. Chief mechanical engineers no longer felt that they were giving away commercial advantage if they freely discussed their work with each other. This was a far cry from the engine kidnapping and deliberate obstruction practised only twenty years earlier, and showed that co-operation paid dividends, just as well as did competition. The actual exchange only involved the Great Western and the London and North Eastern railways, (the LMS 'borrowed' a 'Castle', and lent the GWR a 'Compound' in return, though quite what they were to do with a machine of this kind is not clear).

In the three years after the grouping of 1923, extensive tests were made of the inherited engine resources of the four companies (we will presume that the Great Western tested the engines it inherited before it scrapped them, though there is nothing to suggest that the GWR so much as considered the possibility that any others' products could be on a par with their own). As is the habit in these matters, the way in which those tests were carried out coloured the results, in the case of the LMS at least, to the point where if it had been said that black was white, then the test results would have gone a good way to proving it. What the testing of their own engines on both LMS and LNER did *not* show, was how far adrift even the most modern designs on these railways were from best practice.

To our eyes, accustomed to rigorous testing regimes of the late twentieth century, the way in which testing in the 1920's was carried out seems almost crass in its ignorance of basics. The LMS tested its engines on the long 1 in 100 grades of the Settle and Carlisle, and on the demanding Preston to Carlisle section of the West Coast. Almost nowhere else, south of Perth and east of Offa's Dyke, were there operating conditions on a par with these stretches of railway, the former well aligned and only lightly trafficked, the latter busy to the point of congestion and including two long and severe grades where even expresses were in the habit of 'whistling for a banker'. The chances of determining the best all-round performer from such arbitrary tests on untypical terrain were almost nil. As a data collection exercise it was probably good fun, but that is about as far as the tests went. The use of two routes at least had some moderating effect on the 'home advantage' rule. The subsequent decision to adopt the Midland 'Compound' 4-4-0 as a standard express engine at least shows that if you plan a farce well enough, then the laughter will ultimately be at, not with, you.

The LMS tests of 1925 and 1926

The comparative testing of locomotives was not new in 1925; testing had been developed in the middle of the nineteenth century in an effort to determine the critical factors involved in locomotive performance, with decidedly mixed results. Churchward had imported French locomotives prior to the First World War to test the theories he was advancing on simple versus compound working. What was absent in the tests of 1925-26 was the setting out of appropriate test conditions, and determination of the objectives of the tests. Without these basics, test results are worse than useless, because they represent conditions that are not going to be found in daily practice, and are not in any way representative of the work engines would perform, day in, day out. As with all heat engines, each locomotive will work at maximum efficiency only within a fairly narrow set of parameters, and if obliged to operate outside those parameters will show either a dramatic falling off in performance, or a rise in maintenance costs, and frequently *both*. The key to understanding where the LMS went wrong in its tests is in the assumption that one or more of the locomotives was suitable for the tasks envisaged, whereas it was fairly obvious to a neutral observer that none of them was.

The test route on the Midland involved running express trains from Leeds to Carlisle and vice versa, 113 miles, with loads varying from about 220 to 360 tons, on schedules that demanded average speeds of 42-52 mph. Even in 1925, this sort of performance was seen more as catechism for Catholics rather than rocket science for Rastafarians (and little different from the speeds of the 1870's). From Leeds, the route was both well aligned and four tracked to Shipley, where there was a severe speed restriction, then a mix of double and quadruple track to Keighley and Skipton, both restricted on curves through the stations. Until this latter point gradients are modest, though against the train, but from Skipton to Hellifield the line rises sharply to cross the Aire/Ribble watershed and is somewhat less than straight. After a brief respite to Settle Junction, climbing is then continuous, bar half a mile, to Blea Moor, at 1 in 100. The gradient then eases through Dent and Garsdale, where there were watertroughs, just short of the summit at Aisgill. The downhill run from there to Petteril Bridge, the junction with the Newcasle and Carlisle line, is as fast and straight as anyone could wish. Twenty miles out of the hundred and thirteen were thus steeply graded, and allowing for traffic at both ends, and slowings for Shipley, Keighley and Skipton, a top speed of 60-65mph would see the fastest schedule kept, with ample opportunity to run at 80mph plus from Aisgill northwards, if needed. The southbound run is not significantly different, though the ascending gradients are less steep, but longer.

On such a route, little over 50mph was asked of the five participants, and in retrospect perhaps the most demanding aspect of the test was to reach the watertroughs at Garsdale without an intermediate stop. The two Midland engines were both relatively small 4-4-0's, one a compound, the other an inside-cylindered Johnson derived design. Though superheated, in concept both locomotives were twenty years old, and neither type would see any further development. The two London and North Western designs were both large 4-6-0's, the inside cylindered 'Prince of Wales' class and the four cylinder 'Claughton'. No more of either class would be built despite their relative modernity, though the 'Claughtons' would be modified in an effort to mitigate their many shortcomings in the years prior to the LMS employing William Stanier. The fifth engine was a Caledonian Railway 4-4-0, of outdated design, and so far below the required standard that it only had a single run.

It is tempting to speculate that the entry of this last engine was due to Scottish influence, rather than sheer desperation of finding anything worthy of the term 'express'. The Midland engines had by far the largest numbers of test runs, and were consistently burning less coal than the rest. That 'less coal' was over 30% *more* than the Great Western 'Castle', which would record average speeds of over 80mph in the not too distant future.

The tests on the West Coast were a little more circumspect, in that this was a double track route busy with slow freight, and fifty miles an hour was a fair average speed in such circumstances. The

Midland 'Compounds' again came out on top, this time against Caledonian and Lancashire and Yorkshire Railway 4-6-0's, as well as the 'Prince of Wales' and 'Claughton' classes.

For the purpose of testing the performance of their locomotives, three of the pre-grouping companies, the North Eastern, Great Western, and Lancashire and Yorkshire Railways, had built their own dynamometer cars, the latter company's car coming into the LMS's possession at the grouping, and used on the test trains. The dynamometer car was capable of recording speed, drawbar pull, and by integration, locomotive power output (drawbar horse power, dbhp). Because of water pick up from the troughs at Garsdale (on the Settle and Carlisle) and Dillicar (on the West Coast, south of Tebay), actual evaporation performed by the boiler could only be estimated, though coal consumption was accurately determined, enabling calculation of coal/mile and coal/dbhp/hr, the latter being the only real 'result'. It is a matter of record that checking of the satisfactory operation of the LMS dynamometer car prior to each test was not rigorously carried out, and it was subsequently discovered that the results were less accurate than anticipated owing to parts of the recording mechanism being seized.

Nigel Gresley's Lucky Day

The LMS discovered the error of its ways only too soon, for the real winner of 1925 was Nigel Gresley, who had built a big 'Pacific' in 1922, when he was at Doncaster with the Great Northern, and had not been able to make it go — well, not as well as it should. At the Wembley Exhibition of 1924, Gresley's engine was positioned next to Collett's 'Castle' (*Caerphilly Castle*) and the 'little 'un' was proclaimed the more powerful of the two. In true school yard 'swap yer and prove it' fashion, the two companies did, and proved it was. Once again the tests were not really fair, *Caerphilly Castle* had much the easier time of it on the East Coast main line (straight and not very hilly), while the Great Western chose the curvy switchback of the 'Berks and Hants' (Paddington to Plymouth via Reading, Westbury and Exeter), that could not be learnt in a day, and included South Brent and Hemerdon banks that were far steeper than anything on the engine's home patch. That said, the 'Castle' walked away with the honours in time-keeping and fuel economy, and Nigel Gresley did not need a great deal more paper than the proverbial back of an envelope to show that once again valve design and boiler pressure were the key differences.

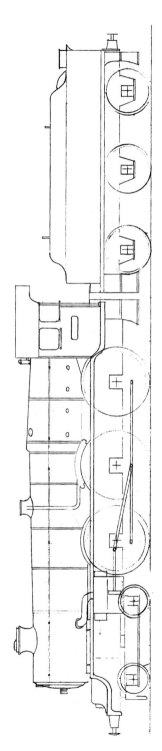

Figure 28: Castle.

Provenance: Post WW1 development of the 'Star' class of 1907 with improved steam distribution and larger boiler.
Designer: C. Collett.

Principal Features: Express 4-6-0 with four cylinders, inside valve gear and divided drive. Sharply coned high pitched boiler.

Principal Dimensions

Cylinders : Four, 16in diameter, 26in stroke.
Working Pressure: 225psi.
Tractive Effor: 31,625lb at 85% boiler pressure.
Driving wheels: 6ft $8^{1}/_{2}$in diameter.
Valve: Piston valves, inside Walschaerts gear with rocking shafts operating the outside valves.
Weight in W. O: 79 tons 17cwt, tender 46tons 14cwt.

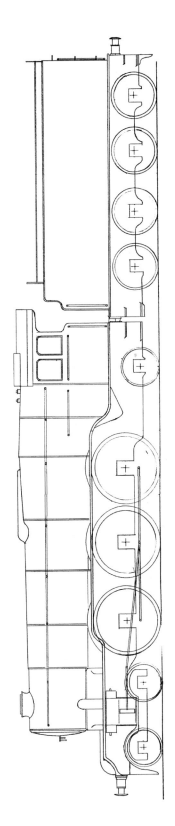

Provenance: Development of Great Northern 'Pacific' of 1922 with higher boiler pressure, and long travel valves.
Designer: H. N. Gresley.

Principal Features: Express locomotive, three cylinders, derived motion inside valve drive, coned boiler and wide firebox.

Principal Dimnsions

Cylinders: Three, 19in diameter, 26in stroke.
Working pressure: 220psi.
Tractive Effort: 32,909lb.
Driving wheels: 6ft 8in diameter.
Valves: Piston valves, Gresley-Holcroft derived.
Walschaerts gear.
Weights in W. O: 96 tons 5cwt.

Figure 29: A3 Pacific

Perhaps this tale is a little too apocryphal for the average man in the street, for there is an alternative version, which runs slightly differently. Nigel Gresley, it has to be admitted, had a reputation for stubbornness, and when an assistant suggested that the use of long lap and travel valves might work a minor miracle on the performance of the new 'Pacifics', Gresley apparently turned it down flat. The chief engineers of the 'Big Four' met informally, the usual venue being Maunsell's office at Waterloo, and as both Maunsell and Collett were already converts to the use of Churchward's valve settings, it seems quite likely that, while Gresley was not the kind of man to take telling from a minion, he was quite prepared to listen to his equals. Such an exchange of locomotives was probably going to need approval at board level, and the Wembley Exhibition probably did no more than provide the excuse Gresley was looking for to put the matter in both the directors', and the public's eyes, where it would be difficult to ignore. There are more ways of killing the cat than an overdose of cream.

Spencer's proposal of 1924, to adopt the revised valve settings of the Great Western, meant quite a major rebuild of the Pacific valve gear, and it was not until 1926 that this took place on a single engine as a trial. The result was a 28% saving in coal, down from 50lb/mile to 36. With results like that, Nigel Gresley's 'conversion on the road to Doncaster' was a foregone conclusion.

Within three years, Gresley had raised the boiler pressure of his 'A1' Pacifics forty pounds to 220psi, and altered their valve motion to replicate the long lap and travel format of the Great Western engine. The result was a locomotive capable of 100mph on service trains, that could run mile after mile on the flat at 80-90 mph, and be pressed up the long 1 in 200 grades north of Peterborough at over 70 mph. Introduction of non-stop working on the East Coast between London and Edinburgh, made possible by that new found coal economy, the strategically placed watertroughs of the pre-grouping Great Northern, and North Eastern railways, double manning and corridor connections in specially built tenders, commenced with the *Flying Scotsman* doing the honours in May 1928.

Watertroughs

The watertrough was invented by John Ramsbottom, when he was locomotive engineer of the 'Premier Line', and the first set installed on the Chester and Holyhead Railway at Mochdre. To pick up water from them, locomotive tenders were fitted with a scoop, hinged at the bottom, leading to a pipe that discharged into the water tank. The velocity of the locomotive forced water up the pipe, and generally water could be picked up by this method at any speed above about fifteen miles an hour. The hinged scoop was moved by a rod and pedestal arrangement, and it was usual for the scoop to be dipped into the water by upwards of half an inch. Tenders could be filled completely, but the level of the water in the trough depended on how much the previous pickup had extracted, because the low head of the feed pipes made for slow refilling.

Watertroughs were installed on the East Coast, West Coast, Great Western and Midland main lines (there were none on the lines of the constituent companies that formed the Southern Railway), and at selected other places where long distance expresses and freight could benefit from the ten to fifteen minute saving of not having to stop for water.

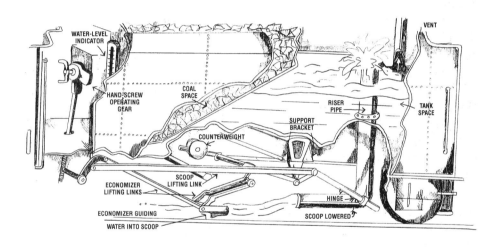

Figure 30: Water Pick-Up.

The location of watertroughs posed a number of problems, for the length of line had to be level and free of junctions, level crossings and crossovers. At either end the line had to rise slightly to avoid having to put a stopend on the trough, which would then be vulnerable to being knocked off by a scoop not being raised in time. Supplying water was a challenge that gravity alone found difficult; pumps were needed to cope with extraction. As up to half of the water would be spilt, four or five thousand gallons, or more, needed to be fed after each pass, and line and ballast drainage had to cope with regular sluicing, which was a major challenge to stability of the permanent way. Ice was always a risk in winter, and the Midland's troughs at Garsdale were both the highest in the world, and steam heated.

The East Coast main line, which as we shall see, put its water troughs to good use, was equipped with troughs at Langley (Stevenage), Werrington (Peterborough), Muskham (Newark) and Scrooby (Bawtry), all fairly evenly spaced on the Great Northern section. There was then a long gap to the first North Eastern troughs at Wiske Moor (Northallerton), followed by a further gap to Lucker (Beal, Northumberland). The North British section was without troughs. While the southern section thus had pickup points at 40-50 mile intervals, this stretched to 80 miles and more north of the Trent, posing a challenge to enginemen in the non-stop era, only partially mitigated by introduction of high capacity eight wheel tenders.

Near-apoplexy resulted on the LMS, when the LNER commenced its non-stop runs. The LMS 'Castle' borrowing in 1926 had shown how poor their locomotives were in comparison. The LMS then proceeded to order, in spite of possessing more works capacity than anyone else, a job lot of fifty, three cylinder express locomotives, on a design and build contract from North British Locomotive Ltd., in 1927. North British (the largest private locomotive builder in Britain after World War One) were left to do most of the detail design, but boiler and firebox layout were dictated by the Derby design office, and the engines looked very much 'Midland' in origin. These engines became known as the 'Royal Scot' class, and saved a lot of red faces on the LMS, as by sheer good fortune they worked 'straight out of the box', and delivered most of what was promised of them. The fact that the engine in both concept and ultimate layout was couched from a set of drawings provided by the Southern Railway's chief engineer, R. E. L. Maunsell, of his four cylinder 4-6-0 'Lord Nelson' class, is an indication of just how badly the LMS had slipped, and of the good work the Southern was putting into its express locomotive design. Fifty locomotives from an outside supplier may have saved the porker from the processor in the short term, but it required a revolution in thinking at the LMS to drag its locomotive design office kicking and screaming into the twentieth century, and that was not to achieved until the 1930's.

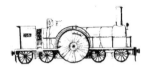

Chapter Fourteen:

Racehorses and a Racetrack:
The East Coast Main Line, 1928-1939

In the grouping of 1923, the LNER had gained three main lines out of London: to Norwich, to Edinburgh/Aberdeen via York, and to Manchester via nowhere and everywhere. In its policy decisions of the late 1920's, the LNER board chose the Great Northern/North Eastern/North British east coast route to be developed to the practical exclusion of the other two, which in effect became secondary routes. To develop the east coast fully needed resources that were probably beyond the means of the company to deliver, but in the field of locomotive design Nigel Gresley was able to deliver the goods (or rather the passengers) in a fashion that was both a spectacular technical success, and did much to salvage the commercial bacon of the LNER. Before we look at these locomotives, it is worth while to cast a glimpse at the route that was the scene of those successes.

The Great Northern main line, from Kings Cross to its junction with the North Eastern six miles north of Doncaster was and is both straight and, except for the start out of Kings Cross, easily graded. Four tracked most of the way to Stoke Summit north of Peterborough, then double to its end on connection with the North Eastern six miles beyond Doncaster. Speed restrictions were few; the curves at Offord, south of Huntingdon, Peterborough, and for the flat crossing at Newark. Watertroughs were in abundance, and gradients to cross watersheds out of/into the London Basin, and the Ouse/Trent, while long, were designed for fast transit. North of

Newark, the east coast was effectively flat to Newton Aycliffe, on the North Eastern section in County Durham, and without speed restriction, Selby and York apart. After Newton Aycliffe gradients and curves dictated speed all the way to Aberdeen. In traffic terms there was a goods and mineral flow to the capital from Newcastle southwards, though alternative routes were available for freight to avoid all the double track sections, which were more numerous then than now. Major traffic flows (including ships!) across the route made Selby to Barlby West Junction, Naburn to York, and others, potential and actual bottlenecks.

The main line then presented a number of problems to the locomotive engineer; long stretches of line, much of it uphill, where sustained high speed would be essential if end to end times were to be reduced for the fastest through journeys. The 1920s eight and a quarter hour schedule for the four hundred (less six and a bit) miles from London to Edinburgh allowed plenty of time to stop and admire the scenery. Secondly, there were slower trains which had to use the main line, and fast tracks on the four track sections, and these included second string passenger and express freight, such as fish, which ran at particular times of the day to suit industry. Thirdly, there was heavy goods and mineral traffic, which out of necessity and economy could not always go by another route; and finally, at the south end, there was an intensive commuter service.

All of these various traffics needed the right motive power. Nigel Gresley's tenure as chief mechanical engineer, for the southern section at least, had commenced in 1911, and included almost a decade in which little new design had been introduced due to the Great War and its aftermath. There was thus a need for the right machines to haul all sorts of traffic in the 1930s, to replace those of his predecessor which were worn out, outdated and/or outclassed.

To haul the heaviest and fastest expresses had been the reason for emergence of the first 'Pacifics' in 1922, and the reasons for the selection of Gresley's design over that of Vincent Raven, the retiring North Eastern engineer, probably centre upon the 'well he would choose his own design, wouldn't he' reason rather than any initial substantial technical superiority. While the locomotives were adequate for the task, it was obvious that there were limits imposed (as we have seen) both in speed and coal consumption, that mitigated against significant acceleration of services in the 1920s, even allowing for the fact that average speeds were hardly pushing 50mph, much less sixty. The school yard swap changed all that.

Transformation of the 'A1' Pacific into the 'A3', with redesigned valves and higher boiler pressure, opened up the prospect of an era of high speed running that the non-stop run of 1928 presented as a first step. Gresley's fastest racehorses also represented the final, mature configuration of Walschaerts' valve gear, the best and most reliable actuation system for express steam locomotive valves in the twentieth century.

Walschaerts' Valve Gear

As briefly discussed in chapter nine, Egide Walschaerts' valve gear stole the show in the first three decades of the twentieth century. That it had not swept Stephenson's Link Motion into the dustbin of history in the nineteenth century was due primarily to the short travel of slide valves then in use. Short travel valves operated by link motion run in full gear made for powerful locomotives, because a lot of steam entered the cylinder. The same locomotive with Walschaerts' gear was more economical because it made better use of the steam, but it could not do the same work, particularly up hills. The one item that throttled Link Motion equipped engines was the variable lead; take the engine out of full gear and the inlet valve for the steam did not open until the out stroke was well under way. Walschaerts gear had constant lead, whatever the 'cut-off', but this was mitigated by the exhaust valves opening earlier as the engine was linked up, and closing earlier as well.

The valve movement of 4in. used on the 'Crewe Type' engines of 1850, was still the norm in 1890. If the valve lap is $1^{1}/_{2}$in, to give some expansive working, then only 1in of travel is generated by the eccentric. Take engines with this setting out of full gear and the steam port is both narrow and only opens slowly. In other words, poor as Stephenson's gear is, it is not marginally worse than Walschaerts' overall, and it has a whopping advantage in full gear because of the large port openings. As we have seen in Chapter twelve, increasing the valve travel transformed Walschaets' gear from second best to second to none.

Fig. 31 demonstrates the effect of two derived motions; as the engine was linked up from the eccentric, the travel of the valve tends to that derived from the piston. If the engine ran on very short cut offs, the inlet valve opening would be less than $^{1}/_{10}$th of an inch, and the exhaust opened after little more than half of the piston stroke.

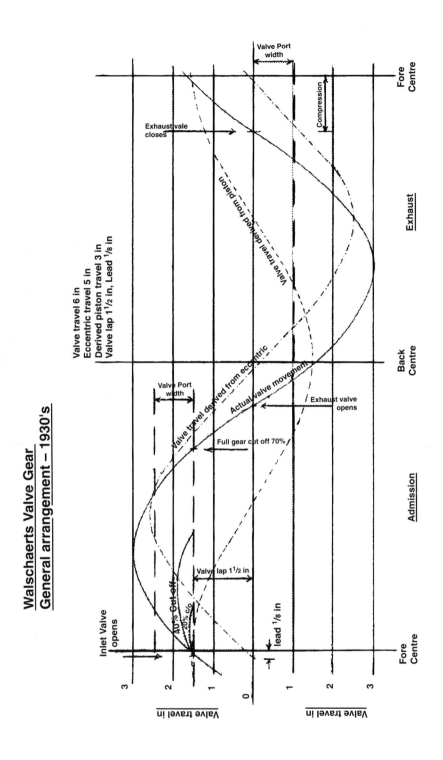

Figure 31: Walschaerts gear, 1930.

Walschaerts' gear in its final form (see Figure 31, opposite) demonstrated the ability to expand steam four or five times in a single cylinder, and was superior to Stephenson's because of the constant 'lead'. It did not offer an ideal exhaust at all cut offs, and the poor exhaust diagram at short cut-offs meant that in the 1930s, the hunt was still on for something better. Likewise, the steam port openings were very narrow at short cut offs, and speed of opening and closing of inlet valves sluggish. The reason for the dominance of this gear was its simplicity, and poppet valves, which were (theoretically at least) much better all round performers, were dogged for many years by poor actuation systems, higher first cost and maintenance, and inferior precision of control.

The adoption of Walschaerts' gear by engineers in the 1920s and 1930s was thus on the grounds of its superiority over the till then dominant Stephenson gear, and its simplicity and lower cost than poppet valves. The general parameters illustrated opposite were not diverged from dramatically; Gresley made his valves travel $5^3/_4$ inches, Bulleid 6.1 inches; Lap varied between $1^1/_4$ and $1^5/_8$ inches, a lead of $^1/_8$th or $^1/_4$ inch was normal. It was this motion, with these critical dimensions, that was to last the steam locomotive for the rest of its days, and it was good enough to be the fastest, too.

With the Holcroft-Gresley derived valve gear for three-cylinder locomotives, graphical representation solves the conundrum of the higher horse power output of the middle cylinder. The motion for the inside cylinder is taken from both outside cylinders. It can be seen, therefore, that the motion of the middle valve is not, as with the outside valves, a compound motion derived from the addition of two sine waves. The compound motion of two sine waves at an angle to each other produces a non-uniform curve. Combining the two non-uniform curves of the outside valves produces a further, but *different*, non-uniform curve. The area under this latter curve is larger than that of the curves it derives from, and the valve admits more steam and delivers more horse power as a consequence. Wear, and poor linkage design, touted as reasons in the past, have nothing to do with this phenomenon.

If initial schedules on the east coast were not a great deal faster than they had been twenty years earlier, then there were good reasons for this (an inter-company time agreement as a result of the 1888 and 1895 races to the North). Prior to 1923, each of the three companies involved in running the east coast joint rolling stock, used their own engines (the North Eastern exercised running powers into Edinburgh, and was not over keen to share with the

North British). Prior to 1906 reversal had been required at Newcastle, making an engine change there a virtual necessity, whichever company provided the traction. The longest run for any locomotive was thus always less than half the total distance from London to Edinburgh. Trains that ran to Leeds (the principal intermediate destination) could have an engine change at Grantham or Peterborough, but that run was well under two hundred miles as well.

When an engine is being run at, or close to, its maximum output for any length of time, the fireman's task becomes progressively more exacting, and there are several factors that determine this. Firstly there is the question of fatigue; with six tons of coal in the tender at the start of a run and perhaps under a ton at the end, the fireman has shovelled over five tons onto the fire, and placed it exactly where it will burn best, all achieved while the engine has bucked and lurched under him. While some tenders carried nine tons of coal, and one type built by British Railways held ten tons, the maximum sustainable hand firing rate over four hours of high speed running was about a ton an hour, and the LNER's first attempts at high speed running illustrated the fact that this sort of effort could not be sustained for a full shift. One fireman could not fire a locomotive all the way from London to Edinburgh, except perhaps as an exceptional one-off.

As the amount of coal in the tender diminished, more effort was needed to ensure that the right size coal was on the shovelling plate, rather than large lumps, slack or dust, and coal may need pulling forward from the back of the bunker as the self trimming effect reduces or ceases. Steam coal pushers were featured on the LMS 'Pacifics', but did not see general use in Britain. Secondly there was the condition of the fire; when newly lit there was little in the way of ash or clinker to foul the bars. Even with low ash coals, a ton yielded up to a hundredweight of ash, and if that ash had a modest fusion temperature, then some of it fused on the fire bars and prevented the fire from drawing. Once this happened, the only way to remedy the situation was to fish the offending red hot lumps off the grate and on to the footplate. Not many firemen were in any hurry to do this, and without a rocking section in the firebars (to dump the clinker into the ashpan) the best that could be done was to use the fire irons to break up the clinker and minimise its effects.

Thirdly there was engine reliability; in addition to feeding the fire, the fireman had to keep the boiler water level within reasonably close limits, by operating both live and exhaust steam injectors. When running, much of the boiler feed was via the exhaust injector, matching the feed rate to the rate of evaporation. To ensure that it worked, and to cope with peak boiler outputs, the live injector was also used on a regular basis. Injectors that would not start consistently were a fact of life, and a lot of effort was put in to produce an 'automatic restarting' injector, as a boiler that could not be filled was a dangerous non-running liability. When an injector played up, it was not infrequently because it had become hot, and would not condense the steam feed to convert latent heat energy to pressure. This could be cured by dousing it with a bucket of cold water, but as most injectors were under the footplate, this remedy could only be applied when stationary.

Finally there was the issue of lubrication; forced feed oil bath lubrication (the system the modern motor car relies on) had only one (disastrous) application to the steam locomotive, and the options in the 1930s were basically oil cups and trimmings, steam displacement lubricators, sight feed (another steam displacement method but in the cab and adjustable) lubrication, and mechanical (pumped non- return) oil feed. Some lightly loaded bearings had balls or rollers with grease lubrication, but plain bearings were the norm, and oil was essential for this type. Oil technology too was in its relative infancy, with viscosities varying wildly with temperature, leading to the risk that bearings could run hot or fail due to poor oil supply if not checked and attended at short intervals.

Gresley's caution then, at not trying to run before walking was mastered, was to be credited with much wisdom for, of all the issues listed above, it was fireman fatigue and state of the fire that figured largest in considerations of long distance non-stop running. The effect of valve modifications in the late 1920s can thus be appreciated; coal consumption down between fifteen and twenty five per cent means a fresher fireman, a less clogged fire and a significant stretching of coal in the tender, itself an absolute limit on how far the engine could travel without running out of fuel. In adverse conditions locomotives on the east coast were arriving at their destinations with virtually empty fuel bunkers, so close to the limit were long distance services.

To run non-stop for nearly four hundred miles, the problem of recrewing while in motion was addressed by construction of a new design of eight wheeled corridor tender, enabling the second crew to travel on the cushions until needed. Only a limited number of corridor tenders were ever built, all by the LNER, and they were allocated to those engines running through services that needed a crew change *en route*.

Having 'cracked the nut' of long distance reliable running, the next step was to increase speed, which, as we have seen, was not exactly electrifying. That the public had to wait until 1934, six years after the start of the London/Edinburgh non-stops, was surprising, and one is tempted to surmise that if the Great Western had not decided to gain a little publicity by accelerating their 'Cheltenham Flyer', then the LNER might not have bothered to speed up their services. Be that as it may, *Flying Scotsman*, by now twelve years old, and still carrying a 180lb boiler, was pressed into service on a special run from Leeds to London, to improve on schedule as it could. The result, a verified 100mph (the first since 1904, thirty years earlier), and an average speed of 73mph, with a locomotive that was not the leading edge of technology, rang a few bells in LNER management, and led to a much more professional and successful run the following year. The way this was done, by a trial run for the press, was a masterpiece of publicity management, and seems to have shaken the '50mph average' brigade out of their complacency.

In March 1935, the 'A3' Pacific *Papyrus* (one of a long tradition of names taken from racehorses of the time) completed a round trip from Kings Cross to Newcastle and back in a time sufficiently under four hours each way, to suggest that a whole hour could be cut from the then five hour scheduled services. Coupled with an average speed of 68/69mph, a top speed of 108mph (a new record), and a twelve mile stretch covered at over 100mph, this sort of performance put the LNER well ahead of its rivals; more was to follow. The A3 was clearly the equal of any express locomotive in the land in 1935, though not nominally as powerful as the Great Western 'King'. In practice, above 70mph, the Pacifics were superior to the 'Kings' in every department, due primarily to modern steam distribution design, particularly the cylinder feed and the exhaust pipes/boiler draughting. Much of that advantage stemmed from cross-fertilisation of ideas, and as with Churchward's foreign foray thirty years earlier, the origin of those ideas was primarily French.

The work of André Chapelon, engineer of the Paris, Lyon and Mediterranné Railway, in appreciating the need for efficient fluid (steam) flows from boiler, through regulator, superheater, steam pipes, piston valves, cylinders and exhaust, had not gone unobserved on the English side of the Channel. Nigel Gresley quickly realised that good fluid dynamics were the key to a 'fat' indicator diagram, with both high initial pressure and good expansion, giving maximum horsepower and efficiency. Gresley was also a firm friend of the car designer Ettore Bugatti (an Italian who had settled in France after a spell in Germany) to whom streamlining the outside of motor cars was a key marketing strategy, and the resulting fusion of these ideas was the ultimate British express locomotive, streamlined inside and out, the 'A4' Pacific.

Introduced as part of a new premium service, initially as a single silver train set (matching the locomotives, *Silver Link* and *Silver Fox*), with a streamlined observation car at the rear, the class was quickly expanded to thirty five engines, thirty four of which ran the top link on the east coast until the arrival of the 'Deltics' in 1961. The thirty fifth suffered a direct hit while in York shed during the 'Baedecker' air raid on that city. In spite of both Edward Thompson and A. H. Peppercorn, Gresley's successors, designing replacements for the 'A4', in accordance with their own ideas, the fact remains that Nigel Gresley's design for the fastest steam locomotive in the world has never been bettered. How that accolade was won is a part of history.

In 1937, the LMS had briefly cornered the speed record, with its new 'Coronation' class Pacific reaching 114mph. The world record however stood at 124mph with the Deutche Bundesbahn, and the LNER was aiming primarily at the British record, when as part of a series of high speed brake tests, the 'A4' *Mallard* was given its head between Grantham and Peterborough on the 3rd July 1938.

Mallard was under eighteen months old, fitted with the improved Kylala-Chapelon front end draughting, and hauling two three coach articulated sets and the ex-North Eastern dynamometer car. The trip was arranged as a return outing from Kings Cross, and to save complex shunting of the dynamometer car, the whole train was reversed on the triangle of lines at Barkston Junction, north of Grantham. The train was driven by a Doncaster crew, driver Joe Duddington and fireman Thomas Bray. The start of the record run was hindered by a 20mph track slowing at Grantham, but from that point on, the engine was driven on full regulator and 40% cut off, accelerating to 75mph at Stoke Summit, and touching 126mph at Little Bytham on the long 1 in 200 down to Peterborough. The effort cost the engine its middle big end, and it limped into Peterborough, where it was replaced. The record seems likely to stand for all time.

While the east coast route is mostly flat and relatively straight, and remained the preserve of the Pacifics, routes in Scotland included the hilly and winding 'road' from the Forth Bridge, across the Kingdom of Fife, to Dundee and onto the LMS metals to Aberdeen. On this section the loads the Pacifics could take were less than the traffic that offered, and to avoid double heading,

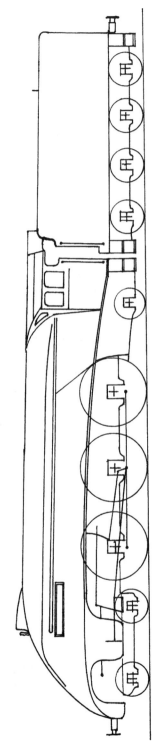

Figure 32: A4 Pacific.

Provenance: Development of 'A3' Pacific, with raised boiler pressure, streamlining, smaller cylinders and larger steam pipes.

Designer: H. N. Gresley.

Principal Features: Bugatti nose, curved running plate, side skirts to driving wheels (since removed, *Mallard* excepted) All fitted with double chimney after WW2.

Principal Dimensions:

Cylinders: Three, 18$^1/_2$in diameter, 26in stroke.

Working Pressure: 250psi.

Tractive Effort: 35,455lb.

Driving wheels: 6ft 8in diameter.

Valves: Piston valves, Gresley-Holcroft derived motion Walschaerts gear.

Weight in W. O: 102 tons 19cwt.

Gresley designed the most powerful express ever to run in Britain, the 'P2' 2-8-2. Two prototypes were built, and to test the merits of poppet valves, one of them (No. 2001 *Cock o' the North*) was thus fitted with Lentz gear and stepped cams, to provide fairly wide cut off variations (the Caprotti version with infinite variability was much more successful). With the grate area of these monsters reaching, no, *exceeding*, the limit for hand firing, this was not too good an idea, as with one cut off the fireman was overtaxed, and on the one shorter, the train lost time. In time the engines, with their long fixed wheelbase, were accused of spreading the track, and Edward Thompson rebuilt them into a new class of Pacific, the 'A2', though fifty square foot grates remained a liability that did little to endear them to their crews.

In two decades then, the fastest trains had moved from a leisurely 50mph average with top speeds in the upper sixties and seventies, to a brisk 70mph for the best and regular, if not everyday, pipping of 100mph. Runs at a mile a minute or more were a feature of services in the 1930s, though the actual number of trains in this rarefied category remained small, primarily because of large volumes of heavy slow moving freight, that dominated the slow lines where there were four tracks, and had to be shunted out of the way on the double track sections. All traffic that was not slow goods and mineral, and this included 'fitted' freight (the ones with brakes), and most passenger trains, had to be pathed around the expresses, or more usually *vice versa*. Most main lines were thus able to offer only a couple of high speed paths a day, without significant disruption to the rest of the traffic. To quote just one example, the 'Cheltenham Flyer' ran in the middle of the day, avoiding the busy morning and evening peaks and minimising the number of train paths needed for a train that was not far short of four times faster than a typical freight. That the LNER could provide a racetrack all the way to Newcastle was due to it having an easily graded alternative route to bypass the double track from Stoke Summit to Doncaster (the 'joint' line via Lincoln and March). North of Doncaster the route was duplicated as far as Newcastle (via the York and North Midland, the Leeds Northern and the Leamside routes) but was further aided by the heaviest of the freight flows being from West to East rather than North/South.

The success of the LNER's high speed train services (the capital cost of the new trains was recovered in under two years) served to underline the complacency that pervaded running of both passenger and freight trains in the 1930s; average speeds were so low as to make all but the fastest services vulnerable to road competition. The bus, car and lorry were in fact already wiping out local branch line loadings, and the start of the road building programme threatened medium distance carryings as well. That the effects of this competition did not show clearly until the late 1940s was the fault of an Austrian corporal-turned-dictator, but the effect on the British steam locomotive was not to stall design, as had been the case in the First War, but to channel it into its final phase, one of utility and economy.

This final era was to last the fifteen years to 1955, and was paradoxically the point at which the appliance of science at last turned the locomotive from an unpredictable and temperamental workhorse into a reliable and tractable machine. Before we tread that road, there is the little matter of the LMS shaking off the torpor of the Webb/Midland influence, by taking several leaves, and a lieutenant, out of Churchward's book.

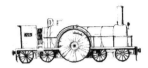

Chapter Fifteen:

Coming up on the Rails:
The LMS catches up 1933-1939

It is nearly fair to say that for ten years after 1923, the largest of the 'Big Four' post grouping companies sat and wrung its collective hands over its locomotive stock. Almost, but not quite. After the trials and 'Castle' borrowing of 1925-6, there was a stark realisation that what the company possessed was not up to the mark in any shape or form, but an almost equal reluctance to take decisive action to remedy the position. In Sir Henry Fowler they had a chief mechanical engineer, but they did not have a creative and innovative designer. Worse still, the domination of locomotive design and manufacturing facilities by the reactionary forces that had caused Deeley to quit twenty five years earlier, were still in place; the Midland had designed small engines with slab-sided fireboxes, and saw no reason why the LMS could not do so too.

Many heads were firmly buried in the sand, to the extent that the 'Royal Scot' class, though designed by contractors, was obliged to incorporate various items of Midland practice, most noticeably that firebox, which was certainly cheap to build, but was not an aid to good steaming. Likewise the 'Garretts', introduced in the 1920s to solve the chronic double (and triple) heading of freight on the Midland Main Line; their effectiveness was considerably reduced by Midland influence. What was needed was a clean break with tradition, a strong leader with lots of design ideas. In the early 1930s it is not surprising that Derby looked to Swindon to secure their man.

William Stanier, as assistant to Charles Collett, was a part of the team that had turned 'Stars' into 'Castles', and then enlarged them into 'Kings', the latter two locomotives being the best of British in 1930. In haulage terms the 'King' was just what the LMS needed, in power output at least. There were other less ideal features of this design, which was dependent both on a supply of good coal, and on painstakingly meticulous firing. Neither of these latter factors could be guaranteed on the LMS, and Stanier's decision to add a wide firebox and rear carrying axle to turn the 'LMS King' into the 'Princess Royal' Pacific ensured its success. Much of the rest was a Swindon *copy*; same cylinder layout, divided drive and (nearly) internal valve gear and rocker drive. At the last moment this was changed to four sets of Walschaerts gear, in a class that ultimately only ran to twelve engines, but was the progenitor of the 'Duchess' or 'Coronation' class, of which more anon. Stanier also brought to the LMS much of the sound basics of constructional details that the Great Western excelled in, and, in addition to raising the steaming and performance capabilities of the locomotive stock, made a big impact on the LMS's chronic reputation for bearing failures and excessive boiler maintenance costs.

Having copied the 'King', Stanier then proceeded to copy the 'Hall', only this time he realised that a much better engine would result if the engine were updated in line with current best practice; out went Stephenson link motion and low temperature superheater, and the result was the mixed traffic class 5, the 'Black Five'. With a scrap and build policy in place, this locomotive class eventually ran to over a thousand engines (841 on the LMS numbering list, and 172 of the slightly differing British Railways model) operating from Wick to Swansea and Bournemouth, lasting to the very end of steam haulage in 1968. Several variations on the same theme were tried, including a batch with stainless steel fireboxes, a very successful application of Caprotti poppet valves, and somewhat perversely, one with outside Stephenson link motion.

Next target was the '2800' class of Great Western heavy freight locomotive, again transformed in the same manner as the 'Black Five' to become the '8F', a locomotive destined to travel to many corners of the globe (there's one in the Turkish National Railway museum, for example). A diversion then followed, with Stanier inventing his own medium weight express passenger class to follow on where the somewhat dated 'Royal Scots' left off. The three cylinder 'Jubilees' were not the runaway success that had been hoped; competent yes, and well ahead of the Midland Compounds, but sparkle they did not, and they were not the equal of Collett's 'Castles', as had been the objective. Two prototype up-rated 'Jubilees', to match the rebuilt 'Royal Scots' and 'Patriots', were turned out in 1942, but the rest were never altered. Stanier's last

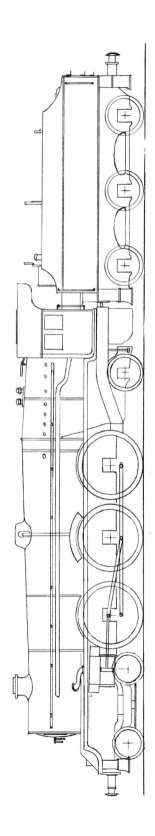

Principal Dimensions:
Cylinders: Four, 16 $\frac{1}{4}$in diameter, 28in stroke.
Working Pressure: 250psi.
Tractive Effort: 40,285lb.
Driving wheels: 6ft 6in diameter.
Valves: Piston valves, four sets of Walschaerts gear.
Weight in W. O: 104 tons 10cwt.

Provenance: Development of GWR 'King' class for service on the LMSR.
Designer: W. A. Stanier.
Principal Features: Four cylinders, divided drive, four sets of valve gear, large taper boiler and wide firebox.

Figure 33: Princess Royal Pacific.

design effort was both biggest and best: the 'Coronation' Pacific, the most powerful locomotive in LMS stock after 1937, and not far short of Gresley's 'P2'.

With just thirteen 'Princess Royal' Pacifics to handle the fastest and heaviest trains in the mid 1930s, the LMS was not awash with top link traction. Copying Swindon had its drawbacks too; Stanier's first 'Pacific' design, while light years ahead of the rest of the LMS locomotive stock, displayed the same sort of performance as the locomotives it plagiarised. Top speed was in the mid nineties, twenty miles an hour less than Gresley's 'A3'. In practice, there were never enough Pacifics to equip both Midland and North Western main lines, and the Midland was deprived to the point of neglect, a state of affairs that was to last for the whole of the twentieth century. In 1937 Crewe works commenced construction of 'Coronation' Pacifics, with larger driving wheels and a modernised front end, to be the equal of the LNER racehorses, but inevitably designed for the very different conditions on the West Coast.

The 'Coronation' was as large and powerful a locomotive as could be fitted into the loading gauge, and at the upper limit of what could be fired by hand. Streamlining was added for publicity, but the locomotives had to do two things very well; run at high speed on the flat-ish metals of the main line south of Carnforth, and possess the 'oomph' to tackle the banks of Grayrigg/Shap and Beattock without either needing a banker, or with speed dropping too low and affecting point to point times.

In speed terms the design was never fully tested; after touching 114mph, a speed that briefly held the UK record, the LMS recognised it had no racetrack suitable for further attempts. In power output, an estimated 3,300hp was achieved on one climb to Beattock, though that figure reduces to perhaps 2500 at the drawbar, the locomotive having to do a lot of work to shift its own weight. With as much modern technology applied as could be reliably incorporated, the 'Coronation' class went a long way to realising the concept of a steam locomotive running 100,000 miles between works overhauls and remaining in front line service for all that time. On the Rugby test plant in 1956, a 'Coronation' was steamed to its limit and proved capable of evaporating 40,000lb of water per hour (nearly eighteen tons), at a firing rate well beyond the capacity of one fireman. One is tempted (but only in a minor burst of megalomania) to speculate what timings could have been achieved on the East Coast main line with a mechanically stoked 'Coronation'. A project for the twenty-first century perhaps?

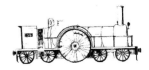

Chapter Sixteen:

War and Nationalisation: An End to All Things

The shock of the Second World War to Britain's railway companies was one from which they would never recover; in 1945 all four companies were effectively insolvent, running a system that in almost every quarter was worn to a threadpaper. The smooth riding, clean, fast and attractive racehorses of the 1930s had turned into grimy worn out nags in the war years. Gresley's three cylinder locomotives (he had designed little else for nearly twenty years), with their wonderfully complex derived valve motion, that needed both time and expert attention to set correctly, were just one of many pre-war designs that found the going tough when staff went off to war. The Great Western found that its engines didn't like second best coal (or inexperienced firemen), and when its fitters were faced with the choice between maintaining the inside valve motion of four cylinder 4-6-0's (a horrible task in extremely cramped conditions), and facing the Hun, 'Jerry' on the whole seemed a better bet.

Of the 'Big Four's' chief mechanical engineers, Gresley was dead by the end of 1941. Stanier retired in 1944. Edward Thompson, long Gresley's understudy, set the tone of a new era by designing a simple two cylinder workhorse 4-6-0, the mixed traffic 'B1'. Out went the Holcroft-Gresley conjugated valve gear and the inside middle cylinder, replacing the front swing link bogie (another over complex item) with a simple side bearer spring controlled design, and abandoning the expensive coned boiler for a cheap and cheerful parallel one. If Thompson could put his shoulder to the wheel of economy with a will, then another of Gresley's assistants, Oliver Bulleid, could not.

Bulleid had taken over as chief engineer on the Southern following R. E. L. Maunsell's retirement in 1937, and just as he had been a key member of the LNER team that was leading the field in the thirties, so also had he a desire to go one better. Bulleid started quietly enough with detail alterations to the 'Lord Nelson' four cylinder 4-6-0's and the smaller 'Schools' 4-4-0, improving the draughting by adding a large bore chimney and a multiple jet blastpipe (the surface area theory of the multitubular boiler applied to smokebox vacuum). The real agenda though was a large Pacific, and detail design was well in hand when war broke out, seemingly scuppering the project. Quite how consent, and materials, were obtained from government to build the first batch of 'air smoothed' Pacifics is a bit of a mystery, as they were only nominally mixed traffic in that their wheel diameter was six foot two. Everything else about them was express pure and, unfortunately, very complicated.

It's impossible not to feel a lot of sympathy for Oliver Bulleid. He saw his opportunity to add his name to history's 'hall of fame' slipping away, and determined to put everything he had into the 'Merchant Navy' class. Without any opportunity to rid the design of its idiosyncrasies, all his ideas went into the one pot, and unlike the 'Royal Scot' of fifteen years earlier, what came out of the box *didn't* work as soon as the fire was lit. Problems abounded from day one; the air smooth casing, specifically designed to lift the exhaust smoke, didn't, leading to several redesigns before a cure was in place. The middle cylinder and the three sets of valve gear ran in an oil bath between the frames, again an idea intended to provide effective lubrication and secure minimum oil consumption. Because the engine was overweight the oil bath plates were thinned to the point where they leaked; oil consumption in the 'Merchant Navy's' was never less than twice that of a comparable Pacific, and the oil got onto the track where it caused severe loss of adhesion.

To compound the problem the valve gear was a variation of Walschaerts', with a chain driven intermediate shaft that merely moved the linkage around. Tests revealed that the cut off varied while the locomotive was in service, quite independently of the reverser in the cab, leading to power surges. Adding to the woes was the high pressure, at 280lb the highest used in Britain (shared with the last GWR design, the 'County' of 1945) large piston valves and short 24in piston stroke, resulting in massive variations in torque on a relatively small wheel diameter. Putting all these negatives together meant that the full output of the excellent boiler (better than that of the 'Coronation') was never reached, because the engine had a tendency to slip, slipping that on more than one occasion was severe enough to bend the coupling rods. Not until 1956 were the defects ironed out and a well designed locomotive emerged from the debacle; by then Bulleid had moved on to Ireland, and five years of proper experimentation had revealed most of the steam locomotive's secrets. Bulleid nonetheless has his place in history, if not exactly as he intended, for his engines sound unlike anything else on the rails, emitting a distinctive soft 'woof' as an exhaust, and true to the idiosyncratic nature of man, of all the representatives that would exemplify best British locomotive design, the National Railway Museum has a sectioned 'Merchant Navy', *Ellerman Lines*, to show how the steam engine works.

If Bulleid did not find great favour after the Second War, then this is true of the other chief engineers of the Great Western, LNER and LMS, for no place at the top was found for them when the inevitable nationalisation took place in 1948. Instead the job went to Robert Riddles, and to him fell the last chapter of British locomotive design. In spite of the restrictions placed upon him by the tendency to design 'by committee', the last twelve years of locomotive construction was at least as busy as the previous dozen, not least because the advent of systematic testing introduced the ways and means of getting the detail design right — well, *almost* right.

Making sure there was an engine at the front of every train, and that it eventually reached its destination, was about as far as the railways went in the war years. The immediate aftermath of the cessation of world-wide hostilities was an end to 'lease-lend', the American blank cheque that had kept Britain afloat for six years, ensuring that the dark days of post-war shortages did not end too soon. Aid to rebuild the exhausted railways came in the form of political dogma; a wondrous scheme to replace home-produced coal with imported oil, so that coal the mines couldn't produce to fire locomotives, could be substituted with oil there was no foreign exchange to buy. Not a good start to the brave new world. Conditions were a world away from ten years earlier, and this hit the steam locomotive where it hurt most; in the firebox.

With the end of hostilities, railway workshops turned their attention away from munitions to the uphill task of six years arrears of maintenance. While in the main this meant overhaul and repair, the erecting shops, when they could obtain materials, made efforts to plug gaps in locomotive stocks, and this meant for the most part more of the same. The LMS continued to build Stanier Pacifics, the Southern 'Merchant Navys', the Great Western 'Castles', a design

159

nearly a quarter of a century old. The LNER, insolvent as it was, broke with convention and designed new 'A1' and 'A2' 'Pacifics', with large grates to burn the rubbish the mines were offering as best locomotive coal. The poor quality of the coal on offer showed that the 'take it or leave it' attitude was no passing phase, and much of the effort of the next decade was aimed at mitigating the effect of this indifference upon the steaming capacity of the top link engines, where main line schedules were now a matter of parliamentary debate, even as the rest of the network slid towards oblivion.

Of all locomotives affected by the changed conditions, Great Western 'Castles' and 'Kings' were perhaps worst off. Twenty five years earlier they had been the cynosure of the locomotive world, fed on the best coal from South Wales collieries, fired and driven with meticulous care by footplatemen who had a tradition to uphold, of keeping the needle on the pressure gauge 'just so', with the safety valves sizzling and the reverser notched back to fifteen or eighteen per cent. With a long, narrow grate and tortuous steam and exhaust passages, anything less than the best meant a rapid fall-off in performance, particularly as the cylinder efficiency was well below the best of the times. Revision of the front end of all the 'Kings', starting with a new (much hotter) superheater and concluding with a double exhaust and chimney, made up for the poor fuel, to a degree. The 'Castles' received the same treatment in a more piecemeal fashion, by no means all of them being attended prior to withdrawal.

The event that led to this systematic assessment of locomotive performance was the completion of the locomotive test plant at Rugby, a joint LMS/LNER project stalled by the war, but completed in time to provide accurate diagnosis of what was wrong with the steam locomotive. After a hundred and twenty five years of development, the answer to that question was still 'quite a lot'. Secondly, the concept of the controlled road test was born, to replicate the way experienced drivers handled their trains (sounds almost revolutionary doesn't it? actually testing in a way that accepted that the driver was not an illiterate ignoramus); and thirdly the use of a mix of locomotives, routes and duties for testing purposes, that were a reflection of the work that was the daily lot of engines and crews concerned.

The results of these tests should surprise few people; most of the engines tested had defects to a greater or lesser degree, and could be made more powerful or more economical, or both, by altering the draught arrangements or redesigning the steam supply and distribution. Basics still being learned at the very last gasp of

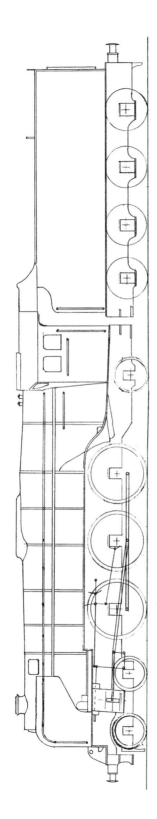

Principal Dimensions:

Cylinders: Three, 19in diameter, 26in stroke.
Working Pressure: 250psi.
Tractive Effort: 40,430lb
Driving wheels: 6ft 2in diameter
Valves: Piston valves, three sets of Walschaerts gear.
Weight in W. O: 101 tons.

Provenance: Rebuild of Sir Nigel Gresley 'P2' 2-8-2 with repositioned outside cylinders and leading bogie (later engines built new).
Designer: E. Thompson/ A. H. Peppercorn.

Principal Features: Similar to 'A3', with larger firebox and smoke deflectors. Unusually placed outside cylinders.

Figure 34: A2 Pacific.

the steam locomotive. The assembled data enabled the best of the 'Big Four's designs to go forward into the new build programme of British Railways, and for the most part this was the details, rather than the concept, which was a simple robust series of two cylinder engines with all the gear outside. This was in fact a new idea; only one express locomotive class with two outside cylinders, the GWR 'County', had been built in the whole of the period of the Grouping, and the design of these engines harked back to the 'Saint' of 1903.

The 'Britannia' class locomotives were on the whole a success; they had their moments (the wheels came loose!), but were not the equals of their pre-war counterparts. The same reasons that made Churchward choose the four cylinder 'Stars' over the 'Saints' fifty years earlier, still pertained in the 1950s; with outside cylinders the 'Brits' were less smooth riding than those with three or four cylinders. Newton's Third Law still applied in the horizontal plane (despite engineers trying to pretend that it had gone out of date) and while the wheelbase was a lot longer than the 'Planets' of the 1830s, the engines were still vulnerable to 'dancing off the track'. As Pacifics, they had wide fireboxes to deal with poor coal, and the boiler was good in terms of output, and economical over a wide range of demand. The class saw service in all parts of the country, and were the last express type to be withdrawn, and the last the author rode behind (from Windermere to Carnforth) in 1966.

The last express built for British Railways was a single locomotive, larger than the 'Britannia', with three cylinders and Caprotti poppet valves. Just to show that designers had yet to be masters of their steeds, the *Duke of Gloucester* didn't go properly; when tested it steamed less well than its smaller brothers, and British Rail promptly lost interest. Withdrawn early and chopped up (its valves spent many years as an unexplained and useless lump of metal in the Science Museum) it was rescued and rebuilt, and has had the TLC lavished upon it to make it perform as its designer intended, thirty years after it was usurped from its duties on the west coast by diesels long since gone and more or less forgotten.

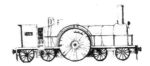

Chapter Seventeen:

No Brakes Please, We're British:
Freight Locomotives 1845 to 1903

We left development of the freight locomotive at the point where Robert Stephenson had brought the 'long boiler' to the stage where it was the definitive heavy hauler, having failed to make its mark as an express to replace the 'Patentee'. While this demotion from top link to the more mundane task of shifting coal was by no means exceptional, and was to be the lot of many engines that did not make the grade until the grouping of 1923 and beyond, it effectively marked the divergence of passenger and freight locomotive design. The reasons for that divergence are both technical and economic, and no analysis of freight locomotives in the nineteenth and twentieth centuries would be complete without a look at the currents in society that provided the formative forces.

The railway had started out, a century before Rainhill, as a low speed haulier of heavy goods. Most of these first railways, using the term in its widest sense, were product-specific, hauling a single class of goods, often coal, from the point of production to the nearest navigable water. Coal had a special place in this early phase of railways; it was indispensable to urban society, and fetched a price that reflected that near monopoly position. Coal mining had started in earnest in the middle of the sixteenth century, and as the towns of Britain grew, that growth was sustained by supplies of coal, a bulky and fairly heavy commodity, whose distribution by horse and cart, even on good roads, was uneconomic over distances as short as four or five miles.

As we have seen, water transport was a much better option, and while coastal and river shipping was both slow, and to our eyes at least, risky and unreliable, costs were lower by a factor of at least ten per ton/mile. The difference between horse and cart, and horse and barge transport costs, enabled two thousand miles of canal to be built between 1757 and 1850, and the horse-drawn railway had not driven either system to the brink of extinction. When the Stockton and Darlington commenced operations in 1825, the economic case for the steam engine was based upon the cost advantage over the horse on the same track, not against the road cart, or the barge or coaster. Rail companies in the middle of the nineteenth century found they could not oust the canal barge from the coal trade on cost, nor was steam totally dominant in the movement of heavy minerals such as iron ore and limestone.

Where railway and canal shared the same route, as was the case of the Glamorganshire Canal and the Taff Vale Railway, both companies found that they could prosper without beggaring their neighbour. Avarice on the part of the shareholders though, meant that a good deal of time and effort was expended on trying to do just that. While the playing field remained fairly even, both canal and railway thrived. With a climb of over four hundred feet in twenty five miles, the canal found it could do some things better than the railway (like carry iron ore uphill), and vice-versa. Rates for carriage of goods were low, barely a penny a ton mile when rates elsewhere could be three or four times this. With high tonnages giving excellent asset utilisation the waterway held its own against the railway for thirty years.

Railway companies killed canals by buying them up and raising their freight charges; but canal carrying *per se* was only given the *coup de grâce* by the plummeting cost of freight transport, courtesy of the motor lorry after the Second World War. In this respect Britain was virtually alone in Europe, and while the forces that killed the commercial canal are beyond the scope of this book, it would not be rocket science to suggest that the cause was the same as led the railways to slaughter at the hands of Richard Beeching; civil servants with cars and roads in their eyes at the Treasury and Ministry of Transport.

Just as the network was built on the vision of fast passenger trains, so was goods transport founded on the economics of freight cost per ton-mile. A market was created by tapping into the latent demand (still not satiated today) of people for more goods of every description, but particularly coal. Substitute 'energy' for 'coal', and this feature of life is as pertinent today as it was two centuries ago. This market place was truly nationwide, unconstrained by proximity of coast or canal, or the unsympathetic geology of the chalklands. The steam powered railway made *affordable* coal available throughout the land. The horse and cart, as local distributors, dictated spacing of stations on the rail network, generally at three to five mile intervals. Having created a new market, railway companies took steps to emasculate the competition, where it existed. Anti-competitive practices (or even a sniff of a monopoly) created decades-long emnity from public bodies. The burghers of both Hull and Cardiff led the campaign by example, battling with the North Eastern and Taff Vale railways, and promoting their own railways (the Hull and Barnsley, and the Cardiff Railway respectively) in an attempt to defy the economics of laissez-faire capitalism.

In freight haulage, railways set out to achieve two objectives: firstly, successful movement of the goods themselves, and secondly, the reduction of the cost of moving those goods to the lowest possible. Speed generally played little part, perishables and livestock apart, until after the First World War, and provision of locomotives centred on the loads that could be moved at fifteen to twenty miles an hour, maximum. Speed actually permitted the transport network to flourish, allowing the goods not only to travel hopefully, but to *arrive.* Large objects, such as oak trees for the naval dockyards, a scarce resource in logged-out lowland Britain, not infrequently took *years* to reach their destination in the eighteenth century. These two statements may seem mutually contradictory, but an average speed of fifteen miles an hour was five times that offered by the competition, where there was any, and even at this pace, most goods reached their destination later in the day on which they were dispatched, at least initially.

From the 'long boiler' six coupled design emerged the first standard mass production machine; the London and North Western's 'DX' goods, a locomotive designed to trundle along on the flat at twenty miles an hour, maximum, with two or three hundred tons of loose-coupled unbraked wagons rattling behind, and possessing just enough 'oomph' to top the hills at walking pace. This picture, well established by 1860, would persist for a hundred years, a leisurely activity that survived because pressure for change was absent prior to the First War, and the industry was too stuck in its groove afterwards. The success of the 'DX' was a lesson well learned by other main line companies, so far as shifting goods was concerned; the six coupled inside cylinder design was copied by all railways with coal to take to London. What was not so universally copied was the simple and robust design that delivered more power per penny, and it is this combination of slow and cheap that drove the freight locomotive for the whole of the nineteenth century, and for a goodly proportion of the twentieth as well.

We have looked briefly at the 'DX' in chapter ten, and recognised that here is the antithesis of the express engine, a locomotive designed to do a modest job at least cost and with utmost reliability. To achieve this in the last forty years of the nineteenth century meant a combination of the essentials and an absence of the frills. Those essentials can be summed up as comprising the following:

- Boiler pressure in the 120psi to 160psi range

- All weight on the six coupled wheels

- Wheels between four feet and five feet in diameter

- Two inside cylinders located under the smokebox and driving the middle axle

- Deep firebox almost square in plan located between the second and third axles

- A relatively short boiler barrel, typically four feet in diameter

- Simple valve gear designed to be run 'flat out'

While boiler pressures were the same as for passenger engines at the start of this period, the general rise in steam pressures at the end of the century passed the 0-6-0 by. For a time at least, without a change in the weight of freight trains, there was little reason to increase the power of the freight locomotive. This inertia occurred because, in the rise to dominance of the railway there was no effective competition, and if existing engines could pull a sixty wagon, three hundred ton freight train at twenty miles an hour, there was no place for an engine that could do the same task at forty miles an hour.

The fast freight, carrying fresh fruit, meat, vegetables and milk from country to town, and fish from the coast, was not an instant phenomenon. Market gardens ringed large towns and cities at daily horse and cart distance, meat could 'hoof it', as had always been the case (cattle wagons just speeded things up) and milk could be supplied from a distance in the form of hay. When such goods eventually took to the rails, the motive power was the failed express, until the twentieth century provided mixed traffic locomotives.

Because the result of speeding up coal and mineral trains would be derailed wagons rather than faster transits, without a complete revision of rolling stock, suspension and braking systems, there was no realistic chance of higher speeds. Likewise, loads could not be increased without lengthening the refuge sidings that were essential to let passenger trains pass. Starting a loose coupled freight was a skill that might not have demanded a great deal from the engine, but was a serious challenge to the driver if broken couplings were to be avoided. If starting was a challenge, what about stopping?

An axiom of any transport system is that your licence to speed is your ability to stop, and freight trains of the lowest kind remained without brakes on the wagons until Richard Beeching was given the job of getting rid of them. The prospect of a freight running at twice normal speed (with four times the kinetic energy), and with only brakes on the engine/tender supplemented by that operated by the guard on ten tons or so of brake van, was one that the Victorians decided they could quite well do without. The fast freight concept, as we shall see, needed something better than the 0-6-0.

If there was little incentive to change on the boiler front, then the same applied to the rest of the locomotive, particularly wheels and motion. The technological challenge of coupling wheels together and making them go for a walk afterwards, was not one addressed lightly in 1860, and was the reason for the idiosyncratic engineer of the Great Northern Railway, Patrick Stirling, having all his express engines *sans* coupling rods. The problem was one of measurement and division; to work properly the coupling rods on opposite sides of the engine have to be at 90 degrees to each other, implying a good degree of exactitude when pressing wheels onto axles. All three axles on a six coupled engine have to be the same to within quite a fine degree of tolerance, no more than a few minutes of arc difference overall. Next, the crank pins on the wheels must have the same 'throw', again to within a thousandth of an inch or so. Finally, the rods themselves must be made to the same fine tolerances, and be capable of accepting vertical and lateral movement of wheels and axles as the engine moves upon the track.

The process of 'quartering', as setting up wheel/axle/crankpin/ side rod relationships was known, was both a skilled task, and one for which a special purpose machine was eventually constructed to produce the desired results. Early locomotives could be upwards of half an inch outside the design dimension in parts of the rolling chassis, leading to the use of enormous adjustable shims and cotters on the side rods and big ends merely to achieve a working fit.

Complete accuracy, building a locomotive to the dimensions specified by the drawing office, and within working tolerances, was not achieved until the last quarter of the nineteenth century, and even then not by every locomotive works.

Practical experiment had shown that even four coupled engines had a lot of internal resistance in their motion compared to 'singles', and for the majority of the nineteenth century, six coupled engines were for freight haulage or other slow work. This recognition of the limits of technology meant that small wheels were no real hindrance to running at speeds that were realistic for trains without effective brakes, and limited wheel diameter meant that nominal tractive effort was as large as was practical given the available adhesion.

This latter factor was a good indication of an engine's ability to start a train, and shift the traffic as a result; it did not matter if a freight took ten minutes to work up to a running speed of fifteen miles an hour. As banking was available on all the steeper sections, hills were only a problem in adverse conditions or if the crew misjudged the task or mishandled the engine. This fine matching of power available to task set led to an extensive system of 'permitted loads', where individual classes of engine were allowed so many empty or loaded wagons on such and such routes, a system that persisted to the end of unfitted freight haulage.

To supply this modest machine needed no more than a modest firebox and boiler: twelve or fifteen square feet of grate, and a boiler ten feet or so between tubeplates, and four foot in diameter. If the physical demands of firing such a machine at forty pounds of coal per square foot of grate per hour were not exacting, the skill needed to keep safety valves sizzling but not wasting precious coal and water was of the first order. The consequences of not firing properly when there was little or no margin on the hills was time lost and traffic delayed, and if a train stalled on an up grade, starting was by no means an assured fact. To compensate for this 'easy life' on the freight footplate, there was an absence of any weather protection, until the advent of rudimentary cabs in the 1870s and 1880s. Bouch's attempts, for the South Durham and Lancashire Union Railway, to introduce cabs on engines designed for the route over Stainmore (by a margin the most hostile through route south of the Scottish border) found no favour in the 1860s and they were removed in short order. Even at the century's end, only the North Eastern Railway provided an effective cab for its footplatemen.

If cabs were minimal then likewise controls were present only in the absolute essentials: regulator, lever reverser and steam brake for the driver, gauge glass and pressure gauge to monitor the boiler, steam and water valves for the injectors, blower valve to provide draught when the regulator was shut, and not a great deal else. Lubrication was by displacement lubricators for cylinders and valve chest, oil cup and trimmings elsewhere, a round of which was made at intervals with the oilcan, not infrequently when running. Driver and fireman were not occupied continuously on the footplate, and with block sections three or four miles long, ten or more minutes between signal sightings was both unexceptional and presented ample opportunities to get 'out and about' on the running plate.

While valves and valve gear had a critical effect on express locomotive performance, the parameters of operation of freight engines were well within the ability of both slide valves and Stephenson link motion, the preferred combination until well into the twentieth century. Use of other gears by Gooch, Allan or Joy was similarly efficacious. The sector plate on the reverser only allowed wide variations of cut off, and typical locomotives in the third quarter of the nineteenth century were worked on fairly long cut offs of 60% plus, and adjustment for speed and gradient made on the regulator. This of course was the way that the valve gear worked best, with wide openings of the valve ports for steam and exhaust, and only limited expansive working. In terms of economy, this arrangement was decidedly *not* best achievable practice, but it was reliable, and the long lives of 'Dean Goods', 'DX', and a host of similar designs, repeated with only minor variations over a period of over seventy years, is testimony to the effectiveness of a design that John Ramsbottom can set alongside the watertrough as the high point of his career.

For companies with a lot of coal or iron ore to shift, and a fair distance to travel, six coupled tender engines were the definitive freight hauler for half a century, nearer seventy years in the case of the Midland Railway. Having adopted the 0-6-0 under Matthew Kirtley, the Midland never built anything else for its own freight for the rest of its independent existence. These conditions did not pertain universally; on the main lines there was a gradual introduction of the eight coupled engine as the Victorian age gave way to an Edwardian high summer, increasing haulage capacity and train weights as wagon sizes grew from five to ten ton capacity. The six-coupled tank engine came to be the prime mover on the shorter haul, and nowhere was this more evident than in South Wales.

The South Wales coalfield was, after David Davies' opening of the first deep mine in the Rhondda, quite exceptional in British railway terms; a host of companies, some more tinpot than others (the Taff Vale was, dividend-wise, the definitive copper-bottomed railway) all scrabbling for a share of the most lucrative traffic the British Isles could offer. The railways the Welsh companies operated all had one thing in common: the loaded runs were downhill, and nowhere more than thirty miles from pit to port. Average gradients with the traffic were sufficient to permit gravity working for long distances, with engines doing no work other than controlling speed.

For these special conditions tank engines were ideal; turning at each end of the short runs involved was unnecessary, little water or coal needed to be carried, and short wheelbase and no tender made marshalling and shunting easy, without having to have special engines just for those duties. When the need to shift volumes of traffic up the grades arose, as with exhaustion of iron ores that supplied the Merthyr Tydfil ironworks in the late 1880s, the task was beyond the means, and the Dowlais Iron Company upped sticks (lock, stock and blast furnace) and went to Cardiff.

Tank engines remained the preferred load shifter in the Valleys until the end of steam, but as we shall see, King Coal attracted other 'foreign' companies to the area, who didn't have the same grasp of gravity as the locals, but adhered to Julie Andrews' maxim when it came to mountains; the engines they built to defy logic and logistics are well worth a quick peek. For the most part though, the nineteenth century remained the domain of the 0-6-0 in tender or tank form, and the reader will have to wait until the twentieth century for a sample of the lumbering leviathans, for the idea of a stretched freight engine, with eight coupled wheels, more power and more adhesive weight, hove into view in the late 1880s. Surprisingly enough, the designer was not a company chief mechanical engineer, but Sharp, Stewart, and Co., the private locomotive builders.

Having realised that the English were having all the fun building railways up South Walian mountains, the native Welsh, led by the redoubtable David Davies Llandinam and the Ocean Coal Company, invented the Barry Railway to prove that the Welsh could haul coal unnecessarily uphill just as well as the English (the Barry Railway was actually born because of frustration over the dominance of Cardiff Docks by the Bute family). Having done so, they found that something a mite larger was needed to work the traffic. Sharp, Stewart and Co. had built a batch of eight coupled engines for export to Scandinavia, and as the Barry (the name of the town, railway and docks, all built for the same, single, coal exporting purpose) neared completion in 1885-9, the Barry Railway took the otherwise unsaleable engines off the manufacturer's hands and became the

Provenance: Contractor export design purchased by the Barry Railway
Designer: Sharp, Stewart & Co.

Principal Features: Extended 'long boiler' design, parallel boiler and round top firebox.

Principal Dimensions:
Cylinders: Two 18^1/$_2$in diameter, 26in stroke, outside frames.
Working Pressure: 140psi.
Tractive Effort: 20,760lb.
Driving wheels: 4ft 3in diameter.
Valves: Slide valves between frames, inside Stephenson Link Motion.

Figure 35: Barry 0-8-0.

first user of the type in Britain. With one remarkable exception, the Barry was on its own until the turn of the century, when H. A. Ivatt at the Great Northern designed his own extra heavy freight locomotive.

The exception of course is what everyone wants to read about, and readers will know what is coming when the name of Francis Webb hoves into view. Taken as a development of the six coupled freight locomotive, the 0-8-0 was a logical extension, giving room for both a longer firebox and boiler, and adding adhesive weight to make haulage of heavier trains a practical reality. With such a simple concept, it took the genius of Webb to turn the design into an unrepeatable fiasco. Having decided on a simple (non compound) chassis, two cylinders of dimensions that were well up to the mark in dimensions and theoretical haulage capacity (tractive effort), Webb used the woeful boiler from his failed 'Greater Britain' express class, and so ensured that there was insufficient steam for the anticipated duties. Almost anything else would have guaranteed success, but it was to be twenty years, on the eve of the First War, before Crewe would replace the six-coupled locomotive at the head of its freight trains with an eight wheeled machine, and by then the North Eastern Railway, and one or two others, had got their oars in first.

At the turn of the century, the North Eastern Railway carried a lot of coal over relatively short distances; the average haul was only just over twenty miles, but the Durham coalfield was the domain of tender freight engines, for a policy of large locomotives, by the standards of the time at any rate, was in force. That policy was due in the main to the need to haul some goods uphill, particularly iron ore, and Wilson Worsdell, succeeding his brother William, introduced the first of the 'T' class of eight coupled mineral engines in 1901. With large boilers, outside cylinders and inside Stephenson valve gear, these engines could lap up any sort of punishment, and the design was quickly improved by the addition of superheaters. This class, and the later 'T2' and three cylinder 'T3', dominated the coal trade of the north east for sixty years, almost to the bitter end in fact, becoming class 'Q6' under the LNER, and only partially surrendering to British Railways standard '9F's', as the 'T3's were displaced from the Consett iron ore hauls.

This latter task was one of the most mystifying examples of industrial inertia. Iron ore was hauled from sea level at Tyne Dock, to 1100 feet above Ordnance Datum at Consett. Latterly, most of the coal the furnaces needed had a similar trek. In its last days, *liquid* iron was hauled from Redcar! As we have seen, the Taff Vale threw in the towel very quickly over the Dowlais works (or rather the Dowlais works couldn't afford what the Taff Vale wanted to charge) but the '9F's' plied a similar trade from Newport to Ebbw Vale into the 1960s, and that trade still limps on in the twenty first century, albeit with semi-finished steel.

As we shift our attention from Victorian to Edwardian, and relocate from Crewe and Darlington to Swindon, a review of the freight locomotive on the eve of Churchward's revolution in design shows that, with the exception of a handful of engines mentioned above, the freight engine of 1904 was not significantly larger than that of forty years earlier. Yes, there were improvements in materials and manufacturing techniques, and steam pressures were generally higher by thirty or forty pounds; steel had replaced iron in boiler and chassis, and lubrication was better, just.

That said, apart from the demise of double frames, and multiplication of individual types, speeds, loads and overall performance had increased by only the slenderest of margins, and most, if not all of that gain had been eroded by the burgeoning congestion that was spawning the first quadruple tracked main lines. That growth of traffic was mostly coal; the eight track railway beckoned (the 'Park Mile' at Tredegar Park, Newport), and before the first decade of the twentieth century was out, the four tracked Taff Vale Railway south of Pontypridd had been joined by six more lines of rails, in the same valley, from three different companies, all hoping for a share in the river of black gold flowing from the proverbial Eden. The pressure for heavier trains worked more economically was growing inexorably.

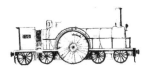

Chapter Eighteen:

The Dinosaur Decades: Freight 1903-1960: Bigger and Heavier is Slower and Worse

History records that those who stand still are soon left behind, and as we have seen, the freight locomotive in 1900 had stood still for nigh on forty years, while passenger speeds and train weights were rising, and the pressure of competition was forever demanding more. On the heavy goods and mineral side, which meant coal, iron ore, and limestone primarily, dumb buffered wagons had given way to those with sprung buffers. Loose-coupled and unbraked, except for a hand brake, the evocative clatter as strings of these wagons were marshalled or pulled into motion, with engine pull rippling through the couplings is, once heard, never forgotten. The five ton wagon gave way slowly to the ten ton, and as the century advanced, sixteen and then twenty one tonners appeared.

Attempts to introduce bogie wagons were stoutly resisted by owners of wagons and goods, as new facilities were needed to load and unload them. Unbraked wagons built out to the full loading gauge never made the grade, and covered vans, for general merchandise, were not designed to be heavy load carriers. Only iron ore, due to its high weight to volume ratio, eventually received wagons that made full use of the railway's axle load, and that was a story still some way in the future. In 1903 the future was bright, Swindon designed and directed, and the pride and joy of George Jackson Churchward.

In 1900 Britain was a long way behind United States railroads in heavy haulage, and there is little doubt that Churchward took the idea of an eight coupled locomotive with a leading pony truck, the 2-8-0 'Consolidation' type, from a plethora of Yankee leviathans. There was no need to invent, only borrow, and adoption of this type, effectively as the standard British twentieth century heavy freight locomotive, while not concluding development, went a good way down that road. There were even fewer new ideas applied to freight locomotives after 1903, when the first engine emerged from Swindon works, than there were to be to Great Western express engines.

To the '2800' class, as the locomotives were called, goes the accolade of being the definitive twentieth century heavy freight locomotive; powerful, a boiler well able to supply two outside cylinders the steam they needed, and heavy enough to provide the all important adhesion. Robustly constructed, these engines lasted the Great Western for almost the rest of its existence (for those of you who fondly believe that God's Wonderful Railway lost its independence in 1948, history records otherwise!) In the light of subsequent developments the design might be accused of an excess of complicated and expensive items, but the sharply-coned boiler and intricately-curved firebox had both long life and top notch steam raising in mind.

Such a design was not cheap to build, but was a long way ahead of the competition in performance, economy and reliability, and the details, with exceptionally long piston stroke and inside Stephenson link motion operating Churchward's ground breaking long lap and travel valves, were ideal for the purpose of starting very heavy trains and keeping them moving up the steepest gradients. The same valve layout that made the two cylinder 'Saints' superior on starting and hill climbing to the four cylinder 'Stars', made the '2800s' master of the hard slog. The cylinder stroke of thirty inches was not to be exceeded on a British locomotive, making for maximum tractive effort, and as with all Great Western two cylinder designs, piston valves under the smokebox meant a very free and sharp exhaust; if ever a locomotive barked at starting, then it was the '2800s'.

In concept and execution, the '2800s' were only superceded by the last of the British Railway standard designs, the '9F' of 1954; for sixty years a single design sufficed to handle heavy goods and mineral traffic, and only in the last decade of steam were they displaced from the heaviest duties. Churchward was first to put the successor to the six-coupled freight locomotive on the rails, and it was by no means clear if others were going to follow in the run-up to 1914. For eight years after 1903, apart from a handful of eight

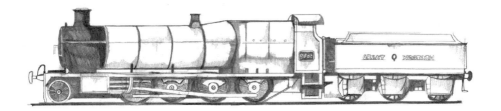

Provenance: GWR 20th Century heavy freight locomotive, concept derived from USA freight designs.
Designer: G. J. Churchward.

Principal Features: Coned boiler, large outside cylinders, inside valves and valve gear.

Principal Dimensions.

Cylinders: 18^1/$_2$in diameter, 30in stroke, outside frames.
Working Pressure: 225psi.
Tractive Effort: 35,380lb.
Driving wheels: 4ft 7 ^{1}/$_2$in diameter.
Valves: Piston valves between frames, inside Stephenson Link Motion.
Weight in W. O: 75 tons 10cwt.

Figure 36: 2800-280.

coupled designs, no company made a move to displace the 0-6-0. This inertia was eventually broken by the Great Central Railway, whose Gorton works produced a '2800' lookalike with a parallel boiler, but effectively to a significantly lower specification than the real thing. When the Railway Operating Department of the Ministry of Munitions opted for this design after 1916, as an engine for the battle zones of France, and ordered far more than were needed, Robinson made a lot of money on royalties, and saw his engines used on many railways, at home and abroad.

The London and North Western made a move to update the six coupled freight engine in 1912, but only with an eight coupled 0-8-0, the only pre-grouping design from that company to survive to the 1960's, and looking very dated after World War Two. Bowen Cooke's 'G1' class was sufficiently robust and effective to be rebuilt with a new boiler and superheater (turning it into a 'G2'), and survive the LMS's critical analysis of cost and performance in the 1930s. By 1960, the 'G2' was one of only two classes of locomotives in British Railway's stock to be equipped with Joy valve gear. Finally, the Great Northern produced its first 2-8-0 to Gresley's design in 1913. Thus at the outbreak of the First War only five of the pre-grouping companies had state of the art heavy freight locomotives on their tracks, and only one had these 'modern' designs in quantity (the Great Northern tally, for example, was just five); their lack of preparedness for the First War (and what the twentieth century was going to deal out in the aftermath) was as universal as was the concept of the war being 'over by Christmas'.

The first of a new breed of fast freight or mixed traffic locomotives, the 'Mogul', 2-6-0 built to Churchward's design at the suggestion of his assistant, Herbert Holcroft, emerged from Swindon works in 1911 as the '4300' class. It was this type of engine that was to be Nigel Gresley's first design (classed 'K1' by the LNER), being built at Doncaster from 1912. As progenitors of true mixed traffic designs, not being 'expresses' that weren't, they and their successors are covered elsewhere. The 'Mogul' as a concept was shamelessly borrowed from North America, where Holcroft had seen it while on holiday.

At the conclusion of the First War, the need for extra power on the front of heavy freight was met to a degree by the War Office hiring out Robinson engines it had ordered but no longer needed. For a single design to be seen on all the major companies' lines (southern companies more or less excepted) was unique at this period; even the Great Western had some. When the time came to dispose of the engines by offering them for sale, while there was no shortage of buyers, there was no long term traffic boom to make it a sellers' market, and it was seven years before the last was sold. The first sales had been at a good price (more than the government paid for them!) but as the years rolled by and the engines deteriorated, prices fell until the remaining few fetched under ten per cent of their original construction cost. With present-day diesel locomotives easily notching up price tags of over a million sterling, it is notable to record that the first cost of a large freight locomotive in 1918, even at inflated wartime prices, was under eight and a half thousand pounds.

With economic conditions in 1920 a world away from the heady days of the run up to 1914, it is perhaps not surprising that there was no major shift to large freight locomotives; what pre-grouping companies contributed to the "Big Four" was a host of six coupled designs more or less adequate for the task. With only two-thirds of the 1914 tonnage of coal being mined, and better asset utilisation of the bigger companies (in theory at least), engine stocks were not in great need of massive replacement or augmentation.

The 1920s, then, did not usher in a brave new world for heavy freight; there was competition for short haul and lightweight goods from the motor lorry, a technology that had advanced by leaps and bounds in the war. For the most part the railways just went belly up; never having had to compete for traffic, they quite simply did not know how to. That the lorry did not, yet, compete for the heavy stuff, did not make the railways sit up and take notice, and efforts made between the wars to hold the lorry at bay were concentrated upon medium and long haul fast freight. The designs of heavy haul engines to emerge in the 1920s were thus the plodders and sloggers of the previous generation; Gresley's first, and somewhat over-complicated, three cylinder freight engine was a 2-8-0, and sixty five of these (LNER class 'O2') would be built, the last emerging in 1943.

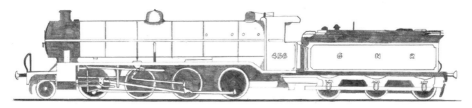

Provenance: Prototype 3 cylinder heavy freight locomotive intended to supercede earlier 0-6-0 and 0-8-0 designs, developed by the LNER in the 1920's.
Designer: H. N. Gresley.

Principal Features: Long parallel boiler and round top firebox, conjugated Gresley-Holcroft valve gear.

Principal Dimensions:
Cylinders: Three, $18^1/_2$in diameter, 26in stroke.
Working Pressure: 180psi.
Tractive Effort: 36,740lb.
Driving wheels: 4ft 8in diameter.
Valves: Piston valves, Walschaerts Motion, with derived action for inside valve.
Weight in W. O: 75 tons 6cwt.

Figure 37: Gresley 2-8-0.

Taking the issue of heavy haul to its logical conclusion was Gresley's next step, with a trailing axle added to the 2-8-0 to make it a 2-8-2, fitted with a boiler and firebox of the same design (they were in fact identical and interchangeable) as that fitted to 'A1' Pacifics. These engines could handle trains larger than could be fitted in block sections and sidings, and were the most powerful engines, bar one, to ever haul a rake of wagons. As wagons generally remained without continuous brakes, the 'P1's' were never given duties that made full use of their haulage capacity, and survived their designer by only four years, the last being withdrawn at the end of the Second World War.

Not to be outdone in dinosaur building, the LMS, being quite unable to design an efficient modern freight locomotive, turned to Beyer Peacock and Co. to sort out its little difficulty. The result was a variation of the low speed articulated 'Beyer Garrett' locomotive, built in numbers for overseas service; two 'Mogul' power units supporting a large boiler and firebox. By adopting many of the LMS's then-standard (mostly pre-war Midland) engineering details, such as poor bearing design (and, of course, that sixty-year-old slab-sided firebox), these engines helped put an end to chronic double heading on the Midland main line, but were displaced and scrapped when a better alternative (the '9F') made an appearance in the 1950s.

William Stanier's definitive heavy freight locomotive, quickly put into production with the LMS in the 1930s to make up for lost time, was in effect an updated Churchward '2800', fast enough to be pressed into passenger service when needed, and doing in the Second War what Robinson's engines had in the First. The '8F's', as they were called after their power classification, found themselves in service in Europe and Asia. Alterations to the design (round top firebox in place of a Belpaire, for example), production methodology and materials turned the '8F' into the 'Austerity' freight locomotive of the Second World War, several hundred of which found their way on to the rails of Britain in the late 1940's.

Finally, and in defiance of the dinosaur theory of twentieth century freight locomotives, E. S. Cox (who didn't really get the credit for the best engine built by British Railways) oversaw design of the '9F', the definitive heavy hauler. Faster than any of its predecessors (90mph down Shap bank on a passenger train), more powerful and versatile than many mixed traffic types, and effectively built to the limit of hand firing. The '9F' 2-10-0 was master of its work (two thousand tons in one train), but came too late to change the way freight was handled, some engines being withdrawn after as little as five years' service. By the time the '9F' was on the rails, the flight of freight from the railways had begun in earnest, and when the last heavy freight locomotives were withdrawn in 1967, their replacements were already short of work, made dinosaurs themselves by a system unable to change.

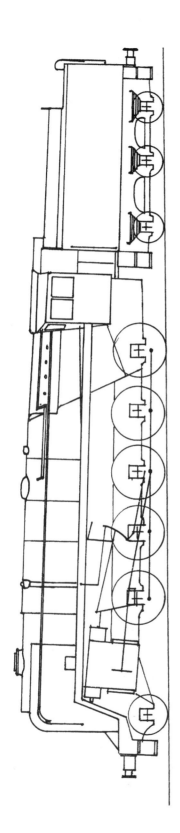

Provenance: 'As large a freight locomotive that would fit the loading gauge and could be fired by hand'. Tenuous relationship with WW2 'Austerity' designs.
Designer: R. Riddles/ E. S. Cox.

Principal Features: Large boiler and firebox, high running plate, large inclined outside cylinders, full cab.

Principal Dimensions:
Cylinders: 20in diameter, 28in stroke, outside frames.
Working Pressure: 250psi.
Tractive Effort: 39,670lb.
Driving wheels: 5ft 0in diameter.
Valves: Piston valves, outside Walschaerts gear.
Weight in W. O: 86 tons 14cwt.

Figure 38: 9F 2-10-0.

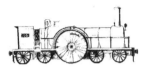

Chapter Nineteen:

Betwixt the Twain:
The Evolution of Mixed Traffic Locomotives

In the last decade of the nineteenth century, mixed traffic locomotives were very much mythical beasts; rumour of their presence abounded, only no-one could agree what they looked like, despite many claiming not only to have seen one, but designed and built them as well. Perhaps this is just a little fanciful, for locomotive engineers had been designing engines for all sorts of traffic, not just express passenger and heavy freight, for many decades, but the truly versatile design, capable of all tasks excluding the very fast and excruciatingly slow, was once again the stuff of dreams. The reason for this was the same as for development of freight and express types; poor valve design.

Sticking large wheels under an engine helped it go fast (provided you got a lot of other details right), just as small wheels enabled the flat out fifteen mile an hour slog. A set of wheels between these extremes however, was quite likely to be neither fish nor fowl; unsuited to grinding along, and unable to muster a gallop. What had evolved in the last quarter of the nineteenth century was a system of hand-me-downs, those locomotives from the top link that were well on their way to needing an overhaul joined the 'never weres', designed for fast services and unable to live up to expectations. Neither of these groups of locomotives was able to deliver, either on cost or quality, and as the gap between fast passenger and slow freight widened, so too did the realisation dawn that something appropriately designed for this growing class of traffic was urgently needed.

A quick trawl of running sheds in the decade prior to the First War gives an idea of the paucity of this type. First stop in this decade has to be Swindon, and true to form, Churchward's adoption of Holcroft's suggestion to build a 'Mogul', 2-6-0, sets the theme for mixed traffic engines; moderate power rating, driving wheel diameter between five foot six and six two, and light weight giving wide availability. Yet the '4300' class did not appear until 1911, and as we have already noted, the 'Mogul' was to be Nigel Gresley's first design in 1912, one he was to develop to suit a wide range of duties, from fast fish to Highland hill climbing.

The North Eastern, too, was 'getting round to it'; its 'S' type, which failed to make the grade as an express 4-6-0, was eventually evolved over a decade into the 'S3' of 1919 (LNER class 'B16'), which passed muster as a true mixed traffic locomotive, hauling intermediate passenger trains and fast goods with an effectiveness that was rewarded with forty years' service, virtually all of it north of the Humber. South of the Thames, the London, Brighton and South Coast Railway weighed in with a small but powerful 'Mogul', Billinton's 'K' class. Like subsequent contributions from the 'Southern' railways in this field, Billinton's engines adhered closely to Henry Morgan's maxim, 'though we be few in number, our hearts be very great'; there was much less plunder to be hauled on southern metals, and mixed traffic types never ran to the hundreds needed by northern companies.

Last to join the numbers of this elite band was a contribution from Derby Works of the Midland Railway, not for itself but for its sibling, the Somerset and Dorset, the rambling railway that was setting records for slow trains long before Flanders and Swann realised there were lyrics to be had in the station names. On any other railway the 2-8-0 would have been a freight engine, but the Somerset and Dorset regarded these as mixed traffic machines, and accordingly used them on everything. This state of affairs lasted into the 1960's when it was still possible to take four hours to travel between Bath and Bournemouth, at an average speed of 25mph. British Railways was proud enough of this achievement to allow the 'Pines Express' headboard to be sported.

To paraphrase George Stephenson a century earlier (giving evidence on the bill for the Great Western Railway), "I could imagine a slower 'express', but I do not know of one". The Midland promptly had nothing further to do with mixed traffic designs for the remainder of its existence.

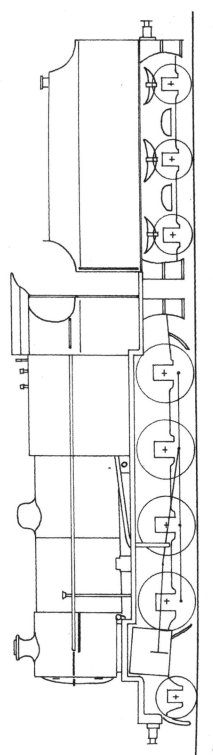

Provenance: Midland design for the Somerset and Dorset Joint Railway.
Designer: H. Fowler.

Principal Features: Freight locomotive used as a mixed traffic engine; small wheels, outside cylinders, large dome, slab sided firebox.

Principal Dimensions:
Cylinders: Two, 21in diameter, 28in stroke, outside frames.
Working Pressure: 190psi.
Tractive Effort: 35,295lb.
Driving wheels: 4ft 8$\frac{1}{2}$in diameter.
Valves: Piston valves outside frames, outside Walschaerts gear.
Weight in W. O: 64 tons 15cwt.

Figure 39: S&D 2-8-0.

New locomotive designs were few and far between during the years of the First World War, but the South Eastern and Chatham Railway was in the front line in hauling cannon fodder to the Western Front, and this gave R. E. L. Maunsell the opportunity to design a new locomotive at the end of 1916. The concept of a mogul with outside cylinders and valve gear was quite in keeping with all subsequent mixed traffic design, Gresley apart, and if the locomotives looked a little on the small side to northern eyes, they embodied much of Maunsell's thinking on design that was quite as advanced as that of Swindon. The first of class 'N' emerged in 1917, surviving the craze for electrification between the wars to achieve a ripe old age.

The start of the 1920s heralded the first of Nigel Gresley's mixed traffic locomotives in which the three cylinder layout with conjugated derived valve motion for the inside cylinder was applied to a high speed engine for the first time. The 'K3' 'Mogul' was a powerful and sprightly machine, well suited to fast fish and intermediate passenger duties, and capable of turning in a reasonable performance on deputy service for express, and slow freight work. For forty years the massive, six foot diameter parallel boiler and round top fireboxes of these engines was a daily sight south of York, sharing work on the east coast with the 'B16s. Smaller versions of the 'K3' came to be built for service in Scotland, where axle loadings were lower and structure gauge less generous, particularly in the Highlands, and the last of these would not be built for a further quarter of a century. If the 'Mogul' defined Gresley's approach to mixed traffic in the 'twenties, then it was Swindon, under C. B. Collett, that defined the true mixed traffic locomotive as a two cylinder 4-6-0.

The lead the Great Western gained in express locomotive design, with production of the first 'Castle', created something of a dilemma in that the two cylinder 'Saint' locomotives were technically only slightly inferior in haulage capacity to both 'Castles' and 'Stars', which were the preferred express types. Having decided upon four cylinder locomotives for express work, the need for something more versatile than the rather light 'Mogul' then in service, to handle fast freight and intermediate passenger work was not met by what was in concept an express engine. Rebuilding the 'Saints' with smaller six foot wheels created the 'Hall', neatly turning a class for which there was no long term future into the epitome of versatility, or nearly so. The 'Hall' class retained the valve and front end layout of twenty years earlier, and were accordingly quick off the mark and impressive up hills. At high speed their performance was limited by a rapid fall-off in drawbar pull caused by poor steam distribution, but the Great Western nearly

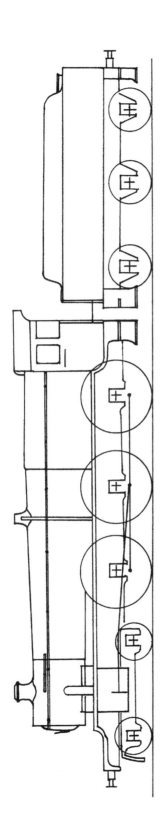

Principal Features: Prototype post WW1 mixed traffic 4-6-0, taper boiler, outside cylinders with long (30in) stroke, and inside valve gear.

Principal Dimensions:
Cylinders: Two, 18½in diameter, 30in stroke, outside frames.
Working Pressure: 225psi.
Tractive Effort: 27,273lb.
Driving wheels: 6ft 0in diameter.
Valves: Piston valves between frames, inside Stephenson Link Motion.
Weight in W. O: 75 tons 0cwt.

Provenance: Rebuild of GWR two cylinder 1907 'Saint' express locomotives with six foot wheels.
Designer: G. J. Churchward/C. Collett.

Figure 40: Hall 4-6-0.

ran out of halls to name them after, so numerous did the class become. If the Great Western was leading the express field in 1923, arrival of the 'Hall' in 1928, to design parameters of nearly twenty five years earlier, while defining the mixed traffic type, could hardly be described as the white heat of technology.

The reason for this seeming inertia, and the 'Halls' were after all a rebuild, not a whole new locomotive, was the spiralling of both British and world economies into a mind-numbing recession. Making do became essential in the short term, and both LNER and LMS had numbers of engines that would 'do' for mixed traffic, if only because they would not do for anything else. The LMS also possessed, seemingly more by accident than design, an excellent mixed traffic locomotive in the shape of the Hughes 2-6-0, turned out by the Horwich Works of the Lancashire and Yorkshire Railway at the 'Grouping' in 1923. With seemingly ridiculously large and steeply inclined outside cylinders, the locomotives were called 'Crabs', and over two hundred were built from 1926, giving nearly forty years' sterling service.

When William Stanier arrived at the LMS in 1932, his first mixed traffic engines, emerging a year later, were an updated copy of this successful design, matched for wheel size and tractive effort. The following year however the prototype 'Black 5', a modernised 'Hall', made its bow, and quickly became the most numerous engine of the twentieth century.

The immediate success of the 'Black 5' was not just due to excellence of both concept and design, but a stark reflection of the paucity of existing motive power. With a modern front end and a free steaming boiler, the mixed traffic 4-6-0 was superior to all LMS pre-grouping express types, equal to the 'Royal Scot' in some respects, and it terms of maintenance and reliability, better. Perhaps no other locomotive performed such a wide range of duties over a 'patch' that extended from Swansea and Bournemouth to Thurso, hauling express trains on lines where heavier engines were not permitted, and maintaining fast schedules on relief services. Likewise all forms of freight were within remit, and it was only the heaviest duties that needed double heading or an '8F'. Having come up trumps with the mixed traffic engine, the LMS experimented with batches of engines with Caprotti poppet valves and roller bearing axleboxes; the latter caught on, though poppet valves did not (the classic example of a better design being unable to oust the *status quo*). In haulage terms the British Railways version was nearly identical, but there were detail differences, and as an aesthetic composition, Stanier's original had a unity lacking in the later copy.

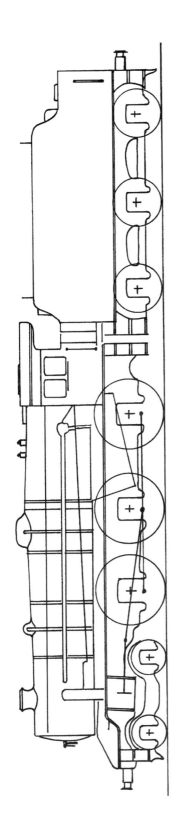

Principal Features: Taper boiler 4-6-0, reverse taper to firebox top, top feed. Some engines equipped with double chimneys and/or Caprotti valves (post 1945 engines only). Numerous other detail differences. Most numerous and widely distributed locomotive on British Railways.

Principal Dimensions:
Cylinders: Two, 18$^{1}/_{2}$in diameter, 28in stroke, outside frames.
Working Pressure: 225psi
Tractive Effort: 25,455lb.
Driving wheels: 6ft 0in diameter.
Valves: Piston valves outside frames, outside Walschaerts Motion.
Weight in W. O: 72 tons 2cwt.

Provenance: 1934 definitive mixed traffic design copying and updating many features of the GWR 'Hall' with the valve gear outside and piston valves moved from between the frames to above the cylinders.

Figure 41: Black 5.

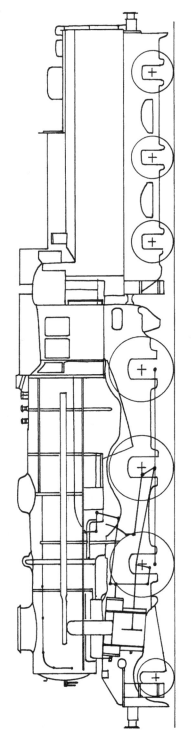

Figure 42: 4MT 2-6-0.

Provenance: 1957 development of 1951 design derived from LMS Stanier/Ivatt mixed traffic locomotives. British Railway's last mixed traffic design.

Designer: Britsh Railways Brighton design office.

Principal Features: 'Standard' locomotive with raised running plate and double chimney.

Principal Dimensions:

Cylinders: Two, 18in diameter, 28in stroke, outside frames.

Working Pressure: 225psi.

Tractive Effort: 25,500lb.

Driving wheels: 5ft 8in diameter.

Valve: Piston valves outside frames, outside Walschaerts Motion.

Weight in W. O: 69 tons 0cwt.

In 1935, both Great Western and LMS railways had a stock of mixed traffic engines that in retrospect were more or less ideal for their purposes. No such equivalent demand for large numbers of mixed traffic engines was to be found on the Southern, where electrification took much of the passenger traffic growth into its bosom. The LNER in contrast was still wedded to the 'Mogul', with a large gap between the 'K3' and the second line express engines, the 'B17' 4-6-0 (the 'B17' was actually designed by North British Locomotive as an engine that would fit the turntables on the former Great Eastern Lines between London and Norwich). Gresley's response to this deficiency was a locomotive not far short of the express 'Pacifics', the 2-6-2 'V2'. Launched as both a fast freight class and an intermediate passenger, the first, and now only surviving, engine was named *Green Arrow,* to publicise the 1936 introduction of the express freight service of the same name.

The locomotives proved themselves master of the heaviest duties, though high axle loads prevented their use over much LNER route mileage, and they were not great wanderers further afield. Good as the 'V2' was, the lack of wide route availability, the 'go anywhere' factor that gives operational flexibility and economy, meant that Edward Thompson had the task during the Second World War of designing a true mixed traffic 4-6-0, turned out as the neat and attractive 'B1' and meeting the operational criteria of 'cheap and cheerful' admirably.

On the formation of British Railways in 1948, while there was need for more of the same in terms of additional mixed traffic locomotives, met for the most part by copying pre-nationalisation designs, divergence caused by increasing train speeds, that had generated the genre, was once more converging. Failure of engineers in the nineteenth century to solve the dilemma over valve gear, and consequential adoption of large wheel/small wheel passenger/freight engines had opened the way for something betwixt the twain. Solving the 'valve problem' narrowed the gap between extremes, with the result that standard designs of express and mixed traffic locomotives after 1950 shared the same six foot two wheel diameter. Production of more than three types of British Railway standard locomotives was due to the realisation that, in the drive to secure economy of working, then boiler output must be matched to duty.

For the time being at least, those duties varied from the leisurely half dozen wagon pick up goods, to moderately timed and quite heavy passenger traffic, and while the half dozen or so true

191

mixed traffic classes could reach perhaps 80% of the system, there were many short lines and one or two longer ones where lighter axle loads were imposed by the civil engineer.

The last mixed traffic locomotives were LMS derived 'Moguls', of lower weight and power output, distinctive in their angular simplicity and diminutive appearance. Their working lives were short as their duties vanished in the late 1950s and early 1960s, displaced first by diesel multiple units from secondary passenger work, and altogether by atrophy of the network. Their working lives were often alongside the other significant motive power source, the tank engine, long the answer to many an insolvent railway company's prayers, but doing much humdrum work out of the limelight.

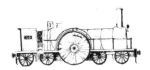

Chapter Twenty:

A Tank for all Reasons : A Century of the Tank Locomotive 1860 - 1960

At the bottom of any heap, the smallest of the breed will always be found, and the idea of making a locomotive carry its own coal and water was attractive from the earliest days. The concept quickly gained a bad press because there are limited places on an engine chassis where bulky and weighty items can be stored, and not only must coal be accessible to the fireman, but water has a tedious habit of sloshing around, and altering the locomotive's centre of gravity as it is used. These factors combined to make design of a fast and stable tank engine a bit of a challenge. As we have seen, there was a long standing obsession with the relationship between the locomotive centre of gravity and the question of stability, particularly at speed. The huge express tank engines on the broad gauge Bristol and Exeter Railway after 1854 had not led to large numbers of high speed tank designs, and on the standard gauge, the type was destined for the back of house role of banking, shunting and branch line work for most of the century under review. Development of a fast main line tank locomotive on the standard gauge had to wait until the 1880s.

Apart from the question of where to store fuel and water, and to resolve the need to make the varying centre of gravity as low as possible, tank engines offered a number of very attractive benefits. There was no particular need for the engine to travel chimney-first; neither was it essential to have turntables, though most footplate staff preferred to point the right way if any appreciable distance was to be run. Shunting and banking were easier as the buffing point was closer, at the rear at least, and the weight of fuel and water added to the available adhesion. In the smaller sizes, and there were plenty of these, engine wheelbase was not much greater than that of the wagons, allowing tight curves in yards and sidings (and not infrequently, on the street as well) to be open to steam traction rather than just the horse shunter.

In 1860, at the start of the career of the tank engine proper, there were a number of unusual, and a few downright odd, designs of tank locomotive. The express tanks on the broad gauge, designed by J. Pearson, the Bristol and Exeter locomotive superintendent, were equipped with driving wheels nine feet in diameter, and a four wheel bogie at each end. There is some doubt as to whether it was intended that the locomotives should run bunker first, but clearly they were heading for the 'Pushmi-Pulyu' look. At this early date the bogie was equipped only with a ball and socket connection to the engine; the principle of secondary springing and lateral control was some way in the future. Combined with no flanges on the driving wheels it is surprising that there were no major derailments with these engines for many years. A crash in 1876 signalled the end of these leviathans as tank engines, being converted to tender locomotives, a not uncommon fate for tanks that were suspected of being unstable.

If the big players in the railway industry had by 1860 all put their locomotive design and building strategies in place, then there were a large number of impecunious little concerns, born on the back of the railway mania, who struggled to complete their line of rails, let alone dabble in the muddy pond of locomotive design. To these hopefuls there was little prospect in the short to medium term of equipping themselves with the motive power they desired; they were obliged to cut their coats to their cloth and buy or hire whatever their empty purses would run to. To satisfy this market, private engine builders offered a number of standard types, and perhaps the first of a classic line of six wheeled 'bargain basement' tank engines was that first produced by Beyer Peacock of Manchester in 1861. Whether they were copying the products of the railway companies, or were themselves being copied is not really at issue, for these were standard engines of unexceptional dimensions. Beyer Peacock's model had a leading axle and four coupled wheels, inside frames and a boiler pressed to 120psi. Designed for modest loads and even more modest speeds, these engines were cheap and cheerful off-the-peg power, and it is not surprising that this product remained in the sales catalogue for twenty years, with only minor modifications. Reversing the wheel

Provenance: 1854 express broad gauge locomotive, taking advantage of the generous loading gauge to dispense with the need for a tender.

Designer: W. Pearson.

Principal Features: Large single driver broad gauge express tank locomotive.

Principal Dimensions:

Cylinders: Two, $16^1/_2$in diameter, 24in stroke, inside frames.
Working Pressure: 120psi.
Tractive Effort: 6,170lb.
Driving wheels: 9ft 0in diameter.
Valves : Slide valves between frames, inside Stephenson Link Motion.
Weight in W. O: 42 tons 0cwt.

Figure 43: Bristol & Exeter 4-2-4 tank.

arrangement and putting a trailing axle in place of the leading one had no real effect on the end result, but both layouts were popular, just as tender engines of this format were in the 1860s.

This mainstream of tank engine life quickly spawned a number of offshoots: a leading bogie; trailing bogies that supported what was more a rigidly attached tender than a tank; coal bunkers behind the footplate or at the side of the firebox; tanks underneath or on top of the boiler, this last variety coming early and staying longest. As one of the first saddle-tank locomotives was for an aggressive and insolvent concern with a *real* mountain to climb as well as the financial one, a look at this pioneer is in order.

In 1865, Sharp, Stewart and Co. designed and built what was basically a Stephenson 'Long Boiler' six-coupled engine, with a saddle-tank over the boiler barrel and smokebox, and side coal bunkers alongside the firebox. The purchasers were the Brecon and Merthyr Railway, whose 'main line' included the seven miles at 1 in 38/40 from Talybont to Torpantau. Other gradients from Bargoed to Fochrhiw and thence to Dowlais Top were only marginally less demanding; it could have been worse, for the seven mile bank was nearly built on the line of the Brynore (Brynoer) Tramway, which had a ruling gradient of 1 in 25. To carry themselves and a modest load up these gradients, a total of about 140 tons, the engines were worked flat out at between six and ten miles an hour, evaporating the 1100 gallons of water in the tank at a rate that required a halt every hour to refill.

Like all long boiler designs, the Brecon and Merthyr engines were not suited to high speed, and speeds down the banks were, circumspectly, no greater than those uphill. Level sections that were straight were few and far between, but these engines were the mainstay of a railway over forty miles long, mostly single track, where meeting the minimum twelve miles an hour average speed of the 'parliamentary' passenger trains was quite a challenge. The success of these engines was paralleled elsewhere, and the saddle-tank (the tank itself occupied various sections of the smokebox, boiler or firebox) became a permanent fixture on the railways of Britain, increasingly on goods, shunting and mineral duties as the century advanced. By the end of the Second World War the type had become standard for all duties on the private mine and quarry systems of Britain, and one of their number was almost certainly the last commercial steam locomotive in service on this island. As a contrast to this extreme working environment, the main line of the London, Brighton and South Coast Railway, was home to William Stroudley's 1872 design of 'Terrier' Tank, perhaps the archetypal six-coupled side tank engine, of excellent proportions best described as 'small but perfectly formed'.

Rebuilt after the turn of the century by Earle Marsh, eleven of these locomotives survived on the stock list of the nationalised railway in 1960, by then making a serious challenge for the title of 'Least Powerful Locomotive' on British Railways, being roundly beaten in tractive effort terms by the two foot gauge Vale of Rheidol engines. When first introduced on a line that long favoured tank engines for even the heaviest duties, the 'Terrier' was a reflection of the contrast between the railways of the North and West, which had a man's job to do, and those of the South, where distances were shorter, loads lighter and the hills were not mountains.

If the 'Terrier' survived on the basis of its good looks, another tank engine, the 2-4-0 well tank design of Joseph Beattie, definitely lands in the ugly duckling class. Emerging onto the London and South Western Railway in 1874, these engines underwent surgery, which does not appear to have improved the engine's beauty points,

Provenance: 1860s bargain basement power for impoverished railways
Designer: Sharp Stewart & Co.

Principal Features: Rudimentary full cab. Saddle tank covering boiler and
smokebox.

Principal Dimensions:

Cylinders: Two, 17in diameter, 24in stroke, inside frames.
Working Pressure: 140psi.
Tractive Effort: 15,284lb.
Driving wheels: 4ft 6in diameter.
Valves: Slide valves between frames.
Weight in W. O: 38 tons 0cwt.

Figure 44: Brecon and Merthyr Tank.

at the hands of successive locomotive engineers: Adams, over the
twelve years after 1884, Urie in 1921, and lastly Maunsell after 1931.
The well tank, where the water tank sits between the plate frames
as close to the track as possible, was a solution to the low centre of
gravity obsession, but meant that the tank competed for space with
the valve gear. By 1960 the three survivors were limited to the
Wenfordbridge branch in deepest Cornwall, where their small size
suited the tight curves and restricted clearances on a line dedicated
to the export of china clay.

The era of the fast tank locomotive, hauling light passenger
trains on the Standard Gauge over short and medium distances,
was born in 1880 with the introduction of the 4-4-2 'Atlantic' tank
on the London Tilbury and Southend Railway. Taking a lead from
the 'Terrier', these were handsome locomotives, though of much
greater haulage capacity on a line that had no gradient much
steeper than level or longer than a few furlongs. Fenchurch Street
station in London was to see a great deal of this type of locomotive,
the trains being hauled by successive generations of tank engines

until electrification eighty years later. The application of tank engines to this kind of brisk work led directly to production of smaller designs for branch lines and for commuting, of which one design, based on the 0-4-4 wheel arrangement, was developed extensively by various engineers, where much of the total weight of the locomotive was borne by the driving wheels and thus available for adhesion.

Provenance: 1880 design for the London, Tilbury and Southend Railway, outside cylinder/inside valve gear, rear tank and bunker. A new design concept when introduced for all classes of traffic.

Designer: Sharp, Stewart & Co.

Principal Features: Small boilered 'Atlantic' tank locomotive with features derived primarily from the 4-4-0 tender engine; leading bogie supporting cylinders and smokebox, deep firebox between coupled axles.

Principal Dimensions:
Cylinders: Two, 17in diameter, 26in stroke, outside frames.
Working Pressure: 160psi.
Tractive Effort: 14,000lb.
Driving wheels: 6ft 1in diameter.
Valves: Slide valves between frames, inside Stephenson Link Motion.
Weight in W. O: 56 tons 3cwt.

Figure 45: LTS 4-4-2 tank.

The North Eastern Railway made wide use of the 0-4-4, designating it as 'BTP' (Bogie Tank Passenger), later LNER class 'G5', the original design by Edward Fletcher having appeared as early as 1874, being modified by Wilson Worsdell after 1890 into a modern locomotive, and only rendered obsolete by the first generation of diesel multiple units after 1955. The London and South

Western Railway developed a similar tank, the 'M7', being one of Dugald Drummond's first locomotives after his appointment in 1895. The Great Western, while attracted to the concept, turned out an engine with just a single trailing axle, the '1400' class, as late as 1932, when it was just a little dated. The main line of tank development, having taken a turn away from the small engine policy of the last quarter of the nineteenth century, once again went through a phase of getting just a mite too big for its wheels, before the emergence of mature designs in the twentieth century.

Having designed a locomotive in the sure knowledge that it was far too small for the growth of train weights at the end of the nineteenth century, the London and Brighton company set about putting the record straight in the years immediately prior to the First War, first with a 'Pacific' tank to the design of D. E. Marsh in 1912, and then with a 4-6-4 weighing in at just a couple of tons under a 'ton', by L.B. Billinton. This was the largest tank engine built for main line service in Britain, and was not destined to survive in the manner of the 'Terrier'. In terms of duty however, the prize for the biggest tank dinosaur goes to the London and North Western Railway, and for once it was not completely the company's doing.

When we looked at the Brecon and Merthyr Railway and its heavy duty practical saddle-tank engines, there is no doubt that they had to deal with one of the longest and steepest inclines in the British Isles. What was also the case was that, like most of their South Walian cousins, most of the traffic was down the grade, not up; coal was hauled up to Torpantau from the South, but the total demand for fuel in the area served by the northern end of the railway was modest owing to a rural hinterland. North of Dowlais a single line of rails sufficed for the whole of the line's existence. The railway that the London and North Western acquired to access the South Wales coalfield was a very different animal; the Merthyr, Tredegar and Abergavenny Railway, and the purpose was much more ambitious than purely local traffic.

The whole concept of the Merthyr to Abergavenny line was to allow coal to be hauled up the valleys rather than down. All traffic generated to and from the Taff, Rhymney, Sirhowy and twin Ebbw valleys fed onto the top of eight miles of 1 in 38/40, down from Brynmawr to the Usk bridge at Abergavenny. Merely operating general merchandise and empty mineral wagons up this grade was a formidable challenge, for the line was tightly curved and not short of tunnels. Operating costs on this eight mile stretch were never less than twice the average for the rest of the London and North Western system.

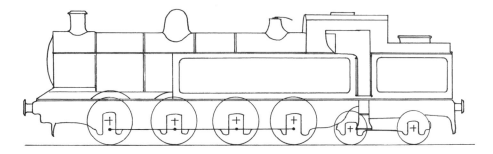

Provenance: Post-WWI heavy shunting and banking locomotive for the LNWR, in many respects a Bowen Cooke 'G2' with extended frame and side tanks.
Designer: H. P. M. Beames.
Principal Features: Long parallel boiler with cylinders, valves and smokebox completely overhanging at the front.
Principal Dimensions:
Cylinders: Two, $20^{1}/_{2}$in diameter, 24in stroke, inside frames.
Working Pressure: 185psi.
Tractive Effort: 29,650lb.
Driving wheels: 4ft $5^{1}/_{2}$in diameter.
Boiler: Large parallel boiler, round topped firebox.
Valve: Piston valves between frames, inside Joy Motion.
Weight in W. O: 88 tons 0cwt.

Figure 46: Beames 0-8-4 tank.

To try and control these costs and provide some heavyweight haulage and braking power, and maximise the line capacity in the immediate post war years, H. P. M. Beames introduced his eight coupled 0-8-4 tank in an effort to get to grips with the task. These locomotives were rendered a little superfluous by the fall-off in freight as recession began to bite in the late 1920 s, and suffered in the same way as any specialised engine; without the traffic for which they were designed they were less economical than more general purpose machines. The schedule for the trip up the bank was an hour, and the spectacle of a locomotive being worked on full regulator and full gear, on this most scenic of routes, is one that is much missed, for British Railways were only too glad to rid themselves of this line, and didn't wait 'til the axeman cometh. Having dealt with the fringe, we can now have a look at the best of the twentieth century designs, which of course means first Swindon, and then Derby and Crewe under the LMS.

The Great Western Railway had a similar need for tank engines as had the railways with which it competed for the coal trade in South Wales; three million tons of coal a year to haul across the level crossing at Gwaun Cae Gurwen and down the precipitous bank into the Amman Valley (the direct line to replace this operating headache was abandoned, part completed, including a handsome curved viaduct that has never carried a train, in 1914). Short runs heavily loaded downhill equals tank engines, and GCG (the locals have always found the full name a mouthful) was only one of a number of locations and routes where the Great Western found tank engines an indispensable aid to shifting the traffic. To this end, Churchward introduced what were basically tank versions of the tender locomotives he designed from 1903 onwards, and if some of the classes were intended for mixed traffic and branch passenger work, the majority were inclined towards the freight locomotive.

Thus the Great Western gained a stock of medium weight 2-6-2 'Prairie' tanks of various detail differences, added to over the years by Charles Collett: a batch of eight-coupled heavy tanks (for the GCG incline, among others), either as 2-8-0's, or later as 2-8-2's with bigger coal bunkers, and as old or inherited six coupled engines went for scrap in the thirties, a design of their own; the pannier tank. The pannier tank was an adaption of the side tank, whereby the running plate and access to the inside motion was maintained by raising the bottom of the tank to a level about one third of the way up the side of the boiler. Old concerns over unstable motion and high centres of gravity were successfully addressed, and several versions were built over twenty years, the last types emerging under British Railways.

As with the tender engine, the Great Western Tank Locomotive was defined in the decade after 1903, and only replicated, panniers excepted, in the years to follow. It was left then to the LMS to set the seal on tank design, and if Sir Henry Fowler could not climb out of the small engine rut (he supervised the building of large numbers of small tank engines, notably the 3F 0-6-0T illustrated overleaf, to complement the numerous small expresses) he could at least lay down ground rules for the definitive tank engines of the mid twentieth century.

Fowler's success with tank engines is in stark contrast to the failure to produce a modern express or freight locomotive, yet despite a dated boiler and firebox, the 2-6-4 tank of 1927 was state-of-the-art in valve design, and accordingly sprightly and economical. Subsequent amended designs by William Stanier, Henry Ivatt and William Fairburn updated the boiler and adjusted the general proportions to suit the intended duties, but the design was still recognisably Sir Henry's. The same can also be said for engines built by British Railways; there really was little more to add in 1950 to the sound principles of 1930-35.

201

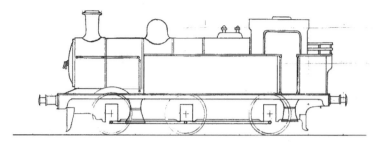

Provenance: 1924 Development of the Midland Railway standard six coupled tank for the LMS, with a history dating back to 1860. Last engines produced 1929.
Designer: H. Fowler.
Principal Features: Inside cylindered six coupled tank engine, smaller than the standard Midland freight locomotive, but similar in almost all other details. Not superheated.

Principal Dimensions
Cylinders: Two, 18in diameter, 26in stroke, inside frames.
Working Pressure: 160psi   Tractive Effort: 20,835lb
Driving wheels: 4ft 7in diameter, Axle load: 16t 10cwt
Boiler: Parallel, with short barrel and small firebox
Valves: Slide valves between frames, inside Stephenson Link Motion.
Weight in W. O: 49 tons 10cwt

Figure 47: LMS 3F 0-6-0 tank

In the decade after nationalisation, LMS style tank engines spread to all the obscure corners of the rail network, performing secondary duties on such lines as the steeply-graded coast route from Scarborough to Whitby, where they replaced the rather dated LNER types. Of the post-grouping railways, the LNER contributed the 'V1' and 'V3' 2-6-2 tanks to the stock of the tank engine and built or rebuilt previous designs, turning the North Eastern's 4-4-4 tanks into 4-6-2s, for example. The Southern Railway, planning wholesale eletrification, had not contributed greatly, after their 'River' class of 2-6-4 tanks had gained a reputation for being unstable at speed and were rebuilt as 'Mogul' tender engines.

In 1960, the most modern design of tank locomotives running in Britain had a pedigree stretching back thirty years. Many were older, all the former Great Western engines dating back in design, if not metal content, to the decade before the First World War. The tank engine's passenger duties were being swept away by diesel multiple units, freight by the road lorry. In contrast to this vanishing role, engines in service on the industrial lines were in fairly robust health; the National Coal Board continued to overhaul steam engines in its area workshops for a further ten years, and to use them for nearly twenty. Most of these engines were saddle-tanks from the private builders, designs little changed from those first engines supplied to the Brecon and Mérthyr a century earlier.

In retrospect the tank engine filled a niche that was generated by the dominance of rail transport and the inflexibility of tender engines. That niche remained only while the steam engine ruled the rails, and was rapidly pinched out after 1960; there was no successful short haul 'go anywhere' diesel or electric replacement. Forty years later the diesel shunter is a rare breed, no new versions having been built since the 1960s, and no design work since the mid-1950s. In design terms the rail system had, after 1945, become virtually an evolution-free zone, even as other transport systems developed rapidly in the same period. Just as the airlines made the express passenger locomotive an extinct species in North America, so too did the bus, car and lorry take the traffic tank engines depended on. If that particular chicken came home to roost on the standard gauge in 1960, then for the narrow gauge the process started fully forty years earlier.

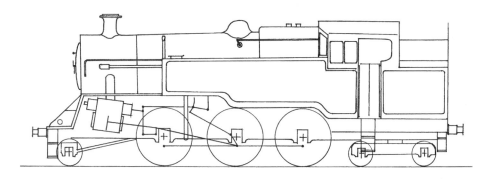

Provenance: Development of the Fowler/Stanier/Fairbairn/Ivatt tanks of the LMS. The last tank engine built in quantity for British Railways.
Designer: R. A. Riddles.
Principal Features: Standard Post Nationalisation tank locomotive, with stepped lower tank sections to clear external motion.
Principal Dimensions:
 Cylinders: Two, 18in diameter, 28in stroke, outside frames.
Working Pressure: 225psi.
Tractive Effort: 25,000lb.
Driving wheels: 5ft 8in diameter.
Boiler: High pitched taper boiler, Belpaire type firebox.
Valves: Piston valves outside frames, Outside Walschaerts gear.
Weight in W. O: 88 tons 10cwt.

Figure 48: BR 2-6-4 tank.

Chapter Twenty-One:

Little Wonders:
Narrow Gauge Locomotives
1860 to 1930.

The Standard Gauge has never been universal; it was adopted as a compromise between those early mineral lines that had never been intended to interconnect, but upon which the steam engine drew its first breath, and the need for a track that was adequate for most purposes, but not excessively expensive to build over distances undreamed of in 1800. Like all compromises, this one did not suit everyone, and here the chief dissenters were the Welsh. Builders of mineral lines in 1800, and for some time afterwards, were aware of the need to provide a track adequate for the traffic but cheap to build; a gauge of five feet might be suitable for coal haulage, but where the mineral 'weighed out' rather than 'cubed out', there was little point in a gauge that gave capacity beyond the power of the horse to shift. Consequently the slate railways of Wales were built to the two foot gauge, or a bit more, and their success as horse-drawn tram and railways down to 1860 meant that sooner or later they were going to fall for the fashion of the steam locomotive, whether they actually needed steam or not.

The technical challenge of building a useful locomotive to fit the two foot gauge in 1860 is one that should not be underestimated. Crewe apart, the standard gauge companies were wedded firmly to inside cylinders, for the reason that lateral turning moments generated by piston thrust were lower, and at a time when vehicle dynamics were in their infancy, this was perceived as a major factor in locomotive stability. The same arrangement was impractical on the two foot gauge, where after frames and axle bearings were allowed for, there was less than a foot width in which to accommodate two cylinders, steam chests, and four eccentrics for the valve gear. Even a single common steam chest for two slide valves was not economy enough to permit a tight fit. Conversion of the Ffestiniog Railway to steam showed that it could be done, and that after thirty years of development, even on the small scale, steam locomotives were cheaper than horses.

George England, one of many private locomotive builders to dabble in the narrow gauge, produced the first engines in 1863, and ability to fit both rails and limited structure gauge of the Ffestiniog, and do the task intended, meant that the horse's number was up. *The Princess* and *Prince* set a theme that was to last for seventy years: small wheels to keep the centre of gravity down; outside cylinders that overhung the track to the full structure gauge width, and tanks, or saddle tanks, as big as would fit. There was not a lot of coal space, but the Ffestiniog added a tender, a course of action few other railways found necessary. The Ffestiniog Railway was the second longest steam-worked two foot gauge railway in Britain (the longest line, the Lynton and Barnstaple found no need for tender engines).

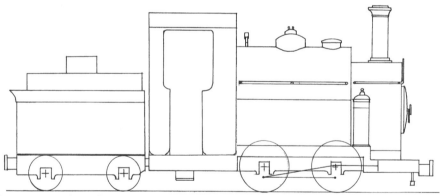

Provenance: One of the pioneer narrow gauge steam locomotives of the Ffestiniog Railway.
Designer: George England Ltd.
Principal Features: narrow gauge saddle tank, originally without cab.
Principal Dimensions:
Cylinders: $8^1/_2$in diameter, 12in stroke, outside frames.
Working Pressure: 160psi (as running in 1983).
Tractive Effort: 4,367lb.
Driving wheels: 2ft 3in diameter.
Boiler: small diameter boiler and small firebox dwarfed by saddle tank
Valves: Slide valves between frames, inside Stephenson Link Motion.
Figure 49: Ffestiniog 'Prince'.

As originally supplied, the George England locomotives (eventually to total six in number) were typical of their times; no cab, not even a spectacle plate to work in one of the wettest climates in Britain, and as the engines aged, rebuilding to match the times they found themselves in changed their appearance. The Ffestiniog was by no means unique in its ability to rebuild its engines, often only contracting out the boiler and firebox work, but the Boston Lodge establishment is one of the few remaining operational nineteenth century locomotive works in the world, and stands a fair chance of being the only one of any gauge within a couple of decades.

Readers will note that the two foot gauge railway was not built to run with steam traction; narrow gauge horse drawn tramroads/railways were relatively common even in 1860, with the Brecon Forest Tramway and the Hay Railway, to quote just two examples (neither of two foot gauge!) extending the line of the Swansea, and Brecon and Abergavenny canals deep into Breconshire. Conversion to standard gauge was the preferred option where passengers were planned to be carried, but after the Ffestiniog showed the way and gained consent from Parliament, steam power on the narrow gauge spread, and prospered, if that is quite the right word.

Application of the locomotive to the Ffestiniog demonstrated the ability of steam to displace the horse and increase line capacity, and the horse-drawn railway, though not the siding, became an outdated anachronism. The proposal to build the Talyllyn Railway in 1865, on the two foot three inch gauge, was for steam power from the start, and the original Fletcher Jennings locomotives are still in use. Seven years earlier, the Talyllyn's neighbour, the Corris Railway, had been incorporated as a horse-drawn tramway; it was not to be the last perhaps, but steam ruled the narrow gauge after 1865.

Diminutive side or saddle tanks on two foot tracks were the smallest practical load hauler, and while there were smaller engines on narrower track (Crewe Works had an eighteen inch system), other smaller than standard railways adopted the saddle tank, usually on four wheels, and frequently turned it into a work of art. The first George England engines lacked a little in grace and proportions, even after several rebuildings, but it was not long before engineer's confidence with this new art form produced the classic diminutive boiler, fronted by a tall chimney of elegant proportions and backed by a cab that it was possible to stand up in, just. With various appendages such as domes, side bunkers, sandboxes and running plates to play with, the Penrhyn, Talyllyn and Corris railways, to name but a well known few, were soon equipped with engines as handsome as the London and Brighton 'Terriers'. While the Penrhyn and Corris lines closed over thirty years ago, some of their original locomotives are still in service, over a century after they were built.

Success of steam on the narrow gauge in Wales led to a spurt of conversions of other railways; narrow tracks were extensively used on industrial sites for internal goods transport, and motive power up to the mid-1860s had been human and animal: horses, donkeys and men, with stationary engine assistance if loads ran uphill. The small steam locomotive, after 1870, became a familiar sight among the mines, furnaces and spoil tips of industrial Britain. The sheer number of these railways takes some believing in the first decade of the third millennium; between 1870 and 1930 there were at least eleven narrow gauge systems, operating steam locomotives on eight different gauges, within fifteen miles of the author's South Wales home. All these systems relied upon the saddle tank, usually with four coupled wheels; if treated reasonably engines in industrial use had a better than even chance of outliving the industry or site they served. Restricted in speed by the state of the track, loads were light, frequently one truck at a time.

Fashion is a fickle animal, and if enthusiasm for narrow gauge steam waxed in the 1870s, then it waned in the 1890s, with the realisation that there were limits to the usefulness of small trucks. While coal needs must be carried in tubs that fit the tunnels below ground, once on the surface, the sooner the stuff is loaded into a wagon that will take it to the consumer, the better. So too was it elsewhere, and recirculation of redundant locomotives reduced demand for new, a demand only temporarily restored by the decision of the War Office to use two foot gauge railways in France in 1914-18, leading to a glut of both track and traction on the second-hand market at the war's end. That glut led to the rich and slightly eccentric building their own railways, such as the short lived Sand Hutton Light Railway near Stamford Bridge in East Yorkshire. By 1930, demand for new industrial narrow gauge steam had evaporated, even though the narrow gauge diesel continued to be built for a further thirty years: an easy first victim of the motor lorry.

The Narrow Gauge was thus set in a mould it found difficult to escape. Construction at less than Standard Gauge almost always implied a lack of cash on the part of promoters. That cash shortage was usually permanent, making re-equipping with new locomotives an undertaking not embarked upon lightly, and worn out or unusable motive power was quite as likely to be set aside rather than scrapped, as it 'might come in useful' at some point in the future. Once again the Ffestiniog Railway proved a temporary exception to this rule of continued poverty, finding that it was in need of greater power to increase capacity on its single line in the 1870s; having obtained powers to double track, the company got cold feet, and were saved from an early demise at the hands of competing standard gauge railways by an inventor of steam locomotives, Robert Fairlie.

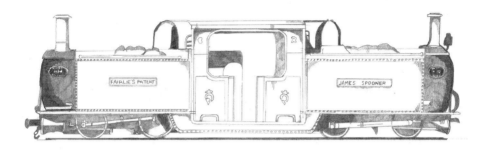

Provenance: Application of the principle of articulation to powered bogies involved steam tight swivelling joints, the 'Double Fairlie' was conceived as providing more haulage power on narrow tracks with a limited structure gauge, and was patented.
Designer: Robert Fairlie.
Principal Features: two four wheel powered bogies , two boilers and fireboxes, centre cab.
Principal Dimensions:
Articulated wheelbase:18ft 8in.
Cylinders: Four: 8 in diameter, 14in stroke, outside frames.
Working Pressure: 140psi (160 in locomotives in service 1983)
Tractive Effort: 7,542lb.
Driving wheels: 2ft 8in diameter.
Axle load: 5t 0cwt (driving axle).
Boiler:Two, with twin central fireboxes, side fired.
Valve: Piston valves between frames, inside Stephenson Link Motion.
Weight in W. O: 20 tons 1cwt.

Figure 50: Double Fairlie.

Fairlie's Patent locomotive was basically two engines in one: two four-coupled engine units, united by a single frame carrying two fireboxes, two boilers and two smokeboxes. This type of locomotive was, and still is, driven and fired from the middle, fireman on one side, driver the other. The design was an excellent way of fitting more than double the power on short-wheelbase four wheel bogies, because the length of the boiler was not limited by that wheelbase. The limit though was coal capacity; there was little space for the fireman, coal could only be stored alongside or on top of the boiler, and there was not enough room to wield a full size shovel. Oil firing to solve this conundrum is a modern phenomenon. The principle of articulation between locomotive frame and power bogies that Fairlie utilised to effect on the narrow gauge was not widely adopted in Britain, nor was the best of the other articulated systems, the Beyer-Garrett. The French system, the 'Mallett', was not used, though adopted extensively in the United States. The first Fairlie appeared on the Ffestiniog in 1869, more followed, with the last being built at their own works over a century later.

If enthusiasm for the narrow gauge waned in the 1890's, coincidentally or not with the end of the main exploration phase of minerals to feed the industrial revolution in Britain, then the last railway built ostensibly for mineral exploitation, the Vale of Rheidol, ordered a single tank locomotive from Davies and Metcalfe that, in size and critical dimensions, put small standard gauge engines in the shade. With long angular side tanks giving the locomotive *Prince of Wales* a distinctive appearance, the railway quickly turned to the tourist trade when the hoped for lead ore failed to materialise. While not first in the tourist field (the Plynlimon and Hafan had got there first and died in the attempt) *Prince of Wales* was a complete success in putting as much traction on lightly laid two foot gauge tracks with sharp curves, without going to the complication and expense of articulation. The Great Western, on gaining control of the Vale of Rheidol at the grouping, built two more of these locomotives to the same general proportions but with an extra half-inch tacked on to the cylinder diameter. All three remain in service, never having been withdrawn. Rebuilding of the original Prince of Wales commenced under Cambrian Railway auspices with larger coal spaces, and later, to match the Great Western Pair, *Llywelyn* and *Owain Glyndwr*, included removal of the cab side window (hardly an improvement!) and substitution of the inside valve gear with outside Walschaerts motion. after the end of steam on the nationalised railway, came conversion to oil firing to minimise fire risk in the occasional dry Welsh summer.

Where one leads, others inevitably follow, and in the English Lake District, the Ravenglass and Eskdale Railway, in its fruitless search for mineral wealth in the area around Boot in Eskdale, met all the necessary criteria for a cash-strapped concern needing to transform itself into a tourist trap to survive. Closure of the three foot gauge line, and disposal of its stock of six coupled side tanks, in 1908, was followed by re-incarnation at fifteen inch gauge, in 1915, initially as a 'proper' narrow gauge railway. In the 1920s and 1930s, in tandem with the Romney, Hythe and Dymchurch Railway, the locomotives used were supplanted by scaled-down versions of the standard gauge, a trend maintained into the second half of the twentieth century. Narrow gauge steam locomotives after 1930 were designed as tourist attractions, but their cousins at the cheap and cheerful end of rail transport, light railway locomotives, came later and stayed only briefly, enjoying little of the success of their continental neighbours.

Finally, just in case the reader thinks that Britain's only rack railway has been missed off the list, design and execution of the Snowdon Mountain Railway was entirely foreign, in this case Swiss. The gauge is metric, the locomotives built at the Swiss Locomotive Works in Winterthur, and the Abt rack system gained no further application on these shores. 'Nuff said!

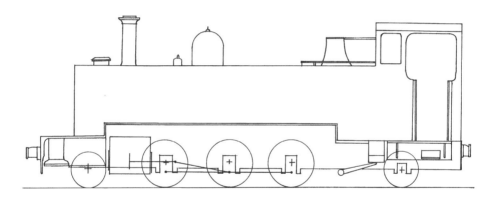

Provenance: Powerful narrow gauge (2ft) locomotive designed to operate on the 1:50 ruling gradient of the Vale of Rheidol Railway.
Designer: Davies and Metcalfe Ltd.
Principal Features: Large side tanks making use of the railway's generous structure gauge, trailing rear truck.
Principal Dimensions:
Cylinders: 11in diameter, 17in stroke, outside frames.
Working Pressure: 165psi.
Tractive Effort: 9,615lb.
Driving wheels: 2ft 6in diameter.
Valves: Piston valves, outside Walschaerts gear.
Weight in W. O: 25 tons 0cwt.

Figure 51: Vale of Rheidol 2-6-2T.

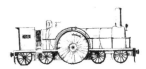

Chapter Twenty-Two:

Crocks and Cast Offs:
The Light Railway Locomotive 1896 - 1968

Legislation to regulate the operation of railways in the nineteenth century was, by the ultimate decade, close to putting the railway companies under a burden of regulation that even government recognised as hindering further system expansion. Problems of transhipment were ones that Westminster was quite happy to foist upon the Irish, but the way forward in mainland Britain, with some exceptions, was seen as a standard gauge railway without encumbrance of severe regulation, but restricted to a maximum speed of twenty-five miles an hour. Thus was the Light Railways Act of 1896 born, and with it a modest mileage of lightly laid track mostly in rural England. To run on these lines, whose finances were as rickety as their tracks quickly became, the companies acquired a motley assortment of the lightest and least powerful locomotives that British manufacturers could offer.

The Act of 1896 did not produce an avalanche of schemes, not least due to the legislation being not as extensive in its relief of restrictions as had been hoped. Thus one of those proposals that was already on the table in 1896, the Mid-Suffolk Light Railway, took seven years to advance to the point at which it had rails to run an engine on. What happened to that engine on the Mid-Suffolk, while probably not unique, was symptomatic of the difficulties of steam on a shoestring. The railway had ordered two six-coupled tank engines from Hudswell Clarke of Leeds, for delivery for the commencement of services; it did not have the means to pay for them outright, and had arranged a form of hire purchase, involving payment by instalments. As locomotives these were unexceptional; handsomely proportioned in the 'Terrier' mould, with small wheels, neat side tanks, and a steam dome that was a little on the large side.

The manufacturer duly delivered the first engine, but without initial payment. Suspicious that the railway company was not possessed of means to pay, Hudswell Clarke not only put the engine on the rails at Haughley Junction, where the Mid-Suffolk met the main line from Ipswich to Norwich, but chained and padlocked it to them as well. Release to the company came only after Hudswell Clarke received some cash. The engine was duly numbered '1' and named *Haughley*. At twenty-nine tons, this engine was the preferred freight locomotive. Engine number two arrived two years later in 1905, fitted with Westinghouse air pumps for passenger traffic, and five tons lighter than *Haughley*. Insolvency and receivership followed, but did not prevent arrival of a third engine in 1908, once again to the same format. In the interim, the railway had hired in a saddle tank to help out: a Manning Wardle engine that had already spent thirty five years on the industrial railways of Britain, and would give at least another ten years of itinerant service, though not on the Mid-Suffolk. And that, as far as the Mid-Suffolk Railway's 'independent' existence was concerned, was that.

Surprising as it might seem, three engines were not always enough to run a ramshackle railway of just under twenty miles in length and two passenger (and freight) mixed trains each way a day; general repairs and boiler washouts meant the Great Eastern Railway supplied on hire one of its own six coupled tank engines, on an 'as required' basis. One of the reasons for this state of affairs was that the light railway was 'light' on earthworks, and the first half-mile of the line was steeply graded at 1 in 50 and limited loads, making the second, lighter engine, less useful than it might otherwise have been. At the 1923 grouping of railways, the line lost its independence, and almost immediately its own engines, gaining the services of locomotives built before the line; six coupled tender engines of LNER class 'J15', heavier by nine tons, larger wheeled and much more powerful. One of these locomotives sufficed for traffic after the mid thirties, and two hours was allowed for the end to end journey, under ten miles an hour inclusive of stops and shunting wagons.

At closure in 1952, the line was under half a century old, operated by locomotives designed in 1883, running to a timetable that was so slow as to offer no competition to any other form of mechanised transport, not even the bicycle. It was neither alone in its obsolescence, nor unusual in its operating methods and single figure average speeds. If the Mid-Suffolk Light Railway has been virtually erased from the face of the earth, then the Kent and East Sussex Railway is both alive and kicking, and a reflection of the talents of a remarkable character in the light railways of Britain, Colonel Holman F. Stephens.

The Kent and East Sussex started life in 1896 as the Rother Valley Railway and, just like its Suffolk cousin, in 1900 placed an order to a locomotive builder, this time Hawthorn Leslie, for two small 2-4-0 tank engines, named in similar fashion *Tenterden* and *Northiam.* The first of these two locomotives had a set of larger driving wheels fitted to cure poor running and wear problems (the engine was so far inside the structure gauge as to need no cutting down of chimney or cab), and alteration to buffers only meant a shift on the buffer beam. In the purchase of new locomotives, this was almost the end of the railway's spending spree, with the only other new purchase being an eight-coupled tank that was too heavy for the southern section of the line, and little used as a consequence. What made the Kent and East Sussex special, along with the other railways run from Colonel Stephens' office in Tonbridge, was the second-hand motive power that was acquired over the next thirty years, down to the Colonel's death in harness in 1931.

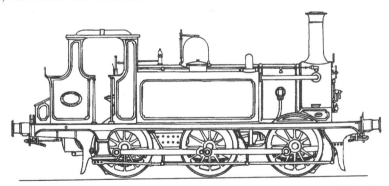

Provenance: 1872 design by W. Stroudley for the London Brighton and South Coast Railway. Light passenger tank locomotive. Rebuilt by Earle Marsh 1911.
Principal Features: Small boilered six wheeled side tank .
Principal Dimensions:Coupled wheelbase: 12ft 0in.
Cylinders: 12in diameter, 20in stroke, inside frames. Enlarged to 14in diameter on some engines.
Working Pressure: 140psi.   Tractive Effort: 7,650lb.
Driving wheels: 4ft 0in diameter Axle load: 8t 4cwt (driving axle).
Boiler:3ft 6in diameter, pitch line 5ft 8 $^3/_4$in above rail level.
Valves: Slide valves between frames, inside Stephenson Link Motion.
Weight in W. O: 24 tons 12cwt, 28t 5cwt rebuilt.
Figure 52: Terrier.

First of the hand-me-downs to arrive was *Bodiam* in 1901, a 'Terrier' tank dating from the 1870s that did sterling service over the next thirty years before retiring to the sidings, whence it was retrieved, rebuilt using parts from other 'Terriers' that had ground to a halt on other light railways, and handed over to British Railways in 1948. This engine survives on the line it has served for the best part of a century. A further 'Terrier' was purchased in 1905, again over thirty years old and destined to provide nearly thirty years' further service. Next to arrive, in 1910, was one of the six coupled tender engines of the London and South Western Railway, known as the 'Ilfracombe Goods', again dating from the 1870s. This, too, ran until worn out twenty years later. The railway continued to purchase locomotives, despite having six and a railmotor, and in 1914 purchased a Manning Wardle saddle tank that had passed into the hands of the Great Western Railway, acquiring Swindon-style dome and safety valve covers in the process. This locomotive was thirty-eight years old when purchased and served on the line until the outbreak of the Second World War, finally going for scrap in 1941. A further 'Ilfracombe Goods' also arrived in 1914, its history and fate mirroring that of the others.

In 1914 the Kent and East Sussex was the owner of eight locomotives to run a single track railway twenty miles long; in practice only six were available, but it is difficult to conceive that more than two were ever needed at any one time, for the line had railmotors for passenger services. The reality of life for a locomotive on this light railway was that engines would be run until they were in need of repair, then be set aside until their replacements were in similar need, at which point a decision would be made as to what would be put back into service. Colonel Stephens was notable for not throwing anything away, and although it is doubtful that such a make do and mend strategy made economic sense, the run-down charm exuded by this method of operation was a feature of all of his railways.

After the Colonel's death the railway was insolvent, and survived only by a complete change of operation, abandoning the ramshackle approach to steam propulsion and hiring in six coupled tanks from the Southern Railway; the engines were dominated by 'Terriers'. Nationalisation brought no change to motive power, until diesels made an appearance just prior to closure in 1961. The preserved locomotive stock, in its variety and tendency to spend long periods out of use, would surely have warmed the cockles of the Colonel's heart.

The shoestring locomotive policy of the Kent and East Sussex, and the numbers of out of use locomotives, was a reflection of the fact that, even in the heyday of the railway, there was a limit to the slenderness of that shoestring. What did not become a regular feature of the rural British railway was the roadside tramway; only the Wisbech and Upwell, the Wantage tramway and a handful of others featured large in their use of tramway type engines, with covered wheels. While Sentinel of Shrewsbury produced a geared vertical-boilered shunter of tramway form, a type that saw limited use on the 'heavyweight' railways, this sort of locomotive was not widely adopted. To the outside observer, the light railway locomotive was just an ordinary locomotive of the smaller size, suited to sharp curves and light track, and in later years, more run-down than most and accomplished at browsing through verdant vegetation. The Derwent Valley Light Railway in East Yorkshire, the only significant Standard Gauge nationalisation escapee, was so grass-grown in the Second World War as to be effectively camouflaged, a state of affairs that persisted until closure in the 1960s and 1970s.

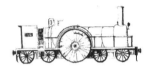

Chapter Twenty-Three:

Unseen and Unloved:
Industrial Steam 1836 to 1980

As we have recounted, the steam locomotive originated as industrial motive power, and made the leap to fame and fortune by virtue of transformation from carthorse to racehorse. The locomotives designed by George Stephenson and Timothy Hackworth, freight haulers *par excellence* in 1829, were not immediately replaced by locomotives in the mould of *Rocket* and its successors. The economics that drove steam locomotive development at breakneck speed in the 1830s did not apply in the same manner to haulage of heavy loads at low speed. The economics of steam haulage over horse power on the iron road were slender, and replacement of the horse was by no means instantaneous. As a shunter of single railway wagons, the horse was employed well into the twentieth century, eliminated as much by the motor lorry as the steam locomotive.

The reality of steam locomotive development was that it was some time before there was a locomotive that was reliable, simple to use, easily reversible and robust, that met the demands of hard headed industrialists unconcerned about un-needed speed, and uninfluenced by the hype surrounding the passenger locomotive. There was also the issue of the track; locomotives needed expensive wrought iron rails to run on, and most industrial railways, even where they were standard gauge, were laid with cast iron track unable to accept locomotives scaling five or more tons. Development of industrial steam locomotives thus had to await the changing economic position of society and, in particular, expansion of industry beyond the ability of the horse to supply motive power.

In some respects it is an easy way out to suggest that the modern industrial steam locomotive is as firmly derived from *Rocket* as is the express passenger locomotive, because the destination of *Rocket*, after its short but crucial service on the Liverpool and Manchester Railway, was industrial use on the Brampton Railway in Cumberland. *Rocket* was sold to operate on the Earl of Carlisle's mineral line in 1836, but saw only limited service over the next four or five years, either because the track was unsuitable or, more likely, because the engine was too light for the task of hauling coal, a factor which had led to its disposal from the Liverpool and Manchester. To have operated efficiently on a mineral railway in 1836 implies, almost certainly wrongly, that the railway was both modern and well maintained. With only limited coal measures available in East Cumberland, and an entirely rural hinterland as a market, *Rocket* was in all probability out of place in every way.

The reality of development of industrial steam locomotives is that it proceeded with limited haste and little speed. Before we look at the locomotives we must recognise, that forces that drove the process of change were different from the world of the passenger railway, and need a brief analysis. Those industries that needed the services of a rail based transport system in 1830 were struggling to justify application of the steam locomotive; in strict economic terms, the Stockton and Darlington Railway presented a case for steam traction over the horse, but not an overwhelming one. That case was between two different forms of power on the same iron road; George Stephenson could not have made an economic case for the locomotive freight railway in preference to the horse-drawn canal, and neither could his son, Robert.

Canals could, and did, compete for long distance freight for the whole of the nineteenth century, to the extent that railways took to anti-competitive practices to deprive canals of trade. Only in particular locations though, was the canal suitable for the short-haul that the mineral railway had made its own. The process of linking coal pits, ironstone patches, furnaces and their stocking grounds, and haulage to the nearest navigable water, had been the *raison d'être* of the tramroad in the first place, and these tracks had been utilising horses as motive power for a century prior to

Rainhill. Horsepower was not going to be ousted immediately, if only because a large capital outlay was needed to change the track, trucks and traction in one go.

These horse-drawn networks were not converted to steam power overnight; most of them were not laid either with edge rails, or to standard gauge. Cast iron was the preferred material; treated properly, it had a service life many times that of wrought iron (the author has a tramplate doing duty as a shelf a hundred and forty years after it last saw service on the Palleg Tramroad, and it is by no means worn out). The life of a wrought iron rail at a busy junction in the 1860s, in contrast, was measured in months. Stone sleepered tracks were laid to curves and gradients unsuited to locomotives, and were fairly crude in design and execution.

The last of these tramroads were still performing their tasks in the first decade of the twentieth century, while the longer routes, like the Monmouthshire Canal Company's, for example, were converted to modern railways from the 1850s onwards. In many instances the demand for greater capacity was the prime driving force; tram wagons held about two tons of cargo, no more than twenty or thirty tons in a train, the canal barge between twenty and seventy tons. Against this the five ton railway wagon was a monster: a train of twenty wagons at fifteen miles an hour delivered the same ton-mileage a day as twenty tram-trains or narrow boats. On the same strip of land a railway could deliver ten million tons of goods a year, a canal or tramroad perhaps only half a million tons. Faced with statistics of this kind, it was only inertia and the cost of re-equipping that enabled the old ways to survive.

Inertia, then, played a large part in the spread of locomotive haulage, and in the decade after the runaway success of *Rocket*, there were few industrialists prepared to dig deep into their profits and lay out on both track and engines to service the short haul from pit mouth to tip or furnace. What changed all this was the economics of the middle of the century: exponential growth of coal and iron output coupled with quantum leaps in the reliability of the steam locomotive. New industrial sites invested in state of the art technologies, and after 1850 that meant the steam locomotive, neatly manufactured and packaged by the private builders: low cost power at the right price.

The ideal specification for an industrial steam locomotive was not a difficult 'wish list' to prepare, and in 1850 it looked something like this:

- Light weight, to be easy on track that would not receive too much maintenance

- Short wheelbase, to navigate tight curves within yards and inside works and go almost anywhere that a truck could.

- All wheels powered to give maximum starting and braking effort

- Simple and precise controls to allow for easy driving and reversing

- No 'frills', just a robust and reliable load-shifter

It is fairly obvious that *Rocket* didn't meet this specification in 1829, and what the main line companies were designing in the subsequent two decades lacked one or more items needed to qualify as definitive industrial motive power, if only because the trunk routes needs were not those of industry. While there was a fortune to be made, or so it seemed, from steam racehorses, by 1850 it was clear that the way forward for expansion of heavy industry was investment in steam power. To substitute for the horse that had sustained trade down the ages, the private locomotive builders were in short order offering the tank locomotive in its many guises.

From the many, it is difficult to select the few that are rightly progenitors of this large and long-lived breed, and here we face the difficulty that many early industrial locomotives have almost as much in common with Timothy Hackworth's *Royal George*, as they do with the genius of Robert Stephenson. A second problem is the regular alteration and rebuilding that was the lot of industrial steam engines, mainly as a result of technological progress and a general reluctance on the part of business to buy new, if the old could be brought up to less than twenty years behind the times. Despite existence of the plate camera in 1860, surviving photographs are few and far between, and records of major work to engines often scant.

In building *Royal George*, Hackworth demonstrated the basics of mineral haulage; weight and power counted more than anything else, for without either there was no work capacity. Speed quite simply was not an issue, and never came into the reckoning. Practically, the six-coupled engine was as big as could be useful under the 'go anywhere' banner, and for most of the period under review the four coupled saddle tank was more numerous than any other industrial power unit. Leading wheels were conspicuous by their absence, and trailing axles rare outside the North East.

For the archetypal industrial locomotive then, we can look at two locomotives built by the Leeds firm of Manning Wardle and Co. in 1863 to consecutive works numbers, the first a four-coupled saddle-tank on small wheels only two foot nine in diameter, and inside cylinders at nine and a half inches by fourteen (stroke) to match. The second, No 80, was six-coupled, again a saddle-tank, with the slightly larger wheels at three foot one (and three eighths!) and twelve by seventeen inch outside cylinders. Fifty years later the company had, more or less, standardised on three foot wheels, six-coupled, with thirteen by eighteen inch cylinders, dimensions effectively settled upon as early as 1882. When we come to look at the company - Peckett - which almost defined the twentieth century industrial saddle tank, we find that story repeated, almost but not quite verbatim.

Peckett and Sons of the Atlas Works in Bristol built substantial numbers of sturdy, long-lived saddle tanks over a period of more than seventy years, concentrating production on the two industrial favourites of four and six-coupled wheels, and over the decades offering a standard product with a list of options in terms of wheel and cylinder sizes.

Thus in the 1880s you could have ten inch cylinders with a fourteen inch stroke, or fourteen by twenty, the latter remaining an option until well after the First War, by which time thirteen by eighteen and sixteen by twenty two inches were also available, as well as fifteen by twenty one, fourteen by twenty two and sixteen by twenty four! Likewise the wheels; starting off in the 1880s as two foot six, three foot two or three foot seven, the advancing decades saw two foot nine, three feet, three foot ten and four feet added to the selection, with the odd half inch tacked on here and there to add interest.

Peckett's last locomotives in the 1950s were generally built out to the loading gauge; as wagon sizes and capacities had increased, so had the need for more tractive effort and adhesive weight. Technologically there was little difference between the products of 1955 and those of 1885. The spectacle plate of the 1850s had grudgingly turned into the half cab and then a full cab to provide reasonable protection for footplatemen. Slide valves had not been ousted, and there was no place either for high boiler pressures or superheaters. Lubrication remained rudimentary, as there was always time to do the rounds with the oilcan. There was little in the way of design input into industrial steam locomotives in the twentieth century, and almost no fresh thought after 1890.

The industrial railways of the North East were exceptional in that they hauled their own coal for greater distances, on average, than did other industrial areas, and as a result the Lambton, Hetton and Joycey Collieries (part of the Grand Allies) had a fleet of six-coupled tank engines with a trailing axle, making them 0-6-2's. The length of some lines tempted mining companies to purchase ex-main line tender engines. Industry generally had a tendency to acquire the cast-offs of others, and while docks, quarries, ironworks and manufacturing provided a steady market for locomotive builders, trade conditions permitting, the second-hand market flourished on the needs of construction and coal mining, even though these industries also bought new on a considerable scale. Fluctuations in trade made the role of the middleman, buying and selling engines, and in slack times holding considerable stocks, an enduring and important one.

While some engines had short lives of twenty or thirty years, many were enduring, often beyond the span of years of several owners. This recycling system started to fall apart after the Second War, as construction turned to road based vehicles and plant, and scrapping started in earnest after 1960, when it was clear that no further use could be found for engines fifty or sixty years old and in need of their third or fourth rebuild. That process was driven by development of the diesel engine, offering power for fractions of the cost of steam; an irresistible force meeting a moveable object.

For over a century from 1850, the industrial steam locomotive was at the heart of all heavy industry, indispensable in the shifting of coal, iron ore and stone. Most docks and harbours had their own shunters, as had numbers of gas works and many other industries, from foodstuffs to textiles and brewing. As the industrial balance shifted after the Second World War, from small low output production units to mechanised megaliths, and the pressure of competition no longer made rail haulage the axiomatic choice, in the space of little more than two decades industrial steam locomotives were swept into the dustbin of history. The last to go was the (by then nationalised) coal industry, always the largest user, just limping into the 1980s.

While there are fewer than twenty collieries at the start of the twenty-first century, and only half a dozen steel works, still users of rail for the most part; a hundred years ago colliery numbers ran to over two thousand, almost all using steam on their rail networks, and ironworks were several hundred strong, again dependent on steam (with a bit of horse) haulage to feed in the coal, ore and limestone and take away steel and slag. Today the lucky few industrial locomotives haul pleasure trips for visitors to preserved lines, or manage the occasional foray onto industrial premises. It is difficult to conceive a more complete eclipse.

Finally, on the industrial scene there were two locomotive types that saw very limited adoption, the Crane Tank, and the Fireless Locomotive, both specialist machines and very few in number. The crane tank was just that: a tank engine modified to include a steam crane on top of the boiler. Given that the whole engine had to fit inside the loading gauge, this meant that the engine was a small one, and the usefulness of such a machine limited, hence the small numbers. The fireless locomotive was strictly speaking not a locomotive at all but the steam equivalent of an electrical battery: a large cylinder for storing steam generated elsewhere, and a locomotive chassis for using it. The attraction of this type of engine was that it could be used safely in places where a locomotive with a furnace could not be tolerated, but where steam was generated for other industrial processes by stationary boiler plant and could readily be supplied for traction. This shore supply was critical, and restricted the fireless locomotive to industrial sites such as paper mills.

Provenance: 1899 model of a design dating back to 1860 with larger boiler and full length saddle tank.
Designer: Peckett and Sons, Bristol.
Principal Features: Six wheel shunting saddle tank engine, with 'full cab'.
Principal Dimensions:
Cylinders: 18in diameter, 24in stroke, inside frames.
Driving wheels: 4ft 0in diameter.
Boiler: Parallel with short, deep firebox between second and third driving axles
Valves: Slide valves between frames, inside Stephenson Link Motion.

Figure 53: Peckett 0-6-0 ST.

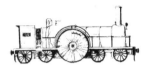

Chapter Twenty-Four:

Might-Have-Beens and Never-Weres:
125 years of Unconventional Locomotives

The Rainhill Trials set a continuing theme that lasted to the bitter end and beyond; there was always someone, somewhere, with an idea for a better mousetrap that would outperform the conventional by a factor of, well, name your own fantasy. The reality of technological development is that the big inventions occur early, and that subsequent improvement is almost always pure graft as opposed to inspiration. The steam locomotive was no exception to this general rule, but it is a matter of history that one hundred and fifty years of locomotive development contains its fair share, and perhaps a little more besides, of allegedly improved 'timorous wee beastie deterrents'.

On the face of it, the idea that only one person's genius should frame mankind's escape from the constraints of history is to deny the vitality of *homo sapiens* in general, and the spirit of the industrial revolution in particular. Nevertheless, the essence of Robert Stephenson's vision maintained its unique primacy until the arrival of Gottlieb Daimler, and on the rails at least, Robert's idea of the steam locomotive was not to be usurped. The reason for this is that in the nineteenth century two methods were developed of releasing the chemical energy stored in coal: straight combustion, heating water to make steam, and destructive distillation, to yield coal gas. Once the combustion/steam-raising method gained a head start, the concept of the portable gas engine, making its own gas and burning it in a form of internal combustion engine, never managed to make it to the starting gate, despite the theoretical efficiency being three or four times that possible with steam. The 'might have beens' and 'never weres', were thus restricted to variations on one theme, that of steam.

In chronological order then, Braithwaite and Ericsson's *Novelty* is without doubt the first might have been, but it was only unconventional in that it was not designed from a rail technology baseline, being an adaptation of the steam road engine/carriage. It was not long, however before the Liverpool and Manchester Railway was approached by the first of what came to be a long line of 'inventors'. In December 1833 the railway was approached by Lord Dundonald, with an idea for a 'revolving engine', an idea originally put to Messrs. Sharp, Roberts, who doubtless not wishing to offend an influential peer, adopted the plan of handing him on to someone else in order to get rid of him. Dundonald, as Lord Cochrane, had, prior to his assuming the Earldom in 1831, been both the hero and the bane of the Royal Navy. Fearless in battle, with a string of prizes and daring feats to his credit, Cochrane's envious enemies had to resort to a prosecution for fraud to have him removed from the Navy List in 1815. Instrumental in securing the independence of Chile, Brazil, Peru and Greece as a mercenary mariner, member of parliament and long-standing promoter of steam power at sea and the screw propellor, the Earl was just as keen to set his seal on the start of the steam age as he had been to serve his country in the Napoleonic Wars. Quite what his lordship was proposing was not clear; an adaption to fit to an existing engine (*Rocket* was apparently proposed) that has not survived the mill of time is the most likely. First, though, among the serious contenders in the unconventional stakes, was Thomas Crampton, whose ideas were realised into working machines.

The Crampton

Crampton was one of the early engineers who secured a patent for his locomotive, based upon the idea that the centre of gravity could be lowered by positioning the single driving axle behind the boiler and firebox, effectively across the footplate front, where its height would not affect the boiler position. Thus positioned, the axle could only be driven by crankpins on the wheels, for there was no room to provide cranks on the axle itself, and the cylinders could not be alongside or underneath the smokebox, their best position. With low piston speeds in the 1840s and 1850s, the only way to achieve high speeds was to have large wheels, and Crampton's idea was one way of producing a stable locomotive. Having no vehicle overhang at the rear helped stability as much, if not more than, keeping the boiler centre of gravity low, and as such, while train weights were modest, the Crampton possessed a charm that led at least two main line railway companies to give the design a try.

The experience of the London and North Western Railway is perhaps typical; one prototype did not lead to a rush of orders. There was nothing intrinsically wrong with the design, not until adhesion weight became critical that is, but there was nothing so obviously superior to the in-house designs of Francis Trevithick and John Ramsbottom that meant preference, and royalty payments,

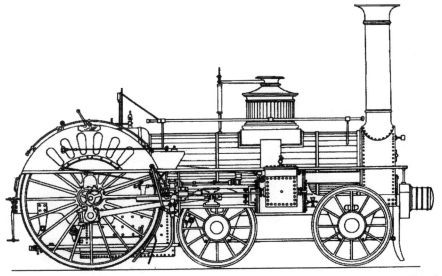

Provenance: Patented alternative to the 'Patentee', Long Boiler', and 'Crewe Type', providing an alternative approach to the idea of large driving wheels and low centre of gravity.
Designer: Thomas Crampton.
Principal Features: Single driving axle mounted across the rear of the firebox, driven by outside cylinders.
Principal Dimensions (1848 engine for the LNWR):
Fixed wheelbase: 18ft 6in.
Cylinders: 16in diameter, 20in stroke, outside frames.
Working Pressure: 90psi.
Tractive Effort: 4,662lb.
Driving wheels: 7ft 0in diameter.
Axle load: 11t 4cwt (driving axle).
Boiler: Oval, pitch line 4ft 7in above rail level.
Valves: Slide valves on top of the cylinders, outside Stephenson Link Motion.
Weight in W. O: 25 tons 12cwt.

Figure 54: Crampton.

should be given to what was basically an interloper. Bearing in mind that Crewe could build anything that was technically possible, from scratch, designing whatever items were needed and then casting, forging, machining and fitting them together and making them haul trains, the idea that this capacity at the leading edge of technology should be set aside for the benefit of Thomas Crampton, or indeed anyone else, is just a little fanciful.

Crampton realised that this preference for in-house designs was going to preclude large orders in Britain, and transferred his attentions to the Continental market, particularly France, where he enjoyed a lasting success. He was not the first engineer to escape the parochialism of his home country, and he was certainly not the last, nor was he alone in having eccentric ideas on locomotive construction; Francis Trevithick had a short fling with unconventionality with the Mk1. *Cornwall.*

Cornwall

There is a clear connection between the design of Thomas Crampton and the genesis of *Cornwall*; they both represent a part of the quest to secure stability in running by lowering locomotive centres of gravity, and if one solution was to put the driving axle behind the firebox, another was to slot it through the boiler. Again this means no cranked axle or inside cylinders, but as it was a step too far to press the wheels on the axle after the axle had been slotted through the boiler, then a notch had to be made in the top of the boiler in which the axle could sit. This is the solution that Trevithick adopted and Crewe Works built, a solution that generated more problems than it solved.

Firstly, it was impossible to slot the bottom section of the boiler, because this is where the tubes are; the slot could only be made in the water and steam space above the tubes. Splitting the steam space meant that collection of steam now had to take place at two points: both behind and in front of the axle. Secondly, the idea of a circular boiler is that it does not need staying across its diameter; cutting a slot in the boiler meant stays or girder plates in the area of the slot, and double longitudinal stays in the two steam and water spaces. Finally, two thirds of the boiler must be under the axle, which with eight foot wheels, means a severe restriction on the boiler diameter, and what is worse a very shallow firebox. Needless to say *Cornwall* was not a success, and was quickly rebuilt to more conventional form. As a locomotive *Cornwall* was on the small side when built, and we can move easily from minnow to monster by moving to the Broad Gauge, and the Bristol and Exeter Railway.

Express Tanks on the Broad Gauge

Theoretically at least, the largest wheel diameter that can be put on the rails is that which is as high as the loading gauge, a little over thirteen feet. In the nineteenth century on the standard gauge eight foot wheels were the largest practically adopted, and as the twentieth century progressed, the largest wheels, all under express locomotives, shrank to a more manageable seven foot, then six foot nine, six foot six, and in the last nationalised designs, six foot two. The wheels of the Bristol and Exeter tank engines managed nine feet in diameter, and the word 'leviathan' was not inappropriate when applied to them, especially when compared to the modest proportions of the locomotives on the standard gauge in the 1850s.

The design, by J. Pearson, the Bristol and Exeter Locomotive Superintendent, built by Rothwell and Company of Bolton, extended to eight engines, and its relative success, for the engines were in service for the best part of twenty years, was in no small part due to the generosity of the broad gauge. With a wheel diameter as large as nine feet, the four foot diameter boiler had a centre line almost seven feet above rail level, the top of the boiler was over nine feet in the air, and in an era when loading gauges were not being particularly challenged, the chimney added a further four feet to make it over thirteen feet from tip to toe. Despite having inside cylinders, there was room to set the cranks at the side of the boiler and have space for double framing and bearings on the driving axle, but the real key to the design's stability was the use of the boiler shell to act both as a stiffener to the frames and as a suspension point for the driving axle springs, pivoted off a huge bracket. In a unique piece of insight, the pivot arm for the two springs, located on top of the wheel, was of unequal length, one pivot point being three quarters of an inch longer than the other. Likewise the springs; the whole assembly thus minimising the risk of the suspension 'dancing' when the engine motion reached the natural frequency of any one of the springs.

It is of course just possible that the design of the springing was accidental, being due to consideration of other factors, but these were machines of a size that set them apart from the crowd, and it is not unlikely that they were regarded as just being a little 'beyond the pale', even for the Broad Gauge. Whatever the reason, they were not multiplied beyond the original eight, and as they grew old and grey, they were withdrawn and shot, to be replaced with four similar engines that lacked this innovative spring design. Derailment of one of these engines in 1876 led directly to their rebuilding as tender engines, reducing their weight and making them similar to the Great Western's stock in trade, whose property they by then were. The Broad Gauge, though, was on the wane, and successors to the 'Iron Duke' were doing all that was needed in express passenger work, including that between Exeter and Bristol. As 'might have beens', these locomotives had a much longer trial than most, but ultimately they were peripheral to the mainstream of locomotive development, not part of it.

Numerous minor inventions graced the last quarter of the nineteenth century; some railways were embroiled in the idea of compounding, and those that weren't actually having a dabble were watching with interest those that were. While the Fairlie came and stayed on the narrow gauge, the Mallett articulated type emerged on to the world stage without actually having a substantive British run . We can thus gallop to the century's end, and beyond, with only a passing reminder to the antics of one Mr Webb, and look at the lesser failure of Sir Cecil Paget.

Paget's Prodigy: Multiple Cylinders and Sleeve Valves

Cecil Paget, as general superintendent of the Midland Railway in 1908, had access to some of the best and most extensive locomotive facilities in the land. Nonetheless, he was not locomotive superintendent, that job being Richard Mountford Deeley's. As a man of influence, and holder of patents for various items of associated steam locomotive hardware, Paget was able to obtain authority to have built an engine that embodied some of his ideas. Deeley's abrupt departure in 1909 probably reflects, among other things, what he thought of the whole affair.

Paget's idea, which on the face of it was entirely sound, was that smoother and faster running could be obtained by balancing the reciprocating parts of the engine and reducing their mass. In addition, the same degree of expansion can be obtained in a cylinder if there are two pistons that drive in opposite directions, but that the stroke, and thus the speed of the pistons, will be halved, dramatically reducing the stress and strain on the bearings, which along with the connecting rods and pistons can be smaller and lighter. This was the concept of Cecil's ten coupled 0-10-0 'Decapod', known somewhat unflatteringly as 'Paget's Prodigy'.

Having two pistons in the same cylinder is not a problem with slide valves, it just means that there is a port in the middle of the cylinder, instead of one at each end. While the pistons can be double acting, the use of exhaust ports opened by the moving pistons is temptingly simple, and the engine then becomes single-acting. Making the pistons single-acting means you need twice as many of them, so some of the advantage is lost, but the connecting rods can run from crank to piston, there is no need for piston rods or slide bars, and the sprung movement of the driving axles is of no consequence. Had Paget stopped at this, then it is quite likely that what emerged from Derby Works would have been a serviceable locomotive. History however records that whilst the boiler was unconventional in only a modest way, the locomotive was equipped with rotary sleeve valves, and these could not be made steam tight.

The sleeve valve is not a complicated device, and was used successfully on aircraft engines for many years in the middle of the twentieth century. Cecil Paget's failure to get his engine to work almost certainly stems from the fact that he had no technical support from the works; he might have been able to instruct on initial construction, but technological ideas are not worth the paper they are written on without the back up of experience and 'know how' to solve the detail design problems. It is difficult to imagine Deeley instructing his design staff to get stuck in and make this interloper work, even if all the works staff were neutral rather than hostile. Parallels with another Derby-based idea sixty years later (the Advanced Passenger Train) can be powerfully drawn. People, as much as any factor in the technical equation that results in innovative design, play a crucial role; an opposing force in the wrong place can spell death to an idea, just as support can make it world-famous. One idea that did take fitfully to the rails over a period of thirty years was the railmotor, of all the 'might have beens', perhaps alone in deserving a better outing than it received.

The Steam Railmotor

As a concept, putting a small steam engine in a coach to make it self-propelled, was really only copying what was happening on the roads in the decade prior to 1914. Firms supplying packaged steam engines for road lorries after the repeal of the Red Flag Act, notably Sentinel and Clayton, joined Gloucester Carriage and Wagon, and Glasgow Railway and Engineering, among others, in realising that these units would do for the railways as well. Thus was born the steam railmotor, a coach in which one bogie was driven either directly as in full size engines, or indirectly from a geared multi cylinder unit. The boiler for these railmotors, while initially a diminutive locomotive type, ultimately resolved itself to copy road practice, and adopted the vertical boiler.

The idea of something cheap to buy and run was attractive to a particular sort of railway company, usually the kind that did not want to put too much effort into meeting its obligations under the Regulation of Railways Acts. Before the First World War, when all the majors were well provided with coaching stock and locomotives of every shape, size and more pertinently, age and condition, it was the smaller concerns, where passengers were a sideline to freight, if not a downright nuisance, that saw an opportunity in the railmotor. Nowhere was this more evident than in a South Wales railway that started life as a dock company, the Alexandra (Newport and South Wales) Docks and Railway Company. Efforts to boost trade at Newport docks led to formation of a sister company, later amalgamated, as the Pontypridd, Caerphilly and Newport Railway. So important to this company was passenger traffic between Pontypridd and Caerphilly (not an inch of rails east of Caerphilly was ever built by the PCN) that on the opening day to passengers in 1887, there were no raised platforms on the line, and passengers had to climb steps from the ground level halts into the carriage (note the singular!)

The two railmotors, delivered in 1904 and 1905, were cheap but hardly cheerful, lasting a full quarter century, shuffling back and forth in obeisance to Parliament and in a parody of a public service. So efficient were these objects in discharging the company passenger obligation, that the Great Western Railway ran them for eight years before putting them out of their misery. By 1930 though, others had seen that railmotors could make a difference to the economics of the branch line, and the LNER invested in a small fleet in an effort to combat competition from the bus. The LNER railmotors were supplied with a Sentinel Wagon packaged vertical steam boiler, driving a six cylinder engine mounted on a four wheeled bogie (a near identical unit drove the Sentinel shunting engine). The units had a cab at each end and could be driven in either direction without the need for a turntable. Reliability proved a problem as they once more sailed close to the wind in the quest for weight saving, and the fact that they had to live in locomotive sheds rather than carriage sidings, meant that they were not always as clean as would have been desirable. The steam railmotor was an endangered species after World War Two, and Nationalisation saw the last of these cars withdrawn after twenty years' service.

The First World War put an end to eccentric experimentation with the steam locomotive, and after formation of the 'Big Four' in 1923, there was no elbow room for the off-beat design. What unconventional designs did ultimately emerge were deliberate experiments to determine if methods of steam propulsion that were successful elsewhere could be transferred to the railway, or to determine the physical limits to which the steam railway locomotive could be built. An experiment in high pressure steam, one of several in this period, is our first port of call, the progenitor the LMS.

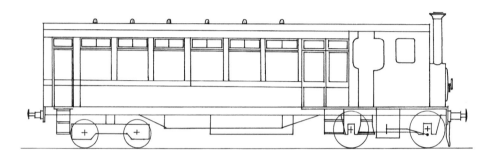

Figure 55: Railmotor

Fury

The principle of raising the boiler pressure to economise on fuel is a sound one; a large slice of the energy needed to turn water into steam is the latent heat of evaporation, heat that is lost when the steam is discharged out of the chimney. Adding heat energy to the steam is energy that can do useful work, and the more energy added, the less water is needed and the smaller the proportion of energy that is wasted as latent heat. After 1900, advent of superheaters had allowed more work to be extracted from each pound of steam, and higher boiler pressures had further advanced locomotive economy, but that economy was still pretty miserable. The concept of the 'Royal Scot' locomotive *Fury*, was that if economies had been gained by raising boiler pressures from 160psi to 225psi over the previous three decades, then the logical conclusion to be drawn was that further economy was to be had, and enhanced performance also, if pressures were raised to the limit of the restraining materials.

The locomotive boiler was formed in compartments, quite unlike the conventional fire tube boiler, with the heart of the system being a water tube arrangement operating a closed circuit containing distilled water at up to 1800psi, and other sections at reduced, but still very high pressures. The engine never entered service, bursting a water tube while on trial and killing a member of the test staff. No further attempt was made to emulate the very high pressure boiler, but the water tube boiler, so successful in marine service, was the target of one attempt to put it on the rails.

Nigel Gresley's Experiments

With nigh on thirty years at the helm, and after 1923, a wealth of both technical design and manufacturing resources at his disposal, Nigel Gresley was able to secure board approval for a number of experiments outside the design mainstream. Of these, the most visually stunning was the water-tube boilered 'hush-hush' locomotive, a massive 4-6-4 whose objective was to test the theory that the water-tube boiler could be made to fit the loading gauge, and do reliable and useful work. With the diameter of the pipes and tubes under pressure being much smaller than in a conventional boiler, and no stayed firebox to cause design problems, opportunity was taken to raise the steam pressure to the practical limit, 450psi. To use this high pressure steam, the engine chassis was made a 'compound'. The locomotive frame was an extended version of the 'A1' Pacific, with which it was intended that it would share duties.

The concept of the water-tube boiler is that the position of water and fire gases is reversed from that of a fire-tube boiler (the conventional Stephensonian arrangement), with water in the tubes and the combustion gases circulating between them. In practice this meant that two or more larger diameter drums were needed to connect all the tubes together and allow for feed water and steam to be collected. In marine service the tubes were usually straight, allowing easy removal and simple cleaning. Marine boilers were also condensing, and thus did not have the same order of problem with scale deposition that beset the steam locomotive. In hush-hush, these ideal relationships could not be obtained; the three steam drums, one at each side and one at the top, were so positioned as not to allow for straight tubes, and of course the boiler was not condensing. Trouble with the curved tubes was thus virtually guaranteed, but there was also trouble with the insulated boiler cladding, which on the inside was exposed to the heat of the furnace. This led to air leaks and these to poor steaming.

Inevitably the locomotive proved more trouble than it was worth, and its boiler was removed, to be replaced by a conventional Pacific boiler, with the Bugatti nose of the streamlined 'A4's'. The boiler was not scrapped, but put into service raising steam as a stationary boiler at Darlington. There it proved its worth, giving many years' further service.

Next on the ideas list was the booster. The East Coast Main Line in the 1920s had a stock of not very old 4-4-2 'Atlantics', displaced from heavy duties by Pacifics, but still capable of many years' good service, and more to the point, equipped with free steaming boilers and wide grates whose steam production, over short periods at least, could be raised significantly above the norm. Added to this was the fact that, while the east coast is fairly flat, there was a nasty four miles of 1 in 96 up to Penmanshiel Tunnel southbound from Dunbar to Berwick, and this had the effect of limiting loads on secondary services. The booster was conceived as a means of giving the Atlantics the extra tractive effort to allow them to shift heavier traffic over Cockburnspath Bank.

The booster was in effect a second 'engine', a geared unit that could be brought into engagement to drive the tender wheels at modest speed, the unit being designed to operate at under thirty mph. A complicated control circuit allowed the booster to cut in and out smoothly, and operation from the footplate was intended to ensure that the work done was in proportion to the locomotive output; a slipping booster would have been worse than useless. As with many improvements, the worth of the booster was not equal to its first cost plus maintenance, and the idea was quickly abandoned.

Nigel Gresley's concept of large locomotives hauling heavy trains then got just a little out of hand with the help of Beyer Peacock and Co., who offered up the concept of the 'Garrett' to the LNER, and with a little help from the three-cylinder obsession, produced the most powerful locomotive ever to run on the rails in Britain. The 'Garrett' is two locomotive chassis with a carrier frame for the boiler slung between them. The boiler can be built to the limits of the loading gauge, without need to avoid the wheels, and feeds the two engine units via flexible pipes. Until the LNER joined the scene, Beyer Peacock had only built two-cylinder chassis; by going for his favourite three-cylinder layout, Gresley was upping the tractive effort by 50%. The result was a locomotive that was quite simply unfit for any normal duty.

Having built such a leviathan, the LNER had to find a use for it; on the east coast it could haul trains longer than the available sidings and loops (it could also exert a drawbar pull that was too close to the tensile strength of the LNER's loose wagon couplings for comfort), and as a last resort it was put to work where it was least suited: banking coal trains up the Worsborough Incline near Barnsley. For this duty it was poorly fitted; buffing up was difficult due to the locomotive's great length and limited view, and the enormous boiler could not be 'turned up' immediately owing to its thermal mass. When steaming freely, it could lift the wagons being pushed off the rails. Banking crews thus came to detest the engine, and found that they could make the tubes leak by a bit of gerrymandering of the controls. The Garrett became a white elephant, and despite a trial on the Lickey incline after nationalisation, never found a suitable niche.

William Stanier's Turbine

William Stanier's arrival at the LMS in 1932 was no bar to that company having a second brief flirtation with the unconventional; the LMS was desperate for an express locomotive worthy of the name, and the first three 'Princess Royal' Pacifics should have been a little bit of the Great Western transferred and updated. Temptation intervened, however, and the third engine was not a four-cylinder machine, but turbine-driven. Given the limited traction resources of the LMS at the time, the decision to invest in a machine that was never likely to be anything other than an experiment is very surprising. Turbines were a very great break from tradition; they needed gears to connect to the driving wheels. Turbines also only ran one way, requiring a separate reverse. As a consequence the locomotive could not haul a train running tender-first owing to the back turbine being of limited power.

Conventional controls and interchangeable parts went some way to mitigate the disadvantages of such an experimental locomotive, but its average annual mileage before the outbreak of the Second World War was under two thirds that of its sister engines. After lying derelict for some time, it was rebuilt as a conventional Pacific in 1952 and named *Princess Anne*. In this form it lasted less than two months, being written off in the multiple collision at Harrow on the West Coast Main Line. The gap in the LMS stock provided the excuse for British Railways to build its sole three-cylinder Pacific, *Duke of Gloucester*.

Not to be beaten on unconventionality, Oliver Bulleid had his fling too, though he was cut short by Nationalisation.

Leaders

The short space between the close of the Second World War and the end of the Big Four in 1948 was not one in which the design and production of something completely different would normally be ruled either desirable or feasible. Bulleid, having had his way with a dubious Pacific express design in the depths of the war, was not put off by the hard times that set in after the end of Lease-Lend, and it is to his lasting credit that he succeeded in both the design and construction of the 'Leader' in conditions that were scarcely auspicious. The 'Leader' was in essence a multi-cylinder steam locomotive running on bogies that took their inspiration from the first main line diesels. Where it came unstuck was in the use of a bodyshell that enclosed the footplate and separated driver and fireman. The fireman was roasted by having to work in an enclosed space, indeed it was only on an experimental basis that any tests were carried out; it was far too hot to work in. The driver had duplicate controls at either end. The 'Leader' was so obviously out of order, that British Railways wanted nothing to do with Bulleid's eccentricity. The whole scheme was quietly dropped and the one completed prototype scrapped. It was almost, but not quite, the last of the oddities.

Crosti Boilers

Five years before the end of steam locomotive production, after the decision had been taken in principle to move over to diesel and electric traction, there appeared on the chassis of the '9F' heavy freight locomotive, a new boiler, the Franco-Crosti. In this boiler, instead of a conventional blastpipe and smokebox, a large pre-heater sat under the boiler proper, into which exhaust gases and steam were directed before being ejected out of a rectangular exhaust halfway down the side of the locomotive. To add interest there was a chimney in the usual place, but it was only used to light the boiler and raise steam, not in traffic. The locomotive thus had a large bulge along both sides of the smokebox, housing the pipes that led to the preheater. Again, the theory of staged heating as a means to economical working is a sound one, but where space is at a premium, making the locomotive larger does not necessarily lead to economy. History thus repeated itself by dispensing with the preheaters quite quickly; their economy was more theoretical than real, and within five years the Crosti boilers had gained blastpipes to operate conventionally.

Having charted the course of the unconventional and unsuccessful and made note that two other bolt-on goodies, the Giesl Ejector (another 'better blastpipe') and a mechanical stoker were also tried on the '9F', we can turn to the add-ons that lived up to their claims, and were more or less widely adopted.

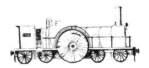

Chapter Twenty-Five:

Bolt-on Technologies:
The ones that worked

The history of the steam locomotive is littered with technologies that didn't work; we have looked at a few, and been amused in passing by the efforts of Francis Webb, who has performed admirably as a butt of criticism. From the very first run of the *Rocket* the idea that the steam locomotive could be made to operate better, faster, cheaper, use less coal, and so on has been the crock of gold at the end of innumerable designers' and inventors' rainbows. Only the very few cracked the puzzle, and for a long time in the nineteenth century there were almost no inventions worth wielding a spanner for. Stationary and marine steam engines quickly ditched much of the hardware the locomotive depended on, in the interests of economy. Notwithstanding this fact, there were some ideas that could be fitted onto wheels, and among the first, and best was that of a Belgian, Egide Walschaerts.

Walschaerts' Valve Gear

The complexities of valve operating mechanisms are disguised by the fact that, on the surface at least, the idea of a set of rods pushing a slide back and forth across the inlet and exhaust ports is very simple. It isn't until you actually examine what the valve is supposed to be doing that the guise of simplicity slips. Egide Walschaerts' understanding of the way a slide valve works, and his design of an operating gear, alone among the nineteenth century locomotive gears, that was both new in concept and much more efficient in operation, is ample evidence of both the difficulty of the topic and the brilliance of the man.

The problem of how to get the right amount of steam into the cylinder, make it do as much work as possible and then get rid of the remains without undoing any of the work performed, centres on the problem of inertia; steam has mass, and while it wasn't important at the start, so too do valves and their operating gear. Steam from the boiler will not instantly fill the cylinder to the same pressure as soon as the valve is only fractionally open; how much steam gets in before the crank turns to where it can exert effective torque, depends entirely on the size of the steam pipes and the valve port openings. The original eccentrics employed by Robert Stephenson to operate slide valves could have their position on the axle relative to the stroke of the piston altered to advance the point at which the valve port started to open, but this is only one of a number of settings that the valves can have. Adding the link motion to adjust the throw or travel of the valve did not enable the locomotive to work expansively, but shortening the travel reduces the valve openings, delays the valve opening and throttles the engine at speed. This feature of Stephenson link motion was the cause of the fashion for large driving wheels on express locomotives, to keep piston and valve speeds as low as possible for the maximum miles per hour.

Walschaerts' idea was that the motion of the valve could be taken, or derived, from more than one source; the stroke of the piston, suitably reduced by unequal arm levers, could provide the majority of the valve movement, while the proportion of expansive working, the 'cut off', could be taken from a separate fly crank or eccentric. Splitting the motion thus allowed more precise setting of the valve characteristics, and meant that taking the engine out of full gear did not throttle the steam supply, either by retarding the point of admission, or by a proportionate reduction in valve travel. Even in mid gear, valve travel was still equal to the full amount derived from the piston stroke. When the ideas of long travel and long lap began to be applied at the start of the twentieth century, Egide Walschaerts' invention was by a margin the favoured gear for express locomotives.

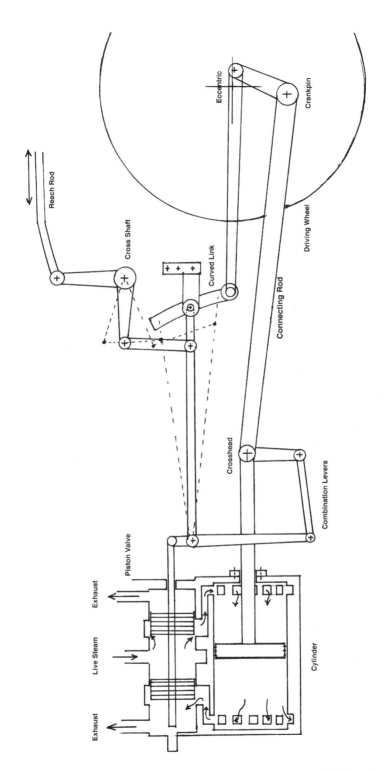

Figure 56: Walschaerts Valve Gear.

243

The Steam Injector

Boiler feed pumps were temperamental beasts at the best of times; Timothy Hackworth had cause to curse at Rainhill, for he was let down by just such a device. Feeding water into a boiler demands that the feed pressure exceeds the boiler pressure, and in 1829, the only way of achieving this was to use a force pump. The force pumps for locomotive use were usually driven by eccentrics from the driving axle, and as such absorbed a significant amount of the engine power.

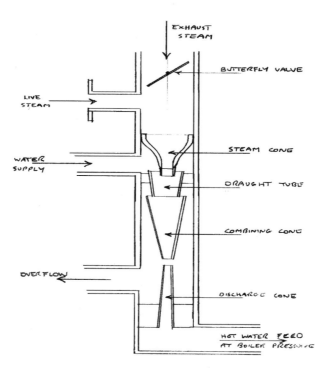

Figure 57: The Steam Injector.

The locomotive injector solved this problem in such an efficient manner that once invented, it was never superseded, and the prize goes to a Frenchman, Henri Giffaud. His claim to fame is that he realised the energy contained in steam at low pressure included the energy of latent heat of evaporation. Condensing steam released this energy and enabled the feed water, which had done the condensing, to be raised to a pressure above that of the boiler from whence the steam came.

Once this feature was realised, it was only a matter of calculating the amount of steam and water needed to condense, devise a means of mixing the two and popping a non-return valve in the circuit in order to prevent the system going in reverse. The practical device employed a steam cone and a water annulus, feeding into a combining cone where the velocity imparted by the steam on the water was converted to pressure. The device worked just as well with live, rather than exhaust steam, and locomotives were fitted with live and exhaust steam injectors, or combination injectors which could use either. Feed capacities of each injector were normally in excess of the boiler steaming rate, and the turndown ratio (maximum to minimum feed rate) was in the order of 2:1. The injector developed slowly; they could be difficult to start, because if the water supply, which had to be turned on first, did not run at the correct rate, when the steam supply was opened there would either be insufficient water to condense the steam, or not enough steam to raise the flow pressure above that of the boiler. Manufacturers advertised their products as 'self starting', but every experienced fireman has wrestled with a recalcitrant injector.

The Superheater

As with injectors, the way superheaters work is not immediately obvious, not even if you can recall school physics lessons and in particular, the general gas equation. Also akin to the injector, the inventor was a foreigner, this time German, Wilhelm Schmidt. Application to the steam locomotive was a trifle delayed after it was recognised as a fundamentally better way of doing things, because the down-side of the idea was a much harsher cylinder environment, which demanded better lubrication than was the norm in 1905. Superheaters did two things: dried the steam being generated in the boiler, and dramatically reduced the quantity of water needed to do the same amount of work.

Steam in contact with boiling water is said to be saturated, that is any fall in temperature will cause condensation to take place and steam pressure to drop, all in accordance with the gas equation: pressure times volume divided by temperature is a constant for a particular gas, viz: $pv/t = c$. Raising the temperature increases the pressure of the steam, but the steam is still 'wet', containing about 10% by mass of fine water droplets in suspension. While a drop in pressure will release some latent heat of condensation, the water in suspension is a passenger; a lot of energy has been put in to feed and heat it, but there is no useful work to be extracted. Separating steam from water and adding heat energy turns most of this water into steam, which is then available to do useful work.' Ah, but,' you say, 'any loss of heat in the pipes and steam chests is still going to result in condensation', which is of course true.

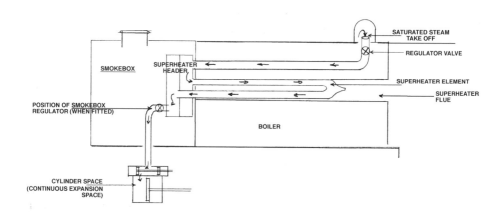

Figure 58: The Superheater.

What the superheater also does is raise the steam temperature well above the dew point, at which point, those of you who are wise to pv/t will say 'how?' If the temperature of the steam rises, then the pressure will also, because you cannot buck the equation. No, but you can cheat, and the way to cheat is to continuously expand the volume of the steam as it is being heated, and the cylinders represent that continuous expansion. Steam entering the cylinders is thus dry, and while containing a lot of energy, contains a lot less water than saturated steam to do the same work. Less water to heat, and less latent heat of evaporation to throw away in the exhaust.

To fit the superheater to the locomotive boiler was a bit of a challenge; there are basically three places where it can go; firebox, boiler or smokebox. The easiest and cheapest place is the smokebox, but it was quickly found that the added heat didn't add up to a great deal, barely performing the 'drying' task. At the turn of the century smokeboxes were not large and there was often not room enough to put more than a few tubes in. There was also the risk of taming draw on the fire and clogging with ash. Likewise the firebox: lots of radiant heat, but an extremely aggressive environment for tubes of steel that do not have any water to cool their insides. The successful design thus used the boiler, and while there were a number of different layouts of tubes, the general arrangement consisted of a series of large diameter 'flues' replacing the top rows of fire tubes, into which were fitted tubes carrying the steam to be heated. A header or collector in the smokebox distributed saturated steam, and collected the superheated steam for delivery to the cylinders.

Low temperature superheaters made their entry onto Britain's railways in 1906, the first users were the Great Western. Really high temperature superheat was not widely used for a further thirty years.

The Better Blastpipe

Robert Stephenson demonstrated, with the first production batch of service locomotives for the Liverpool and Manchester Railway, that the effect of a tapered blastpipe on the fire at the other end of a six foot long boiler was to pull it off the grate and throw it out of the chimney, if that was what was wanted. Longer boilers with more tubes followed until by 1920, there were boilers in use six feet in diameter, and fifteen feet, and more, between tubeplates, capable of evaporating ten plus tons of water an hour when working flat out. Positioning a single blastpipe under the chimney was then seen not to be the best way of making a boiler steam. It was realised that to give of its best, boilers had to draw evenly through all firetubes and superheater flues, rather than most of the gases taking the easy route through the upper tubes. Introduction of the petticoat pipe was an early solution: an open topped bell positioned over the blast pipe to help both draw the lower tubes and eject ashes from the smokebox. Churchward added a loose ring on the top, a 'jumper', to moderate the blast at full output. The jumper ring was lifted automatically by the blast when working hard. This was by way of an improvement, but as locomotives grew larger and more powerful, the single blastpipe did not give optimum steaming and the search was on for a better arrangement.

Perhaps the most visually and audibly impressive of the revised draughting ideas was that adopted by the Southern Railway; the multiple jet blastpipe, where the single nozzle was replaced by a ring of five smaller jets discharging through a large diameter chimney. The visible chimney on the 'Lord Nelson', 'West Country' and 'Merchant Navy' classes was perhaps the best proportioned chimney ever seen on a locomotive, and the soft 'woof' of these engines starting, the most delightfully evocative of sounds. As a system it was not to be widely adopted, because the simpler double chimney was preferred by the nationalised railway.

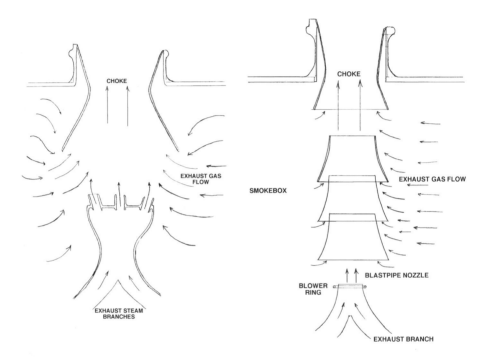

Figure 59: Multi-Jet and Kylala-Chapelon Blastpipes.

The blastpipe that blew *Mallard* to 126mph was a variation of both petticoat pipe and double chimney, in fact a combination of the two known as the Kylala-Chapelon or Kylchap blastpipe. This system comprised a stack of three concentric petticoat pipes under each chimney, the idea being that the draw on the tubes would be both maximised and even, avoiding lifting of the fire. For maximum performance, this system was the best by a margin, but use was limited due to the restricted duties that required the utmost of locomotives. Second best generally proved good enough, and the double chimney thus found far wider favour than the ultimate blastpipe, once again proving the theory that additional performance or economy of an improvement does not guarantee adoption, when placed against first cost plus extra maintenance.

It comes as a bit of a shock to realise that in 1950, only a decade from the end of steam locomotive production in Britain, the design principles of locomotive draughting were still being determined. The double chimney had been adopted by both LNER and LMS in the 1930s for their most powerful express types; rebuilt 'Royal Scots' received the treatment to boost their steam production, but it was not until the 1950s that practical experiment on the new testing plant at Rugby showed just how hit and miss design of existing front end draughting was. The results of those tests showed up weaknesses in many locomotive types, leading to redesign of chimneys and blastpipes; the Great Western 'Kings' were all altered to a double blastpipe and chimney, and were much the better for it. A well designed exhaust system, though, paid other dividends; less wear on plates and tubes, more even steaming, and less ash accumulation (the self-cleaning smokebox became a standard feature).

Gauge Glasses

Quite how the steam locomotive boiler was monitored before the invention of the gauge glass is not a mystery; there was a test cock, which when opened blew off either water or steam. If steam emerged then the boiler feed pump was turned on until it blew off water. The gauge glass put an end to this hit or miss arrangement, and is still used today on modern stationary steam plant. What made the gauge glass possible in the nineteenth century was development of a modern glass industry, whereby it was possible to manufacture glass to close tolerances and specific forms. Up to that point manufacture of glass had been a struggle, for glass can be made in hundreds of ways in terms of mix of ingredients, but forming it into useful objects had always been difficult. That said, gauge glasses would not have found their way onto the steam locomotive but for a little bit of technological wizardry.

Glass generally is quite brittle; not the ideal material for withstanding the considerable pressures and temperatures of a locomotive boiler. There was, unfortunately, not really any alternative to glass in the nineteenth century, and the way that it was used in the water gauge paid due respect to the material's inherent weakness. Firstly, the tube diameter was kept small to minimise the total pressure on the glass, and the tube wall thickness was proportionally great. Secondly, special gaskets, glands and nuts

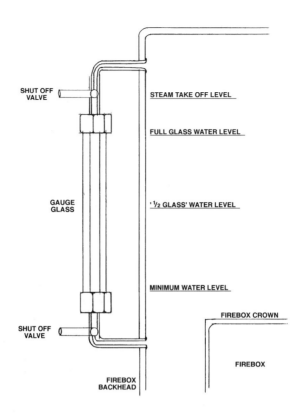

Figure 60: Gauge Glass.

were developed to prevent the brass or steel pipes from the firebox backhead exerting any point loads that might cause failure. Thirdly, the whole unit was encased in a further glass screen to contain any blow-out, and the whole arrangement protected by self-sealing ball valves, that cut off the steam in the event of a failure. While failure of gauge glasses was thus a fairly common occurrence, spare glasses could be fitted while the engine was in service, and risk of scalding from escaping steam or water was minimised.

The real problem with any mechanism for displaying boiler water level, and particularly with a short glass tube, was the risk both of a false reading, and of narrow limits within which the boiler could be safely operated. Filling the boiler to the top of the glass ran the risk that water would carry over into the cylinders, with the attendant risk of damaged valves or pistons. There was accordingly reluctance to run with a continuously full glass, and turning injectors on and off on a regular basis was usually planned to keep the water level in the middle third of the glass, though the last section of a hard climb might be executed on a falling glass, in knowledge that there would be plenty of time to refill on the downgrade after the summit, where steam demand would be minimal.

False readings due to poor maintenance were fortunately rare, but priming due to excessive salt concentration when a boiler washout was due could also expose the firebox crown. Most boiler failures in the twentieth century were due to overheating of the top of the firebox, and the subsequent failure of the stays and crown plates. Gauge glasses were not total proof against this catastrophe, and neither was the other device, the fusible plug.

Mechanical lubrication

Oil pots and trimmings lasted to the end of steam. If, by the turn of the nineteenth century, they were a little dated, the effort of providing a dedicated oil supply to those parts of the engine motion that were difficult to provide with fixed pipes was often found just not to be worthwhile, and the way the steam locomotive was lubricated in 1960 was not wildly different from the means employed in 1860. Between those times there were a number of inventions, more or less widely adopted, that supplied oil to the parts of the motion that a pipe could reach.

Oiling a steam locomotive involves every moving part; regulator, reverser, cylinders, crossheads, big ends, valve motion, axle bearings, valves. While it is possible to pipe oil under pressure to all of these bearings, the concept of forced lubrication and filtered sump supply was only adopted as a whim by Oliver Bulleid, and it was not a conspicuous success, rather the reverse. Oil could be pumped to where it was needed, the method eventually favoured by the nationalised railway, but the first idea for forced lubrication was to use steam pressure to provide the motive power, and the result was first the displacement lubricator, and then the sight feed lubricator, so called because the driver could monitor and, to a degree, control, the oil supply from the cab. With oils of variable quality (we would describe most of the lubricating oils of the nineteenth century as 'unfit for purpose' today) one way of ensuring a supply was to heat the oil, and the steam could do just that, before it was used in the cylinder, valve chest and regulator, areas where dashpots and trimmings were unsuitable.

The principle behind the displacement lubricator was that it was possible to use steam to directly heat oil and, because oil floats on water, condense steam in an oilpot at a given rate, which would then cause oil to overflow down the feed pipe to the surface to be lubricated.

The sight feed lubricator merely shifted the oil to the cab (the Great Western's system had a condenser coil mounted on the underside of the cab roof), where the flow rate could be observed and adjusted before being piped to the point of use.

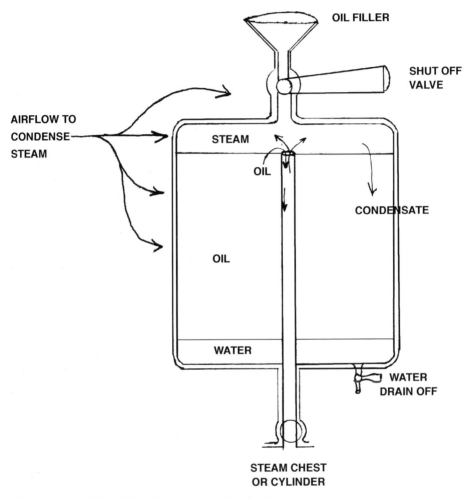

Figure 61: The Displacement Lubricator.

The Great Central's chief engineer, J. G. Robinson, patented his 'Intensifore' sight feed lubricator in the years before the First World War, and obtained royalties on this item fitted on every '8K' 2-8-0 supplied to his design to the Railway Operating Department of the War Office. This was not the only sight feed lubricator on the market, but patents were not always granted at that time on the exclusivity of the idea. Later mechanical lubricators, such as the 'Wakefield', were driven from the engine motion, and comprised separate ram pumps for each feed pipe, a method that avoided the risk of a central pump not feeding all destinations evenly, allowing bearings to go dry.

The Blower

Despite the name, this item has nothing to do with telephones and everything to do with safety. As boilers grew longer and fireboxes larger, so the inertia of the combustion system in the steam locomotive increased. In particular, the volume of hot gases being produced by the fire when it was being drawn hard by the blast in the smokebox did not cease as soon as the regulator was shut. When an engine is working, exhaust steam is drawing the fire through the smoke tubes and combustion air through grate and firehole door, which will be partly or fully ajar: fully ajar if the fireman is firing the grate, and partially ajar at other times to admit combustion air over the firebed. Shutting the regulator cuts off the blast, but the fire does not die down instantly, and if not prevented, searing hot gas will blow back through the firehole door as it looks for a way to escape that is easier than through the boiler. Accidental blowbacks were a perennial risk, causing numerous injuries to footplate staff, for the blower is a manual rather than an automatic device, and wordless and seamfree co-ordination between driver and fireman essential for safe operation.

The blower then was an auxiliary steam jet, or rather a ring of jets, positioned around the lip of the blastpipe and designed to draw the fire when the regulator was shut and blastpipe idle. Controlled by a steam valve on the firebox backhead, it allowed the fireman to keep some draw on the fire while the firebed temperature dropped and rate of combustion slowed. Dropping the dampers on the ashpan cut off much of the combustion air, but the heat of the firebed could be 1200deg.F or more at full output, and only 600deg.F or so at idle.

Sanding Gear

The idea that sand applied to the wheel/rail interface would improve adhesion was a sound one. Actually putting sand on the rails proved a little more troublesome. Wet sand will not run to where it is needed, and despite all running sheds being equipped with sand furnaces (to dry the stuff before it was installed in locomotives sandboxes) gravity sanding was unreliable, tending to fail in wet weather, just when it was wanted most. The solution, devised by the Midland Railway, was the steam sander, where use of a jet of steam to blow sand onto the rails in front of the driving wheels produced a system that was as reliable as the gravity arrangement was not. The result in the 1880s was a new lease of life for the single driver locomotive, enabling the 'single' to make it to the start of the twentieth century, and giving a good helping hand to the steam locomotive's biggest bugbear, poor adhesion, particularly on starting. When track circuits were introduced, the steam sander had a rail washer added to clean the rails after the driving wheels had passed. Steam sanding was adopted world-wide, perhaps the most comprehensively adopted of the add-ons.

Chapter Twenty-Six:

The Kingdom of the Chief Mechanical Engineer: The Railway Locomotive Works

When Buddicom put in hand the instructions of his directors, to build a new locomotive works on a greenfield site on the Cheshire Plain, he may indeed have had the vision that Crewe Works would grow to be the largest in the land; that it would rank in terms of technical expertise and production capacity alongside the largest engineering works of Britain (and by implication, the world), was probably not on the agenda, at least not at first. Crewe Works was born out of necessity; the Grand Junction Railway needed to keep its trains running, needed to feed back the experience of running trains into its own systems, to improve quality and reliability, and to control costs. So inescapable was this logic, that other large companies, as we have seen, followed in short order. Over a period of less than twenty years, the railway companies that could afford the capital outlay went from buying trains and running them, to designing, building, running and repairing them, and the heart of that system was the 'Works'.

Perhaps contrary to expectations, most locomotive works did not build new locomotives as their primary activity. The actual bits that wore out were quite small, and development of the locomotive between 1830 and 1850 was as much concerned with repairability and increased mileage between 'shopping' as it was with performance; better methods of construction to make parts last longer, and better assembly techniques that shortened the time and reduced the expense needed to turn a worn out engine into a rebuilt one, ready for the rails. Buying new motive power from the rapidly expanding private industry was always competitive, and throughout the history of the steam locomotive, this procurement method was used by almost every company, whether they had a works and new build capacity or not.

Over a period of eighty years to the grouping in 1923, the numbers and size of the locomotive works in Britain grew steadily, but at the grouping, while there was no immediate change, the main works that had either an actual or a theoretical new build capability shrank from about twenty five to a modest dozen by the time British Railways was formed, viz:

> Swindon (GWR)
> Crewe (LNW)
> Derby (Midland)
> Doncaster (Great Northern)
> Darlington (North Eastern)
> Horwich (Lancashire and Yorkshire)
> Brighton (London, Brighton and South Coast)
> Eastleigh (London and South Western)
> Ashford (South Eastern)
> St Rollox (Caledonian)
> Cowlairs (North British)
> Stratford (Great Eastern)

Of these, the last three were to be downgraded quite quickly to join Gorton (Great Central) and Inverurie (Great North of Scotland) as repairers rather than builders, a fate that had already befallen a number of works in the rationalisations of the 1920s and 1930s.

The basic plan of a locomotive works in the middle of the nineteenth century was that of a production line; while it was possible to crane whole locomotives around, it was far easier to roll them on their own wheels, and as a locomotive might receive heavy repairs every two years, depending upon its duties, and a rebuild at ten or twenty years, the layout reflected the fact that repairs were the works' bread and butter. Locomotives in need of an overhaul would thus arrive at the works in one piece (on occasion there were parts missing due to out of course events), and the first task, before any repair work commenced, was to remove coal, ashes, grime and water, none of which have any place in metal bashing.

The engine then had to be assessed for the extent of the proposed overhaul and allocated a space on the repair line. Component stripping then commenced, the boiler being craned to the boiler shop for major attention, if needed, and other components to their various overhaul points in the works. Wheels were sent to the lathe for reprofiling of tyres and turning of journals back to circular; bearings for remetalling; cylinders for skimming or reboring. If the work was particularly extensive, there might be little more than the frames on the repair line after the rest had been dismantled.

The amount of work an engine needed is perhaps a little beyond what we would expect to comprise an economic repair today. Boilers, to take just one example, could just be inspected and left on the frames, or they could be renewed complete. Between these extremes a boiler could have a few tubes replaced, a complete retube, partial or complete re-staying of the firebox, new tubeplates, a new firebox inner, a wasted corner cut out and replaced, a new brick arch or foundation ring, firebar carriers or ashpan. Superheater flues or elements, steam pipes, regulator valves, smokebox plates, safety valves or whistle would come up for repair or renewal in their turn. All of these would be regarded as normal parts of an overhaul rather than a reason for scrapping. Boilers treated reasonably by their home sheds, given regular washouts and warmed up and cooled down gently, and not hammered by their crews driving or firing badly, would often be in need of overhaul only one third or a quarter as often as the chassis.

For a long period, the reason for scrapping an engine would centre upon its suitability for the traffic that was on offer. Locomotives that were expensive to repair, poor on reliability and not up to the intended task were much more likely to be withdrawn than a long in the tooth but reliable freight shifter. A large class, such as the Midland/LMSR '4F' 0-6-0, originally introduced in 1911, with large numbers built in 1922-24, and still over five hundred strong in 1960, would see occasional withdrawals if an individual engine had a large number of serious defects (especially frame, wheel or cylinder problems). Those withdrawals would be exceptions though, and would only occur after a policy decision had been made, either to cease making new components, such as cylinder and valve castings, or to place a cost limit on repairs, again usually for traffic reasons. Rebuilding, to improve performance and reliability, or to make use of updated standard boiler and firebox, for example, was a regular occurrence. In 1960, a fifty year old engine might well have part or all of the main frames, and perhaps the wheel centres and some of the motion rods, made of the original metal. The rest would have been replaced, and usually on more than one occasion.

This repairability was both the steam locomotive's strength and its weakness; the idea of an engine eighty years old and still in revenue-earning service was not unthinkable in the 1950s, nor was the concept of overhaul and return to traffic without limit of useful life. Long life and low cost added to the idea of nil depreciation equalled an asset on the balance sheet that was difficult to justify replacing with something 'modern'. Even replacing old steam locomotives with new ones significantly better at the task and cheaper to run was an accounting challenge. When diesels cost ten times a new steam engine, biting that bullet was not easy for the nationalised railway. After a century of building in repairability to the steam locomotive, the railway works had in effect justified their existence by stretching unit life to as long as was required by the traffic department. Built in obsolescence was unheard of.

The steam locomotive was always unique; in design it pre-dated tolerance-defined interchangeability, and when that arrived from the USA, no-one attempted to apply it to locomotive construction, with the exception of boilers and fireboxes, and bolt-on accessories such as injectors and lubricators. Engine parts such as wheels, bearing housings, motion, valves and cylinders were unique to each locomotive, and if they were capable of being removed, then they had to carry the loco number with them, even though they were superficially identical with the same part on the next member of the same class. The reason is that locomotives were not assembled but fitted, and when fitted, a locomotive gained its own unique valve setting table to which reference was made each time valves had to be set after removal or overhaul, and those settings depended on all the motion parts and the chassis, not just the valve rods.

As locomotives grew in physical size and technical complexity, so too did the works that maintained them; bigger boilers could only be handled by larger cranes, and if the same number were to be overhauled each year, the workshop had to be bigger in proportion. More wheels meant more work in the wheel shop and tyre department, and of course the train mileage grew in line with track mileage and traffic. There was seemingly no end to this process of growth, and by the First World War, all the major railway works were spread over many acres, threaded with railway tracks and surrounded by sidings stuffed with everything from raw materials to withdrawn engines.

While heavy repair shops could be used for new locomotive building, it was far from an ideal location; there were work items, such as frame cutting and assembly, that were just not a normal part of the repair process. Thus by the time of the grouping, those companies with extensive in-house build programmes followed the lead of the Great Western at Swindon and had a separate erecting shop or shops. Here the delicate work of turning one inch thick rolled steel plates into main frames and assembling them so that they were absolutely true could be carried out on a surface plate set in the floor, giving a datum to the required accuracy.

With almost everything done either by hand or by a machine under manual supervision, the numbers employed, from the drawing office to the fitters, boilersmiths, labourers and canteen staff, ran into thousands, with all the major works dominating employment in the towns which had grown up around them. In effect the whole life of these towns revolved around the works; schooling and further education, which was mostly technical, was aimed at the job in prospect, be it a start at the works, or a better job later on in life. While the steam locomotive lived and breathed, so too did it breathe life into the towns that served it.

The early engines of the 1840s were limited in life and quickly superseded, but after 1860, while power outputs grew and the total number of locomotives increased to perhaps 45,000 in 1900, the equation between miles run and overhauls required did not change significantly until steam's day was seen to be drawing to a close. The steam locomotive's demand for the services of the works was thus fairly constant, dipping when trade recessions reduced freight services, and increasing to fever pitch at times of high demand, but overall providing a guarantee of employment for many, and in a large number of instances, a lifetime's work for three or four consecutive generations of the same family.

Not every railway company went to the extreme of the London and North Western and built their own steel works, but the independence of locomotive works from what we would now regard as a normal supply chain takes a little understanding. All works bought raw materials: iron, steel, coal, copper, and the other rarer metals that they needed. These materials were supplied as ingots or plate, for melting and casting, machining, forging and turning. Everything from turning a set screw to casting cylinders and valve chests could be, and was, done in-house; as engines grew in complexity, the 'Big Four' developed techniques that were special to their own products and could not have been produced elsewhere to order. Gorton Works in Manchester, for example, produced the monobloc cylinder castings for the three cylinder locomotives of the LNER, casting cylinders, valves and all the steam and exhaust passages in one go. Swindon developed the bending and forming of heavy copper plate for inner firebox wrappers to a standard that belongs perhaps as much to art as engineering.

It was only for those items that were specialised or patented by others (injectors, brake valves, and, later, items such as roller bearings, where the patents or special production methods meant that buying in was the best or only option) that the railway works were reliant on others for finished goods.

Having the capacity to make something implies the ability to design it as well, and everything the works made was designed in the drawing office, from the material specification, through running tolerances to the form and pitch of the threads on the nuts and bolts that held the finished job together. All were drawn out by hand, and until the era of the first copiers (the origin of the concept of the 'blueprint', for the first machine-made copies were blue), the drawings were then all laboriously traced by hand to produce copies for foundry or boiler shop to work from. It is as well to record at this point that what the works dealt in was technology; science played a back of house role. Doing, at least initially, was more important than theorising. Making a design work was more important than understanding the science of why it worked. The inventions that produced first mild steel in quantity and then a myriad of special steels, to quote just one example, were adopted by the railway works, not invented there. Machinery to perform tasks special to the locomotive was about as far as the works went in inventions. Locomotive works built and repaired locomotives; toolmakers made machine tools; steelmakers special steels, even if they were to the works' specifications.

Capacity to produce the practical necessities of the locomotive meant also the capacity to design and produce embellishments, and almost everyone, from the chief engineer down to the shop foremen and fitters could not resist the temptation to add a little joy to their work; Francis Webb had a fling with an intricately embellished chimney, and when the LNER built identical locomotives at Doncaster and Darlington, you only had to look at the cylinder covers or count the wheel spokes to tell where they were built. The cynic of the nineteenth century would have said that engineers were obliged to make their engines look good in an attempt to deceive the public that they performed well, too, but the dominance of the steam locomotive as a transport form led to inevitable beauty contests, and it is perhaps a reflection of the relative good taste of Victorian Britain in this respect, if not in others, that the excesses of the Americans were avoided, and the Continent was foreign: good to go and look at, but to copy? No.

The works, then, was as self-contained as need made it, no less in the installed equipment than in the skills of its workers. Metal bashing in the steam era meant big technology; steam hammers to forge connecting rods, lathes to turn eight-foot-diameter driving wheels, melting and casting shops capable of handling several tons of liquid steel for a single pour, annealing and quenching furnaces, presses to drive wheels onto axles, plate forgers and flangers to bend boiler plates. For all of these machines high-pressure steam or compressed air was needed, distributed round the works by pipeline from the engine house. For smaller lathes and milling and grinding, until the advent of electricity in the first decades of the twentieth century, line shafting and belt drives festooned workshops, a mass of whirling and creaking movement. Above this hive of activity rumbled the works cranes, running on tracks attached to the building stanchions at high level, and capable of moving any item the works made or repaired, supplementing the smaller fixed jibs and hoists used to load and manipulate work items onto and off lathe beds and forges.

The end of the locomotive works crept up slowly; as engineering works par excellence, they demonstrated their ability to match industry in general and government armouries and arsenals in particular, when war demanded that they turn aside from their prime purpose. Thus when the first diesels and electrics took to the rails, some of them were built in the works that had hitherto been the sole preserve of the steam locomotive, and when diesels needed overhaul, well, the works were up to that too. The decline and fall of steam did not result in the instant closure of the works that served them, but 20,000 steam locomotives were replaced with 2,000 diesels, and ultimately most of the works found, like the private locomotive builders, that the market for their products had evaporated.

Where also the steam locomotive had progressed over the century from 1850 from running 50,000 or so miles between overhaul, and perhaps a million miles to scrapping, to double these figures, the diesel in the twentieth century's second half moved from overhaul at 10,000 running hours to twice that. This equates to between 400,000 and a million miles in front line service, and many million miles before withdrawal, depending on the duty, running sixteen hours plus a day and covering perhaps fifteen hundred miles in that period, three to four times the distance of the best steam performance. By degrees the works faded away, closing their doors in the last decades of the twentieth century, some of them, like Darlington, having spent quite a lot of their final years in cutting up the engines they had built and maintained.

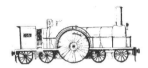

Chapter Twenty-Seven:

The Running Shed:
Feeding, Watering and Maintenance

If works were few, running sheds were legion; almost every railway company saw construction of a locomotive running shed as part and parcel of the infrastructure needed to run a railway. Just as you could not own a horse without a stable to keep it in, it seemed unthinkable not to have a suitable home for each and every steam locomotive. The outcome of this principle being adopted by virtually everyone (including those who couldn't afford to buy their own locomotives) was that there were generally more running sheds than were needed for the efficient running of the railways. As strategies for handling goods and passenger traffic developed and matured in the second half of the nineteenth century, sheds were closed, reopened and closed again as traffic demanded. While running sheds were often capable of a range of repairs, their purpose was day to day operation and maintenance of traction, the cleaning, fuelling and watering of engines required for service, performing boiler washouts, oiling, renewing oil trimmings, adjusting bearings to take up wear, changing worn firebars and brick arches, adjusting packings and attending to minor faults in boilers and fireboxes.

When sheds received the new or newly overhauled locomotive from the works it was not in steam; oiled up yes, filled with coal and water, no. To put the locomotive into service the running shed foreman had to deploy his human resources as manager of a system supplying power to the railway. The yard shunter would take the engine to the coaling stage to fill the tender or bunker, and then to the water column to fill the tanks. On completion of these tasks, the engine would be placed 'on shed', under a chimney, and the boiler filled to 'half glass' with hot water and handed to the 'lighter up'. The use of hot water to fill the boiler was an important item in the maintenance regime, as it raised the temperature of the firebox and boiler tubes above the dew point of the combustion gases, which were strongly acidic, and would cause severe corrosion if allowed to condense on cold boiler plates.

The 'lighter up' was one of the team, whose ultimate ambition was to be a driver, responsible for the locomotive prior to it being handed over to the rostered crew. As the name implies the 'lighter up' had the by no means unskilled task of lighting the locomotive fire, and to assist in this, the blower could be connected to the shed steam supply to provide some draught. The importance of careful lighting up, in building the fire steadily and evenly to prevent uneven thermal stresses causing boiler leaks, and in providing the fireman with a good start to his day's labour, was not to be underestimated. Raising enough steam to start work took time; at least an hour on the smallest engines, over two on the largest, and while this was in train, the foreman would have a fitter check the motion to ensure that none of the bearings was overtight or too slack. This action would be repeated by the driver when he arrived, and he would also check the oil pots and trimmings to see that all was well.

Once the fire was making steam, the crew could take over, and in the case of a new or overhauled locomotive, the turn allocated would be an easy 'running in' one. The aim of the 'lighter up' was to have the engine able to move off shed in time for the duty, with enough fire on the grate to enable the fireman to make up a good blaze in time for the start of work, which may be some time after leaving the shed and involve a fair distance running 'light'. An engine that had a full head of steam in the yard, and either blew off on the safety valves, which could be a nuisance if there were nearby residents, or had the boiler filled to the top of the glass to stop it blowing off, was an engine mismanaged.

When the engine returned from its turn on the road, it would be somewhat less clean than when it went out: ashpan and smokebox full of ash, firebed more or less choked with clinker, boiler tubes dirty, and the water in the boiler retaining all those impurities that were left behind on evaporation. The first stop for the engine on its return to the shed would thus be the ash disposal road, where the fire was dropped, the ashpan emptied and smokebox ash evicted. If the engine was to be kept in steam for the next day's duty, the fire would be made up again and the loco moved to the shed to be cleaned. The cleaners were the bottom of the promotion ladder of hopeful drivers, and hand cleaning the only way to do the job properly. At the end of the week, or longer if the local water supplies were good, there would be so much sludge in the boiler that it needed a washout, hot or cold, depending on the company policy. Washing out the boiler involved drawing off the dirty boiler water (recovering the heat in the process) removing the washout plugs and mudhole covers and using water under moderate pressure to flush out the muck that gathers from the water. If a cold wash was used then the locomotive would have to cool for five or six hours before the task could begin.

While out of steam, other tasks could be attended; firebars got worn and bent and running sheds kept large stocks as consumables, to be fitted as required; loose and worn packing glands and stuffing boxes on piston rods and regulators could be renewed or adjusted, big end cotters tightened to take up wear and the motion taken down for cleaning and adjustment if needed, and if there were any weeping tubes, stays or seams in the boiler or firebox, they could be repaired or renewed. Brake blocks needed regular checks and renewal, injectors cleaning, oil trimmings renewing, and the round of oiling and greasing was of course ceaseless.

In addition to the engines allocated to the shed, the running foreman had to cope with a constant stream of engines that, visiting as part of their duties, needing de-ashing and coal and water as a matter of course, and the occasional running repair also. If the shed was close to a terminus then there would be a queue of locomotives heading for the turntable, all potentially obstructions to the smooth running of the shed yard.

Keeping the running shed supplied with coal was a very visible task, particularly as the coaling towers of the twentieth century replaced the stages of the nineteenth. When the steam locomotive reigned supreme, eight million tons of coal a year was shovelled into fireboxes nationwide. Water, too, was needed in quantity, and all sheds had a supply commensurate with their demand, not infrequently from the company's own borehole. The vast shed at Hull Dairycoates, for example, was supplied from a borehole, pumping station and treatment works three miles away in the goods yard at Hessle.

With large volumes needed, a tank store close to the point of use was an absolute necessity, and gravity supply essential, a fact that led to the vicinity of sheds and stations being populated with large water tanks on plinths or stilts (the concrete one at Cardiff General has gained a decor of giant daffodils in recent years). Feed pipes to the water columns were large bore pipes controlled by a wheel-operated gate valve at the column base. A brazier was precaution against freezing. The quality of the water was important too; the Hessle treatment plant was needed to remove temporary hardness of water drawn from the chalk. At the other end of the scale, the small supply and tank at Parracombe on the Lynton and Barnstaple Railway existed because it was both convenient to the railway (but not necessarily for train operation) and of excellent quality.

Smaller quantities of other materials were equally important; cotton waste was extensively used as a cleaning material, and cloths were standard issue to footplate staff who used them to insulate their hands from hot controls. Shovels wore out, as did the fire irons used to keep up a good fire. Overalls were essential, and stocks of kindling for lighting up, oil and cotton trimmings for lamps and lubrication all kept the storeman busy. At the back of the shed the 'shore' steam supply was often a landlocked locomotive, tied to the building with water feed and steam supply pipes.

All this was repeated at scores of sheds up and down the land, but at the other end of the scale, there was the single- or two-road shed for one or two engines, at the terminus of a country branch line. Perhaps the most remote one was on the incline isolated Rosedale Branch on top of the North Yorkshire Moors. Sheds were often without allocation of locomotives or permanent staff, at a junction such as Market Weighton, where occasional use of the facility during the summer holiday period justified its retention. Here, the most that could be obtained in supplies was water, occasionally coal.

The Market Weighton shed existed only because it had been a terminus for twenty years after opening, and when the lines to Driffield and Beverley opened after the railway king's demise, both had stiff gradients on which banking was occasionally needed. In later years banking holiday trains was effected by attaching a pilot engine much further west, at Gascoigne Wood; as many of the trains were excursions from distant industrial towns, whose crews did not know the route beyond Selby, the pilot engine crew were needed, and both crews then got a day out on the beach at Bridlington or Filey, before having to take the day trippers home in the evening. Nonetheless, Market Weighton's shed survived to the closure of the four lines in 1965, and it was by no means alone.

The running shed was primarily a supplier of what all the world desired: power, yet that supply was augmented by the fact that, being strategically located, the shed was the most logical place for the winter essential that now appears optional; the snow plough. Snow ploughs came in two forms; the small plough mounted on the front buffer beam, and the independent wheeled plough that was the full height of the loading gauge. In many ways the steam locomotive was the ideal form of propulsion, the crew directing operations, like generals in war, from a position well to the rear. There were plenty of the full size ploughs; the Great Western had thirty two on the books in 1936, distributed around God's Own Country (Wales) and western England. Wales had a disproportionate share, but there was even one at London (Southall).

As the twentieth century advanced, concern over being able to offer a home to every locomotive waned, particularly in the drier east of Britain. Sheds lost their roofs owing to fires and were not repaired, or were demolished completely and the engines left out in the open air when not needed. If maintenance was not carried out at the shed, rather it was just a stabling and signing-on point: unless there were good reasons for housing engines, such as the lack of security on evenings and weekends, there was little point in building anew. When steam came to be displaced by diesel and electric traction, it was quickly realised that the steam shed was not the ideal place to call home. The running shed thus declined in line with the steam stock over the decade to 1968, though there were times when over-enthusiasm for the new leapt ahead of the need for the old. Windermere lost its turntable before the shed supplying traction for the branch, Carnforth, lost its steam allocation.

Today the few running sheds to survive the sweeping away of most things steam-powered, and the system atrophy of the last forty years, are as yet endangered species, without recognition of their historical importance and groaning under a burden of half a century of near zero maintenance. One or two sheds have gone on to other things: York is now the National Railway Museum, polished and gleaming; Camden Roundhouse had a modest career as an arts venue. Aberystwyth and Carnforth have survived, the one by conversion to Narrow Gauge traffic, the other as a base for preserved steam locomotives.

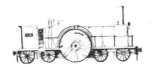

Chapter Twenty-Eight:

Immortals on the Footplate:
Driving and Firing - A Way of Life

In the beginning, railway pioneers drove and fired the engines they had designed and built, before entrusting their fire-breathing dragons to the tender mercies of a new breed of Briton, the engineman. As befitted the spirit of the age of high speed travel, footplate staff took their cue from the 'free and easy life' of the stage coach drivers, who cut a dash on the turnpikes, driving four in hand on schedules that were as demanding as the age could make them. Driving a steam locomotive in top hat and 'weskit', while fine for the opening celebrations, was quickly realised to be inappropriate for day-to-day footplate service. Handling a steam engine with the carefree abandon of a whip-cracking coach driver also bit the dust in short order; for one thing, horses did what was needed most of the time without having to be rigorously controlled, and the voice of command was the prime mover, rather than the reins. The steam locomotive had to be watched every inch of the way, and death was the reward for an excess of neglect.

The payment-by-results system used on the Stockton and Darlington Railway led to abuses: breaking the speed limit, scuffles with horse-hauliers, neglect and mishandling of engines. Such a system on a railway that had trains running at forty miles an hour without any effective signalling (or brakes!) was a recipe for disaster, and it was a measure of the infant railway companies that they took the issue of safety seriously and created a profession that could be trusted with these new responsibilities. The fancy dress soon gave way to a more practical uniform of working jacket and trousers, and a flat cap that wouldn't blow off the open footplate. The casual approach was a little more difficult to weed out. In an era when most working men needed to drink quantities of water to replace that lost in manual labour, beer, ale and porter were the preferred fluid intakes, none of them appropriate to the railway's required level of sobriety. Travel had been associated with the rise of roadside and canalside inns in the latter half of the eighteenth century; a similar state of affairs arose on the Stockton and Darlington Railway, where hauliers were not going to change habits of generations just because their carts now ran on iron rails. Liquid (alcoholic) refreshment during the working day remained the norm.

Such was the problem of drunkenness in the nineteenth century that disciplinary action up to and including dismissal, was a regular occurrence; whatever the risks old habits died hard. Professionalism of footplate staff grew by degrees to emerge into a distinctive band of workers after 1850, where entry was controlled by a mix of required experience, expertise and seniority. Locomotives might well be designed and built by mere mortals, but the skill and courage needed to handle them on the rails was the preserve of the few, whose elevation to the footplate put them on a par with the gods. Even among the footplate staff themselves there were clear lines of promotion, from firing on shunting locomotives to driving the top link express passenger engines, and to get from the one to t'other was both a long road and a demanding one.

The key to footplate service was both knowledge and experience; as a cleaner on the running shed staff it was part of the service to learn the duties of fireman; how to manage fire and water, learn the detailed operation of the locomotive both in theory and practice, to the point where they could be 'passed' for duty as a fireman, firstly on the shed yard, then on shunting duties further afield. Progression to fireman on freight locomotives was again by accruing the experience and knowledge required, forging the bond with the driver to work as a team, and learning routes to the point where firing the grate and operating boiler feed and water pickup became a seamless and efficient piece of clockwork, knowing where and when to do the right thing every time.

The skill of firing included that of timing the use of the shovel to allow for the inertia of the combustion system; coal thrown in the firebox actually reduces steam production for a short period as heat is absorbed by the new fuel prior to ignition. Firing thus commenced before the steam was needed, and ceased before steam was shut off for a station or down grade. Manipulating fire irons was better done where there were no overbridges, as they could be difficult to operate within the loading gauge. Putting down the water scoop at the right place, rather than half way along the watertrough, was important if extra water stops were to be avoided. Once learnt, the whole process had to be gone through again to progress into the passenger link, where running trains to time depended absolutely on the fireman's handling of steam production.

Having arrived at the top of the fireman's tree, the next step was to become a driver, again starting on shunting locomotives. There was a very good reason for this: after about the age of forty-five, the physical requirements of firing the largest engines were more than the average body could sustain for a full shift, and those who could not make the grade as drivers had to take lesser duties as they grew older. Having fulfilled the requirements of good eyesight and physique, the driver's promotion route was similar to that of fireman: shunting, freight and then passenger work. To the driver fell the dual responsibility of being in command on the footplate, responsible for the observance of signals, speed limits (usually without a speedometer), timings, both point to point and overall, and the safety of train and locomotive. To the driver also fell the skill of persuading the locomotive to do its duty, in the face of anything that the weather, track or other traffic could offer as hindrance. Here the driver's experience was the difference between the work being done, perhaps, and being done properly and regularly.

The demands of driving anything other than the lightest of trains were considerable; train loads were calculated to reflect locomotive capacity on the worst or most demanding section of the route. Two or three horsepower per ton of trailing load was the maximum normally available, often much less, and drawbar pulls of two or three tons, to overcome starting resistance, were only marginally less than the adhesion available at the driving wheel/rail interface. The basic challenges to the driver were thus to start the train without excessive slipping (bent side rods and motion were a serious risk of uncontrolled slips) maintain a high enough speed to keep time, to manage the train up the steepest gradients without stalling, and keep enough of a grip on speed downhill to maintain effective control. With freight trains the lack of continuous brakes and presence of loose couplings meant added care over starts and descents.

At busy junctions and station throats there was the added challenge of picking the right signal for the road; the North Eastern Railway had a penchant for forests of signals controlling every possible movement at station throats, the gantry at Bridlington South offering a challenge to the driver into the 1960s long after the worst ones, at York and Newcastle, had surrendered to colour lights.

The driver then had three basic controls to do his deed of skill; regulator, reverser, and brakes, and while driving techniques varied down the years, there was a basic approach that held good for all. Having collected his engine for the day's duty, the driver did a round of all the oiling points, making sure that there were no problems, and if there were faults booked from the previous outing, checking as far as was possible that these had been remedied. If the run was a long one, the next port of call would be the coaling stage, where as much coal as could be reasonably stacked on the tender would be taken on, followed by a fill of the tanks at the water column. With a whistle for the road, the driver would then put as much forward gear on the reverser as he deemed necessary to ensure a move in the right direction, open the cylinder drain cocks to free any trapped condensate, crack open the regulator and release the brakes. After a few seconds the drain cocks could be closed, the reverser pulled back to a minimal cut off and the engine then driven on the regulator to the siding or station to collect its train. While this was going on the fireman would be busy making sure the fire was right and the boiler making steam.

Backing down onto a train that was loaded or full of passengers was always done with the utmost care; a hundred tons plus of engine and tender packs quite a bump even at low speed, and approach was accordingly circumspect. Buffering up needed just enough momentum to compress the buffers and make the shunter's task of coupling up easy, and in the case of a passenger train, screwing up the drawhook, and connecting steam heating and vacuum brake pipes. A full brake test to check on the coaches then followed, fixing of reporting code numbers, name or destination board if appropriate, and headlamp code, and a chat with the guard to confirm journey and train loading details. The guard, it should be noted, was responsible for the train, the driver the locomotive only.

With the train ready and the starter signal cleared, the guard gave the 'right away' with his green flag, and the day's work began in earnest. The procedure for starting is repeated; whistle, drain cocks, reverser, regulator and brakes off, only this time there is a slight delay as the brake release takes place down the length of the train, and in order to make the full load overcome its starting resistance, the regulator has to be opened a little more. In wet conditions this would often lead to slipping, and the steam sander was then brought into play to help the wheels get a grip.

Wheel slip had to be corrected by closing the regulator immediately, only opening up again when the slip was ended. Once the train was moving at a modest speed, the driver could, if he wished, open up the regulator progressively, matching the power delivery to the available adhesion, and setting the reverser to the chosen cut off. Once running speed was achieved, if the reverser could be wound back without causing problems, then cut off would be reduced to somewhere between fifteen and twenty five per cent, and the regulator partially closed to prevent excess speed. At this point the experienced driver who knew the road thoroughly would have chosen a speed to keep time, and a steaming rate that his fireman could maintain with comparative ease, letting the train make its way up hill and down dale without further adjustment of the controls.

On a long run the only alterations the driver had to make would be to comply with speed restrictions and out of course slowings, such as checks at signals, but on a particularly severe gradient of modest duration, he could choose to have a run at the bank, or if time pressed, may need the recovery margin which a spirited attack on the gradient would grant. The locomotive would then be pressed to its limit: full regulator and forty or fifty per cent cut-off, or more on occasion. If the fireman was well prepared he would be able to hold the boiler pressure at just below blowing off, and provided there were no adhesion problems, speed would tail off slowly until a balancing speed was reached for the gradient. Even on express trains, that speed with a maximum load was quite likely to be under thirty miles an hour on the steeper banks.

Loads were calculated on what would reach the top, rather than at what speed the summit would be passed. In service terms this was quite acceptable; the following train was probably going to be a freight, and was unlikely to do any catching up. On the down grade, gravity did most of the work, steam often being shut off, and the fireman had a chance to pull coal forward to the shovelling plate, or relax and take a look at the route with a view to the day when he might be the driver. The fireman's prime duty, after seeing to the needs of the locomotive, was to assist the driver in the observance of signals, a duty not unattractive with its connotations of future promotion.

Once the journey was done, it was uncouple and away to the shed for turning and watering and topping up the tender, before returning for the home run after a brief rest. When back at the home shed, the engine would be handed over to the shed staff, a report filed on any observed defects for attention before the next turn, and the crew signed off for home. On occasion the turn for the crew would involve lodging away, and railway companies provided hostels for crews who were unable to work 'out and home'. At first there was no real control over the hours that footplate crews could work; the twelve hour shift was not by any means exceptional, and in the 1850s and 1860s life on the footplate, with only a spectacle plate for protection from the weather, was hard, but perhaps appearing more arduous to us than to the crews of the time, for there was real resistance to enclosed cabs.

The eight hour day was a product of trade union pressure; as railway unions gained strength and influence at the end of the nineteenth century, bitter disputes about hours, pay and working conditions arose, and the end result was often crews driving for less than half their shift. The influence of footplate staff was considerable, to the point where a deputation could demand an interview with the Chief Mechanical Engineer, and get one. If crews did not like a particular class of locomotive, then they possessed the power to have it sent elsewhere. After nationalisation there was a considerable 'trade' in unpopular locomotives, and the disparaging comment of a driver in respect of the top speed (only 90mph!) of the prototype 'Deltic' diesel, was enough to have the production batch regeared. Picture that happening today!

Night work and weekend working remained part and parcel of footplate staff's lot; the railway ran seven days a week and often twenty four hours a day. Some traffic, notably mail and fish trains, ran overnight on a regular basis, and on busier routes freight ran whenever there was an available path. On the footplate at night, there was illumination from the fire, and oil lighting for the gauges, which would otherwise be difficult to see, but the work was done mainly in the dark. Even with no light in the cab, sighting signals frequently required the driver to look out of the side window, owing to reflection of the fireglow in the window spoiling the view forward. Driving in winter time meant one side of the face was often painfully cold.

Operating conditions improved with the adoption of full cabs (the Great Western was a notable exception and never built its tender engines with decent weather protection) but the crew always had a howling gale at its back and searing heat to the front, and as the engine ran more miles, bucking and swaying of the footplate increased to the point where crews could be driven to complain. Some engines were rough riding from the off, the noise was enough to make conversation well-nigh impossible, exhaust blast gave background to the clank of the rods, but when the engine was worked hard, the dominant noise was the roar of air through the firedoor, feeding the fire's insatiable demand.

That bass roar was a constant reminder of how dangerous a place the footplate was; no driver, fireman or inspector was under any illusion as to the perils that lurked, waiting for a moment's slackness or distraction. If the fire and risk of a blowback presented the most obvious danger, then it was followed in short order by the possibility of a burst tube or collapsed firebox crown, and these by a broken gauge glass or blowing steam joint. When wide fireboxes arrived with 'Atlantic' express engines in the decade prior to the First War, the challenge of firing to the firebox corners led to complaints of burnt hands, and controls on the firebox backhead grew hot enough to ward off an unwary hand, hence the need for cloths. As quality control and boiler testing improved, the risk of boiler explosions diminished, but footplate conditions remained robust, and nowhere on the line was this more pertinent than in tunnels, especially those on a gradient.

Perhaps the worst conditions to be found on this island were in the single track bores of the original Woodhead Tunnels, where the wrong weather conditions could prevent smoke clearance, leading to crews being deprived of oxygen and forced to breathe in the air path of the fire, at low level on the footplate. On a slow freight, transit times of ten minutes were unexceptional, frequently a slow roasting and choking torment. Contrariwise, conditions in Britains longest tunnel, under the Severn, could be poor due to the lack of ventilation shafts. That concern paled in the face of the regular and gory task faced by footplate staff, of checking the motion for the remains of those run down in the darkness as they tried to walk through and save the train or ferry fare. Severn Tunnel Junction shed had more than its fair share of this unpleasant duty, only ended by opening of the road toll bridge, which included a free footpath with the object of cutting these casualties.

If this was the lot of the crew out on the main line, then life was certainly a lot different for those destined for the lesser roles of shunting and banking. Not untypical of these duties was that of station pilot, a duty that has bit the dust completely in the past decade. In one critical respect the job was different in winter than it was in summer, because, for much of the twentieth century, coaches had to be steam-heated, and the source of that steam was the locomotive boiler. In winter, the station pilot had to be attached to the coaches, and having brought its charge from the carriage sidings, remain attached to them until the train engine arrived and took over the heating role. Steam heating was quite efficient, but warm up times were usually around half an hour, of which twenty minutes or so would be the pilot's lot, during which the crew would have little to do.

In summer it was different, for the pilot need only dump the coaches at the platform before returning for the next rake, and didn't have to attach at the 'wrong end', or wait to be released from the buffer stops. On summer Saturdays at seaside resorts, the station pilot was the hardest working engine and crew, removing stock and releasing train engines as quickly as possible, to maximise platform space and minimise delays when the system was being worked to capacity. Just occasionally, the authorities had an idea that the train engines could shunt their own stock; a period of near-chaos would then ensue, before the station pilot was restored to office.

If station pilot work varied with the seasons, then the lot of the banker was short bursts of activity in long periods of doing very little; for they also serve who mostly stand and wait, and waiting is what banking freight and passenger trains up the shorter banks, such as Worsborough or Shap, was all about. To be fair, the lot of banking crews varied considerably. Hellifield shed banked freight to Blea Moor, a journey that was the best part of an hour in length, flat out for the whole time, but the four miles up Shap needed but twenty minutes to half an hour. When an engine 'dropped off' at the top, it was into the refuge siding before waiting to cross over to the other line; there might well then be a fair wait for a path down the bank, followed by more waiting to cross back and buffer up to the next train. Banking was however supplied on the basis that it was cheaper than double heading for the whole journey, for where the run was all uphill/down dale, a double load was a better way of working, and that meant a pilot engine on the front, rather than a banker on the rear.

Perhaps the least sociable turns on the footplate were the running of the auto trains, a sort of half-way house from the railmotor, where a train of limited length could be hauled by a tank engine attached at one end, or in the middle, but capable of being driven from the ends. This curious arrangement left the fireman in command of the engine when the driver was in a remote cab, and meant that the footplate team spent at least half a turn at opposite ends of the same train. The driver was able to operate the regulator, brake and whistle, but the fireman had to handle the reverser as well as carry out the duties of firing. Most auto trains were branch line or stopping services, and not noted for speed, but the concept still left a burden of responsibility on the fireman that was absent in more conventional operations.

The sheer variety of duty across the driving links was matched by the vagaries of the traction; it is true to say that each and every locomotive behaved differently, sounded differently and gave a performance on a day-to-day basis that could vary between sluggish and brilliant. For most of the nineteenth century, this fact of variability was acknowledged by allocation of crews to only one engine, 'out of course' events notwithstanding. The harsher economic climate after 1914 led to locomotives being diagrammed for many crews, making it difficult to predict what kind of trip the footplate staff were going to enjoy, or otherwise, each time they signed on. As economies elsewhere bit into the time and resources devoted to keeping engines in good fettle, and multiple manning of engines became the norm, pride in the immaculate engine and footplate dimmed to the point where engines were turned out into traffic uncleaned and obviously unloved.

If an engine was not steaming properly, and there were many reasons why they did not perform as required, then the hunt for the reason could be a long one. Here are a few of the most obvious:-

• Air leaks round the smokebox door

• Blastpipe/petticoat pipe not concentric with the chimney

• Leaking tubes

• Leaking stays

• Boiler washout overdue

• Poor coal: wrong size (too much slack and dust), too high ash content, too friable, non caking, too old (lost its volatiles)

• Fire choked with clinker

• Ashpan full

• Damaged brick arch

• Dirty tubes and flues

• Poor firing technique

This is just a short list as to why a boiler won't make steam; there were just as many reasons why a locomotive would waste steam after the boiler had produced it. Then there is the issue of driving techniques; an engine driven on full regulator with maximum expansion of steam will be more economical than one where steam chest pressure is only half that in the boiler and there is little pressure drop in the cylinders. Then there are all those niggly bits like recalcitrant injectors, inconsistent sight feed lubricators, worn packing glands on piston rods, bent firebars that fill up the ashpan with half burnt coal, regulators so stiff that both driver and fireman have to battle to move it at all, and engines and tenders so rough riding that there is more coal on the footplate than in the bunker after half an hour on the road. It is no wonder then, that when the Victorians came to measure the performance of the steam railway locomotive, they found it quite a challenge.

Chapter Twenty-Nine:

Locomotive Performance: Recording and Measuring, the Pro-Am Double Act

In recording locomotive performances, the public took an active, even a professional, interest, and a considerable proportion of the railway press devoted time and attention to the performance of individual locomotives on top link express passenger trains. At the same time, railway companies were bitten by the Victorian urge to measure everything in the hope or expectation that it would tell them something worthwhile. Strange as it may seem the companies also found time to get into bed with 'amateur' recorders (several of whom were professionals, but not employed by the railway companies) recognising that when it came to publicity, the use of an independent observer was, especially when confirming feats or records that the companies needed to boost their profile, an extremely useful tool.

On the one hand then, there were the professionals, who spent a lot of time and effort in the nineteenth century devising methods of analysis that would tell them just what the steam locomotive was doing, while on the other, there were a number of individuals, like Charles Rous-Martin, whose primary interest was the recording of train and engine performance in service. It is probably fair to say that both parties had a lot of fun, but the history of recording locomotive performance and output paid back relatively meagre rewards until George Jackson Churchward assumed the helm at Swindon. Both independent observers and railway companies were of one mind over the value of publicity, though; almost any feat short of a derailment or collision was perceived to be positive to the marketing department, and the 'races' to the north in 1888 and 1895, were perceived as just that, with drivers effectively encouraged to take risks to arrive at Edinburgh or Aberdeen first.

With emergence of the steam engine as prime mover of the industrial revolution, divergence, (in the shape of large engines for stationary duties, somewhat more compact versions for marine service, maximum power per unit of weight on the railways, and so on) quickly demonstrated that the various types of installation were dramatically different in the efficiency they delivered. By 1850 the marine engine had drawn ahead of the field, owing to the need for economy of fuel on long sea voyages. Understanding of the theoretical basis of heat engines was emerging, and it was realised that the basic equation for steam engine efficiency was thus:-

Useful Energy Output (Work) = Energy Content of Fuel - System Losses

An hour or two's work with a calorimeter, and a calibrated drawbar spring (that's a trifle unfair, for the research work took decades rather than hours, but the idea is easy enough to grasp) was enough to bring home the fact that energy losses on a railway locomotive were in fact over 90%. Further calculation and experimentation showed that these losses occurred in a number of areas, viz:

- Unburnt fuel (dropped into the ashpan or thrown out the chimney)

- Incomplete combustion (unburnt volatiles and carbon monoxide)

- Poor gas/water heat exchange

- Heat wasted on raising water to boiling point

- Latent heat of evaporation

- Condensation

- Water carry-over as droplets in the steam

- Internal resistance due to poor cylinder/valve design

- Steam discharge to atmosphere under pressure

- Heat discharged from the chimney as combustion products

Each and every one of these losses came under the microscope as engineers in the second half of the century grappled with demands for heavier trains and higher speeds. The issue of unburnt fuel was one that came round with regularity; patent furnaces with some new improved combustion technology had only just run their course in 1914, but the real development work had been done sixty years earlier, allowing the switch from coke to steam coal to be made in the 1860s. This had been achieved by the use of deflector plate and brick arch, the arch supplying heat to ignite the evolved gases, and deflector plate directing air from the firehole into the fire to provide the necessary oxygen.

The effort to persuade steam coals to burn smokelessly had been made in tandem with the battle of the coal owners, particularly those in South Wales, to break the stranglehold the Grand Allies had on the supply of coals to the Admiralty. This had brought in the concept of comparative trials, where different coals were burnt in the same engine and the work recorded, giving the calorific value of the fuel and its evaporative power. The standards of performance for the steam engine from this point on were pounds of water evaporated per pound of coal burnt, and pounds of coal per drawbar horse power/hour (lb/dbhp/hr); in other words how much water was evaporated, and how much useful work could be done for each pound of coal. It is a matter of record that the steam-raising qualities of best Welsh steam coal were well in advance of all other British coals, with carbon contents in excess of 90% and very limited volatiles, though this advantage was mitigated by friability and limited shelf life.

The low volatiles meant low smoke production, allowing much lower excess air ratios (the air that has to be admitted over the firebed in addition to that needed to ensure combustion of volatiles) than the competition, and this was reflected in evaporation rates. The long narrow grates of the Great Western 4-6-0s were markedly more exacting to fire, and less effective to boot, when not fed with their preferred Welsh fuel, because the ratio of firebox to boiler heating surfaces meant that the engines relied on radiant heat in the firebox to a greater degree than locomotives designed for more volatile fuel.

The issue of maximising gas/water heat exchange was one that Robert Stephenson addressed in his first rearrangement of the fire tubes in the immediate post-*Rocket* engines. Rearranging the smoke tubes in the boiler, and when superheaters were introduced, altering the number of flues as well, was an occupation most chief engineers indulged in. The LMS 'Pacifics', totalling no more than fifty one locomotives, managed five different patterns of boiler, with numbers of tubes varying between 170 and 101, in two different sizes (a whole 1/8th of an inch different!) and 16, 32 or 40 flues, and this ignores variations that did not affect heating surface, of which there were several. Superheaters suffered in the same way, with two or three forward and backward passes of the steam, or the fluid flow split on the backward pass and returned to a common pipe for the forward pass. The only certainty of this sort of hit and miss experimentation, is that engineers were guessing instead of calculating and testing.

There is a limit to the amount of heat that can be transferred between two fluids; the final temperature of the heating fluid cannot be lower than the lowest temperature of the fluid being heated. In a boiler where there is no staged heating process, that limit is the temperature of the steam under pressure. This is a fundamental limiting factor of single stage heating, one that the Crosti boiler of the 1950s attempted to address. The reason that no successful attempts on multi-stage heating were made in the nineteenth century is that the steam injector was a very simple and effective preheater, and simplicity beat complexity every time when reliable locomotives were needed.

The technical complexity of the locomotive boiler meant that issues of construction very often impinged upon those of efficiency; the multi-tubular boiler, in terms of its heat transfer per square foot and per ton, was not desperately good. Much more heat was obtained in the firebox owing to a combination of higher temperatures and radiant, as well as conducted and convected, heat. This fact was recognised in the United States after 1875, and boiler dimensions in proportion to the firebox began to shrink. The classic slab-sided firebox that the Midland Railway hung onto for over fifty years was adopted because it was not technically difficult to construct. That it was not very efficient was a secondary consideration. When George Jackson Churchward began his experiments on boiler design at the turn of the century, he set out to determine how water circulated round firebox and boiler, recognising that the key to good heat exchange was vigorous water circulation, promoted by allowing large water spaces with low resistance to thermo-syphonic action. Pumping water round the boiler does not seem ever to have been considered.

The result of Churchward's experiments was the sharply coned boiler and complex curved firebox, expensive to build, but as efficient a steam-raiser as could be put on a locomotive chassis. Such a boiler was low on maintenance costs due to good water circulation, giving lower metal temperatures, more even heating, lower thermal stresses, and much less work for firebox stays and boiler tubes to do in holding the whole edifice together. By raising steam pressures to forty pounds above the average of the times, Churchward addressed the issue of minimising energy inputs for heating water and supplying latent heat. The adoption of the superheater over the next decade reduced water and latent heat inputs further: less water to do the same work. In the quest for more power, boiler pressures for express locomotives would be raised over the next four decades to 280psi, but the gains in thermal efficiency were to a degree offset by raising the discharge temperature of the exhaust gases.

The last two elements in the quest for more efficiency, cylinder and valve design, and the discharge of the exhaust to atmosphere were linked, and more than a little effort was directed to this area because it dictated locomotive performance. Once speeds reached sixty miles an hour on eight foot drivers, it slowly emerged that the steam locomotive of the 1850s and succeeding decades was being throttled by poor cylinder and valve design. The difficulty was that finding out what happened in cylinder and valve chests at speed was not easy; any recording system with even minimal inertia was incapable of producing the data needed in the quarter of a second that the wheels took to perform a single revolution.

For slow speed engines, the indicator diagram produced a reasonably accurate graph of the work done in a cylinder, but how to apply this machine to a high speed locomotive? The recording machine, being mechanical, had to be close to the cylinder, and a way had to be found of reducing the movement of the recording pen so that its inertia did not affect the result. The first problem was solved by design of a shelter that could be bolted on the engine front, known for obvious reasons as an indicator shelter, and the second, by tracing the indicator diagram in a series of small movements, building up the whole diagram over many revolutions.

The results told designers of locomotives much that they could have found out by asking the drivers. At low speed and long cut-offs, steam pressure in the cylinders approached that in the boiler, providing the regulator was fully open. The resulting expansion after the valve port closed was minimal. Worked in this manner, the steam locomotive was uneconomical and very hard work for the fireman. To run at a reasonable speed in the second half of the nineteenth century meant leaving the cut-off in a wide setting, and shutting the regulator to throttle the cylinder steam supply. Worked this way, there was little point in high boiler pressures, because there was little expansion and only modest pressure drop in the cylinder. This fact led directly to experiments with compound propulsion.

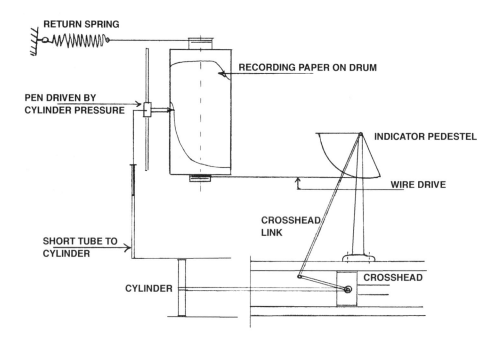

Figure 62: Indicator.

Having obtained a method of assessing cylinder performance, engineers were no nearer a solution until Churchward showed how changes to valve travel and lead could mitigate the disadvantages of Stephenson's and Walschaerts' link motions (analysis of other motions showed that they did nothing that was not done as well or better by these two). This allowed cut off to be shortened so that pressure drop in the cylinders could be fivefold rather than half.

While these technical developments were almost painfully slow to feed through (it was over twenty years before the importance of Churchward's work was fully recognised and adopted elsewhere) there had grown up an amateur interest in timing of trains which served the public, and the railway companies, by providing information on the relative merits and performances of top link engines in service on the main lines. Despite the superficiality of the information, for train timing was as often done from the coach as the footplate, top speeds, overall journey and point to point times, and performance up the steepest gradients were all discussed in detail most minute. This information was a valuable spur for competing companies to sharpen their performance, but in assessing power outputs and locomotive thermal efficiency it was virtually useless, and to address these issues two further recording and analysis methods were introduced: the dynamometer car and the stationary test plant.

By the time of the grouping in 1923, three railway companies had invested in dynamometer cars: The North Eastern, Great Western and Lancashire and Yorkshire Railways. The Great Western was also owner of the only static testing plant in the country. Dynamometer cars enabled the power output of a locomotive in normal service to be calculated and displayed graphically. This was a big step forward; coal and water consumption could be monitored, overall thermal efficiency calculated. With indicator diagrams, a near complete picture of the totality of a locomotive's performance was emerging, and with it the option to alter operating parameters one at a time and monitor the effect. The static test plant enabled modifications to be made during tests, speeding up arrival at a solution of any one problem, and when the test plant at Rugby was completed at nationalisation, it was this method of analysis that allowed major improvements in locomotive front end design, particularly draughting, to be made to many engine classes.

The effect of the blastpipe on a locomotive is to pull the combustion products from the firebox through the fire tubes. On superheated locomotives of the twentieth century, the combustion products had a choice of passing either the superheater flues or the ordinary tubes, but it was realised that the draw through each tube or flue was not equal, nor could it be; with the blast applied at right angles to the gas flow, no conceivable arrangement would square that circle. With gas flow in the smokebox violently turbulent, the vacuum generated would cause those gases that encountered the least resistance, in practice those travelling through the upper tubes of the boiler, to move fastest.

The petticoat pipe and the Kylala-Chapelon triple petticoat could only mitigate this effect, and stationary tests for the development of smokebox vacuum served to emphasise the critical effect of the blast nozzle being concentric with the chimney, and the right distance from the actual choke, as opposed to the constructed choke (the choke is the narrowest point in the convergent/divergent chimney). Nonetheless, even with all the parameters for an efficient locomotive blast in place, it proved impossible to either measure the gas flow in every tube and flue, or to do more than a passably good job at drawing the fire evenly.

As with the blastpipe, so too with the fluid (steam) flow from regulator to cylinder, in principle just a straightforward application of fluid mechanics. Fluid flow in pipes is broken down into two types, laminar and turbulent. Turbulent flow requires much more energy to push the same amount of fluid down a pipe than smooth or laminar flow, and the pressure drop between boiler and steam/valve chest is a function of the length of the pipe, its diameter, and how many bends it has along the way. Making the pipe large enough to avoid turbulent flow, and keeping the bends of large radius, was the only way to make the steam pressure in the boiler apply in the cylinder when the engine was being worked at high speed. Both Nigel Gresley and William Stanier used this knowledge to effect in their express 'Pacifics' of the 1930s. Testing of existing express types on the Rugby Plant after nationalisation led to rebuilding of the steam and exhaust layouts of several locomotive classes to alleviate pressure drop in the steam pipes, and minimising of back pressure/optimising draught from the exhaust.

The one fact that was starkly elucidated by the measurements of the late nineteenth century was that while losses due to unburnt fuel and poor heat exchange could be minimised, there was no way round the conundrum of losses in the form of latent heat. Water might be an ideal fluid in many respects for conversion of chemical energy into useful work, but if you could not recover the energy needed to turn water at 212deg.F to steam at the same temperature, then your overall thermal efficiency would always be very low. Even with an exhaust steam injector heating the boiler feed water (that is, all of the heat being supplied by heat recovery up to boiling point, which at 200psi is 388deg.F), the latent heat lost to atmosphere still amounts to two thirds of the total heat supplied to the steam.

Train recording by independent observers grew by leaps and bounds after 1900, mainly due to continued interest in a rail system that for the first half of the twentieth century boasted the fastest trains in the world, and aided not a little by development to maturity of the stop watch. With mile and quarter mile posts, and stations and signal boxes every three or four miles on almost all routes, accurate timings were fairly easy. When it was dark, the real professionals could work out speed over short distances by counting the beats on the rail joints, provided you knew what lengths of rail were used on which railway. What the amateurs showed was that observance of speed limits was not by any means universal; few locomotives had speedometers, and recorders found themselves obliged to omit dates of logs when they were published in order to avoid landing blame on the crew for breaking speed limits.

The amateur 'log', effectively that developed by Charles Rous-Martin, recorded point to point and overall times as well as maximum and minimum speeds and time gained or lost. The real difficulty in determining anything relevant from these performances was the narrowness of the information recorded; there was little publicity mileage in anything other than the top link expresses. Thus there are endless logs of ascents of Shap, Grayrigg and Beattock banks on the West Coast, or Whiteball, Dainton and Rattery on the Great Western, or of the high speeds on the East Coast. Move even a little out of the limelight, say to Llanfihangel, between Abergavenny and Hereford, or to any of the routes on the flat lands of the east, and the number of records plummets. Of freight, which had to be recorded from the footplate or brake van, the pages are virtually blank.

This imbalance colours the written record in a quite inappropriate way, for the skill needed to persuade an ex-North Eastern Railway run down 'H class' 4-4-4 tank to haul four coaches up the twisting 1 in 39 to Ravenscar on a typical wet and windy summer's day, was of the same order, if not greater, than that needed to extract a top line performance from the most modern express.

As the steam locomotive bowed out in the early 1960s, the Waterloo to Bournemouth route, as the last steam operated main line, was extensively recorded, with several observers claiming 'tons' from the rebuilt Bulleid Pacifics, in spite of their somewhat neglected condition. In more than one aspect, these extensively rebuilt locomotives were beneficiaries of the testing regime of the post war years, which showed just how far short of Bulleid's original plans the engines in their original form were. That testing regime, including both the controlled road test and the stationary plants at Rugby and Swindon, was developed over the seven years after 1948, and is a classic illustration of how the dynamics of change will blow away an institution literally overnight.

The need to get things right, after decades of guessing at the right ingredients for the perfect steam locomotive, led to testing being at long last rational and systematic. Yet of the improvements decided upon, only those locomotive classes that were few in number had all engines modified, as with the 'Kings' and 'Merchant Navys'. The second line expresses, being numerous, were withdrawn and scrapped before they could be modernised; diesels delivered and didn't need this kind of test procedure (some people will believe anything!)

Chapter Thirty:

A Lasting Obsession:
Names and Numbers

There is something deeply rooted in the psychology of the human being, in that there appears to be an inherent need to name important lumps of hardware, and from the off, steam locomotives have been named, all the important ones at any rate, with only the odd exception. It is thus a measure of Richard Trevithick's detachment from the human race, in that, of all the early engines, his were the only ones built that appear not to have received names. We have seen fit to allocate them names in the decades since, as *Catch Me Who Can* and *The Penydarren Locomotive*, but Trevithick's engines, the original concepts that in effect launched the age of the steam locomotive, never received a name from their creator.

Names, then, played an important part in the mystique surrounding the steam locomotive, and the names used are a fair reflection of the hopes and aspirations of their designers, their sponsors, and later, in praise of famous and not so famous men and women, battles and the spoils of conquest. Obscurity is a common feature; not many outside Scotland (or inside for that matter) would 'ken' the origin of *Luckie Mucklebackit*, and while General Blucher may have had some fame before Waterloo, and lasting fame after the battle, today only a few historians would be able to tell you anything of the man, his command, and his role in the defeat of Napoleon.

The first christenings then were Blenkinsop's *Prince Royal* followed by the two engines *Wylam Dilly*, and the *Blucher*. When the Stockton and Darlington Railway was nearing completion, George Stephenson may well have had the idea to set the seal on his proprietorship of the steam locomotive. *Locomotion No.1* could not have been more inaccurately named on a global stage, even though the 'globe' as far as the steam locomotive of the time was concerned did not extend more than fifty miles in any direction from Darlington. *Locomotion No 1* was only 'number one' on its own railway, but it was a fine way for George to nail his colours to the mast.

Naming of engines in the years 1825-29 followed no particular pattern. *Royal George* was patriotic but hardly ground breaking, and if *Lancashire Witch* was a little more innovative, it too was not destined for a high profile in the history books. The competitors at Rainhill achieved immortality only because of the name of the victor. *Novelty* and *Sans Pareil* were certainly *sans* point, but they bask in the shadow of the *Rocket*, which shares the topmost plinth of fame with only two others, of which more anon. Robert Stephenson's decision to name his engine after the fastest man-made object of the time (barring the bullet) was a touch of commercial genius. Compared to the rest of the competition, it lived up to its name in a manner no-one expected.

With the first production engines for the Liverpool and Manchester Railway, we see the emergence of themes; first the 'Meteor' class, and then the 'Planets', of which the heavy freight versions received the appropriate names of *Samson* and *Goliath*. Less obvious were names for other early engines; the Canterbury and Whitstable Railway's first was named *Invicta*; while it may be an easy one for Latin scholars to decipher (Unconquered), it is also the motto of the county of Kent, but probably meant little more to the average man in the street then than it would today. Names alone were however destined for a very short life; as traffic grew, so did the numbers of engines to handle it, and there came the necessity of identifying locomotives for repair and overhaul, the keeping of repair cards, records of valve settings, and stamping of non-interchangeable components with numbers, to prevent them from being put back on the wrong engine following repair. For these purposes it became essential that every engine had a number, and it was not long before names became optional.

If names on individual engines became less than universal in the 1850s, then proliferation of engine designs meant that it became convention to name or number the class to which an engine belonged. By no means every class received official names; it is difficult to see the directors of the London and North Western Railway going with the 'Bloomers' (rational dress for ladies), as McConnell's express engines were named. The Midland Railway went some way to take the gloss off the general trend of romantic or quirky names, and refused to name its classes, numbering them instead '260 Class' or '999 Class'. Doubtless it saved a fortune in nameplates and naming ceremonies (engines were not named either), but if that led to economies of a sort, the company could not be accused of skimping on the paint, with the most magnificent crimson lake livery the nation has ever seen.

When individual companies got around to numbering their engines, they generally found it difficult to start with '1', if only because they already had a stock of whose history they were more than a bit hazy. Stock lists tended to be a bit haphazard, and as the engine number was for the purposes of identification, rather than an indication of age or chronological sequence, companies had a widespread habit of giving new engines vacant numbers in the stock list, rather than a new one. The result was a numbering chaos, and by the end of the nineteenth century, most of the larger railways were probably not sure to the nearest half dozen how many engines they possessed. For the amateur observer this was a nightmare, particularly with engines that were superficially the same, and without any reference document, knowing what was what was more than a trifle difficult.

At the grouping in 1923, the 'Big Four' realised that something needed doing in respect of both names and numbers; Naming engines was good business sense, as you could invite some 'big wig' to perform the ceremony, and garner not a little publicity for a new service or engine type. Renumbering of engines into numerical sequences made life easier for everyone; if engines 5108, 5109 and 5110 were a light shunter, express and mixed traffic types respectively, then even the shed foreman who maintained them had to think twice before allocating duties; if they were all 'Black Fives', then it was easy.

All of the 'Big Four' thus got round to renumbering their stock, though the LNER managed to put the ordeal off until the last year of its existence. The Great Western managed to fall neatly between two stools by not allocating enough numbers to certain classes, and being obliged to muddy the water by adding batches of numbers further down the list to cope with the surplus. In naming, though, this company was systematic and comprehensive, both with the choice of names for locomotive classes that could be as long as was needed, and with the naming of almost all of those engines that were in regular express or secondary passenger duties. The Great Western started the twentieth century with 'Atbara' and 'City' classes, quickly moving on to the 'Saints' and the 'Stars'. An example of rapid obsolescence, the 'Atbara' name, after the Battle of Atbara River, part of a campaign to subdue the Sudan in 1898, was one of those excessively patriotic, even jingoistic names that hide a murky tale of mass murder to gain an empire. Two years later Kitchener was to face an enemy as well armed as he, and the British were then the lambs at the slaughter. Paardeberg scarcely made the history books: certainly no locomotive class ever 'Boer' that name!

Of these four pre-war Great Western classes, only the 'City' was really marketable, but after World War One came the 'Castle', 'Hall', 'King', 'Manor' and 'Grange' classes, and with each locomotive there were a number of people, often many, who could identify with 'their' engine. Identification thus became fairly simple to even the slightly interested, and while the 'Castles' were ultimately patriotically renamed to include a batch of Earls, a regiment or two and a whole host of World War II aircraft, the remainder were true to their type, with no Queens in the 'Kings', and only a little bending of the hall concept to include Westminster and Albert.

If the Great Western got it right commercially, then the LNER, while wandering in the wilderness, chanced upon the two remaining gems in the crown of locomotive names, names remembered by reputation and deeds. Logic struck in the naming of locomotive classes, and was not to be shifted. The LNER denoted each of its locomotive classes with a single letter, which gave the wheel arrangement, and a number, to distinguish each class with the same wheels. Thus all the Pacifics were 'A', as in A3 and A4, and all the four wheel shunters were in 'Y', with the rest in between. To know a locomotive class on the LNER involved not a name but a code, and the general public were thus excluded, logical though the system was.

Only a handful of the LNER pre-grouping types, such as the Great Central 'Directors' kept their names in the face of modernity. Naming of individual engines was too important to ignore, but once again the LNER passed up the opportunity of consistency, and dotted its express Pacifics with names of racehorses, birds (*Mallard* is the one remembered, of course), company directors, countries of the British Empire, locomotive engineers, the odd novelist, and the original *Flying Scotsman*, now perhaps the most famous locomotive in the world, and certainly the most widely travelled.

The Southern saw what the Great Western was about and copied the style, though not quite so well, with 'King Arthur', 'Schools', 'Merchant Navy' and 'West Country' classes. The 'King Arthurs' were not desperately memorable, and some of the 'Merchant Navy' a bit obscure, but the 'West Country' names went down well, as did the 'Battle of Britain' air squadron names for those locomotives in the 'Battle of Britain' West Country sub class. The LMS, while arriving last at the inter-war 'name the locomotive' competition owing to not having any engines worth naming prior to 1927, did its bit commercially and patriotically over the next twenty years.

The LMS started out in good form by naming the first 'Royal Scot' just that, and continued to press its claim for the most patriotic railway company by naming most of the rest after regiments, such as the no-longer-aptly-named *The Scottish Horse*, and not forgetting the junior corps or the ones that got away, with both *The Boy Scout*, and *British Legion*. With the 'Patriot' class, the name was good, but the locomotives were not consistently patriotic; *Private W. Wood, VC*, was joined by both *Blackpool*, and *Bangor*, and their contribution to British jingoism seems a trifle dubious. When the 'Jubilee' class emerged in 1934, after naming the first one *Silver Jubilee*, the names trawled through every corner of the British Empire, from Aden to Zanzibar via India and Australia, with perhaps the best sounding one being the Indian states of *Bihar and Orissa*. Unfortunately for the LMS, it needed more Jubilees than it could find place names for, and after surreptitiously including *Eire*, which had seceded by virtual brute force, and *Palestine*, to which nobody in their right mind would have laid claim in the twentieth century, was obliged to lose the plot in a mass of admirals and warships, or warships named after admirals.

British Railways adopted a similar stance when it came to names in the 1950s, starting off brightly with the 'Britannia' class and '*Britannia*', and hitting intellectual heights with *John Bunyan* and *William Shakespeare,* before spoiling things with a grotesque misspelling of Owain Glyndwr (*Owen Glendower*). After that it was all downhill, though the 'Clans' all received clan names. There was a start made on naming mixed traffic engines, but this trailed off after a few Arthurian legend characters had taken to the rails (to replace the 'King Arthur' class withdrawals on the Southern Region) and, apart from the solitary 'Duke' (of Gloucester), and *Evening Star*, that was that.

To bring some sense to this chaos, Ian Allan had started his stock lists while working for the Southern Railway as a junior, extracting information from a reluctant management with a tact and skill that quickly turned collecting locomotive numbers into a widely practised hobby. With the publication of the first 'ABC's, as they were called, the hobby threatened to get out of hand in the 1950s, with hordes of 'spotters' (a very apt term, in more ways than one) descending on the more popular locations on Saturdays to add more 'captures', duly underlined, to their books. The more affluent ones joined regular organised weekend 'shed bashes', an aspect of the hobby that involved marathon tours round the country to such unlikely venues as Annesley or Woodford Halse, to capture locomotives whose daily itinerary meant normal obscurity except for the few local enthusiasts.

The pace of these number chases takes some believing; many sheds were some distance from the nearest station, and the time allowed per shed was usually measured in minutes rather than hours, reducing the information gleaned to numbers only. It is probably fair to say that had railway management been possessed of foreknowledge of what would result from the publication of information they had supplied, then the clerk would probably have been given his marching orders and banned from every station, works and shed in the land. History, however, records otherwise, and the habit lives on, despite the almost total inaccessibility of most privatised railway works and maintenance depots, and the severely limited variety of present day traction.

In conclusion, more locomotive engineers have had locomotives named after them than most directors and other company servants, and names have tended to favour the famous, especially royalty. Of the last three chief mechanical engineers of the LNER, not one missed out on having an engine named after himself, but in manipulation of a valuable marketing tool, the Great Western stands head and shoulders above the rest in originality and consistency; after all, almost no one remembers a number (OK, the author admits to remembering *lots* of numbers), but a name can be something special.

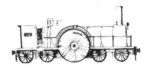

Chapter Thirty-One;

Proportion, Line and Liveries:
The Locomotive as an Art Form

Few people who are in possession of the means to make their workplace individual and attractive pass up that opportunity, and the steam locomotive quickly succumbed to this most basic of human traits. We can only guess whether Richard Trevithick decorated his pioneers with gaudy colours, and in the absence of good evidence it seems likely that he did not. It is quite clear though that all the participants at the Rainhill Trials regarded the appearance of their entries as almost as important as their mechanical reliability. *Rocket* was outshone, literally, by the polished and gaily decorated *Novelty*, even though the former was about as garish as any locomotive that subsequently took to the rails in Britain. Casual spectators, then as now, cared little and understood less about the mechanical intricacies of what they were watching, and cast their favours in a way basically no different from any other beauty contest.

Once the steam locomotive's success was assured, and profits began to roll in, on the more important routes at any rate, there was money to spare to put some serious effort into making engines shine, and in not a few instances where the engines were not up to the task, their designers sought to disguise the fact with embellishment and decoration. There are in fact a number of ways in which the overall proportions of a locomotive can be adjusted to make the best impression, without altering the basic critical dimensions, and creditable efforts were made to make a picture by adopting the strategies of the ancient Greeks in massing and proportion. With his task of design made easy by the generosity of the Broad Gauge, Daniel Gooch rapidly turned the 'Iron Duke' class into an object lesson; the engines looked as good as they performed.

The 'Iron Duke' was a careful essay in proportion, line, massing and colour; the top of the main outside frames was carried through from front buffer beam to the tender rear, with a graceful curve over the driving axlebox. This upward sweep was reflected by similar downward curves of the plates supporting the remaining engine and tender axleboxes, the line of the running plate emphasised by painting the frame plates bright red. The copper-capped chimney was already there, green boiler and firebox cladding set off by polished brasswork and wheel splashers, smokebox and firebox backhead burnished black. The Great Western Railway was, in its own eyes at least, great in locomotive aesthetics from the very first, and over the next hundred years, gave no hint that it had any intention of surrendering this primacy.

If the Midland Railway had nothing to equal the style of the Broad Gauge in the era of Kirtley's tenure at Derby Works, when Samuel Waite Johnson took control he showed that the transformation of the outside framed locomotive from something vaguely and messily French to a sleek showstopper, was really only a sleight of hand. The Midland's crimson lake livery was not really shown off to best effect until the engine lines had been cleaned up, and Johnson went to some length to hide all pipes and rods under boiler cladding or inside the frames. The result, in the single driver 'Spinners' of 1887, was a superbly proportioned locomotive set off by vibrant colour, unified by delicate yellow-gold lining out and diminishing heights of chimney, steam dome and safety valve cover, evenly set out along the smokebox/boiler/firebox barrel top. These machines enriched the landscape they passed through, and the lives of the people who had the privilege to witness them, and it is difficult to imagine their being turned out in anything other than gleaming immaculacy.

Twenty years later Richard Mountford Deeley turned his famous 'Compounds' out in the same livery; with running number in large letters on the tender the effect was even more impressive, and while they were not the best locomotives in the country, they were quite simply a marketing man's dream: something for the soul to drool over. As a high water mark of locomotive aesthetics,

Deeley's efforts may stand unequalled. Not every railway company was possessed of such good taste and fortune, and at the opposite end of the same spectrum was the London and North Western Railway, for widely different reasons.

The reason why the London and North Western Railway decided to paint its locomotives black is one of those stories that verges on the apocryphal. The tale goes that, in the search for further economies, the general manager Richard Moon had it suggested to him that it would be cheaper to paint engines black, and that he at once picked this up and said 'so be it'. For seventy years the company painted all its engines black, and in their efforts to make black a statement, made the colour gleam with a quality and style of finish that was almost certainly as costly as the more vibrant colours preferred elsewhere. The real problem however was that after Ramsbottom, the next decently proportioned express engines to emerge from Crewe were the 'George the Fifth' 4-4-0's in the first decade of the twentieth century.

Francis Webb was not insensible to the concept of aesthetics, he just appears not to have had any idea how to put the various elements together into a coherent composition. While the six coupled goods and the coal tanks held their own by a general lack of poor detail, rather than any really good beauty points, when the last of the London and North Western designs, the 'Claughtons', and H. P. Beames' large tanks, took to the rails, the marketing department must have felt near suicidal. Colour can disguise, lining out and contrast work perform miracles, as any club-bound young lady will instantly affirm; but to ignore the basics of good design, was to shrink from the real world.

The Caledonian Railway on the other hand, put a lot of effort into its stunning blue livery, adding lining out, using the black smokebox as a contrast, putting handsomely curved wing plates to smooth the line between smokebox and running plate; and while it was not the builder of the famous 'single' No 123, Dugald Drummonds' 4-4-0's were still in the same aesthetic league, which even included the big express 4-6-0's as in *Cardean*. As a big-boilered inside cylinder express locomotive, *Cardean* could easily have been a disaster in terms of appearance; as locomotives their performances were barely adequate, and in massing and proportions had little to put them in the top flight of good lookers. The combination of blue and black and the delicate lining out, however, were enough to make the locomotive and its sisters favourites on the northern section of the West Coast.

In the rest of the country, most companies made an adequate fist of combining colour and detail in a way that was generally pleasing to the eye; some locomotives, like the London and South Western 'T9' 4-4-0's, the 'Terrier' tanks, and the North Eastern equivalent, which was to become the 'J72', were so well proportioned and detailed that lining out and full colour livery was just gilding the lily. The Great Northern always seemed to be one step ahead of its East Coast partners in that its express engines were consistently the better looking, but in the colourful variety that preceded the First World War, the locomotive was a canvas that few refused to decorate.

If a lot of work went into decoration and proportions, then the amount of attention lavished upon the external appearance of the locomotive chimney was nearly beyond belief. The Great Western's love of the curved copper chimney lip, always immaculately polished, was reflected elsewhere; Francis Webb designed a curved and slotted masterpiece that had no relevance to the function it was supposed to perform, and it was not until boilers grew to be close to the limits of the loading gauge, that chimney design ceased to be an obsession. Even through the days of severe austerity after 1939 it was rare to find a purely functional 'stovepipe'; on the lowliest locomotives chimney casting continued to be a labour of love.

The location of the running plate, originally dictated by the top of the outside frame plates, was further excuse for much intricate work. On express types, driving and coupled wheels projected above the running plate, and were housed usually in individual curved and slotted splashers; the slots were ostensibly to allow for access for lubrication, but became a work of art, suitably lined out and losing any hint of practicality. And so it went on: curved cab-side sheets with coats of arms; domes and safety valve covers curved and polished to outgleam all comers; brightly painted wheel spokes, rims and centres; burnished copper cylinder drain pipes; nuts and bolts tightened so that their heads aligned with those of their neighbours.

In the changed times of the 1920s, it might have been supposed that these habits fell quickly by the wayside, but it seemed that, while pure decoration went into a decline, the concept of the locomotive as a work of art did not. Running plates, like hemlines, began to ease upwards, enabling most of the motion to be displayed; with the general adoption of outside valve gear this was sensible, and did nothing to compromise the looks of the locomotive. On the Great Western, which would have nothing to do with outside valve gear, running plates had lifted to a position they would retain for the next forty years, with the introduction of the 'Stars' and 'Saints'. In aesthetics, as in many other aspects, the Great Western led in the years leading to the First War, and was not followed until the decade after it. Unseemly pipework and fittings were stuffed out of sight beneath boiler cladding or inside frames, despite the maintenance headaches this caused, and designers still considered it their duty to produce a locomotive that looked good, irrespective of how it performed.

With the actual number of companies down from scores to four, the variety of liveries declined rapidly, and economy was sought in the labour of cleaning by the increasing use of black for those engines that were not too often in the public eye. Thus after 1923, colour schemes came down to green (Great Western), green (Southern), green (LNER), red (LMS) and black. Having said that, even black liveries were lined out to make them attractive, and there were a few deviations from this basic pattern, and the greens were all different anyway. What made the liveries between the wars different was the adoption of streamlining after 1935, and it was the LNER that led the way.

Smoothing airflow over aircraft, where performance was critically dependent upon minimising wind resistance, had taken centre stage in the late 1920s and early 1930s, as aviation emerged from the shadow of the First World War and began to attract the attention of commercial and, to a lesser degree in Britain at least, military operators. These ideas were taken up by designers of motor cars, notably Ettore Bugatti. Bugatti realised that appearance sold motors, and one of the selling points of Bugatti's cars, apart from their exclusivity, was the imagined benefit of streamlining the front end compared to conventional designs. Gresley and Bugatti were on good terms, and the cross fertilisation of ideas between the two men led to streamlining of the first 'A4' Pacifics, with wedge-shaped noses, and a similar raking applied to the cab front.

The first four engines, *Silver Link, Silver Fox, Silver King* and *Quicksilver*, were turned out in appropriate livery and attached to a new 'Silver Jubilee' train, also in silver paint. The stunt was probably the most successful commercial venture the LNER put on, but in style and colour terms silver was not an ideal livery; dirt tended to show around hinges and plate joints and was difficult to clean and impossible to keep clean for long. Similarly, elaborate side skirts concealed the wheels and were a retrograde step, the engines looking much more the part when for maintenance reasons the skirts were later removed.

Tacit admission that silver livery was not a good idea came as further engines of the class were turned out, first in LNER apple-green, and then in a deep garter blue, set off by red wheels, but the engines, as the Great Western had shown thirty years earlier, looked their best in dark green, a livery later applied by British Railways, of which more anon. Where one company leads, there are always sheep to follow; the Great Western 'streamlined' a 'Castle' *(Manorbier Castle)* and a 'King' *(King Henry VII)* and then promptly wished it hadn't, for the attempt was ham-fisted and half-hearted. The LMS though, was determined not to be beaten, and when its ultimate design of Pacific (the 'Coronation') hit the rails in 1937, it too was streamlined from the running plate up, and like the 'Silver Jubilee' train, carried the livery (red with gold 'go faster' stripes) down the coaches. The LMS also painted its streamlined trains in a blue and white striped livery, but slowly dispensed with the streamlined casings during the 1940s, a tacit admission that energy saved by such means was not worth the tin needed to provide it. Last to try his hand at the streamline game was Oliver Bulleid, but he was on a different planet.

It is difficult to consider the 'air smoothed' casing Bulleid applied to his 'Merchant Navy' and 'West Country' Pacifics as streamlining; true, the idea behind smoke deflectors was lifting of exhaust away from the driver's line of sight, but the reduced resistance to motion was virtually nil. Aesthetically though, the final form was both attractive and, had the thought occurred (which apparently it did, but it was not acted upon) amenable to mechanical washing. The effect was somewhat spoilt by the Southern's rather insipid Malachite Green, but overall the impression was certainly modern and well up with the competition, even if locomotive performance was not. More eye catching was the makeover applied to the heavy freight class 'Q1': no running plate, monobloc wheels (without spokes, as in the Pacifics), and armadillo-like sectioned boiler cladding, reputedly on the basis that it was cheap. The effect was really to predate punk styling thirty years ahead of the Sex Pistols; love it or hate it, you just had to admit that it was radically different.

To their lasting credit, British Railways was not home to, or ruled by, a group of latter day philistines, and tried really hard to put forward both good, sound, aesthetically pleasing locomotive designs, and to give both them and their existing stock liveries that would enhance their appearance. Accordingly, a number of locomotives were turned out in a variety of liveries, including LNER garter blue, and very creditable reproductions of Great Western and LMS colour schemes. The decision to go for general Brunswick Green for express locomotives was a wise one, though the 'A4's' looked good in black or garter blue, and application of crimson lake to ex-LMS 'Pacifics' was fine until no one bothered to clean them or repaint them when they faded. The design department turned out very pleasing aesthetics on all three classes of Pacifics, with the 'Britannia' just edging ahead of the field for cleanness of lines and general proportions. The 'Mickey Mouse' light traffic engines were charming derivatives of LMS designs, and the last of the '9F's,' *Evening Star,* showed just how much difference a coat of paint makes to an already well thought out locomotive.

Last, but by no means least, rebuilding of locomotive classes down the years has been an exercise in uglification; the conversion of Gresley's 'P2's' into Pacifics being a case in point. Alteration of Bullied's temperamental express engines after 1956 was an exercise equivalent to both radical corrective and cosmetic surgery. The rebuilt engines, all beefy well thought out and executed curves from footplate to smokebox door, were everything in both aesthetics and performance they had not been for the previous fifteen years. Not everyone, on the other hand, was unqualified in their praise of the design of smoke deflectors fitted to the Gresley 'A3' Pacifics, to cure downbeat of exhaust after fitting of double blastpipes and chimneys. On the whole though, alterations and amendments were carried out with a good eye for detail during the British Railways era, which was overshadowed aesthetically by the decline, and ultimate cessation, of the age-old practice of keeping locomotives clean and painted.

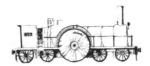

Chapter Thirty-Two:

Death and Rebirth:
The Preservation Movement

The glamour that failed to disperse from the steam locomotive after the conclusion of the Second World War can be seen, in retrospect, to be part of a wider human attachment to the machine that was first to free mankind from the shackles of the past. If anything could sever that affection in Britain, then surely travel on a worn out, grimy and depressed rail system, with late running and overcrowded trains, would have effected a cure. When the first round of closures were proposed and implemented less than two years after nationalisation, there were the first of many emotional 'last trains'. Fortunately for the history of the steam locomotive, there was a hard core of campaigners who not only saw what the future heralded, but determined to do something about it.

Death came to the railway before it came to the steam locomotive; the branch line closures of 1950 (the Ministry of Transport counterpoint to the relaunch of the road construction programme two years earlier) resulted in withdrawal of only modest numbers of the oldest engines, and a thinning of the serried ranks of locomotive classes that numerically ran into hundreds. Line closures did not mean an end of steam, except on the narrow gauge. The narrow gauge railways of Wales were still nominally commercial in 1939; by 1945 they had all but shut up shop. First to go was the Welsh Highland Railway, dismantled in 1941 for scrap, after closing in the late 1930s. This was rapidly followed by the Ffestiniog, which failed to reopen after the quarry summer holiday in 1946. The Corris Railway was next, not surviving a flood that washed away its Dovey Bridge in 1948. The tide seemed unstoppable in 1950, when the

Talyllyn Railway put up the shutters. The remoteness of these lines meant that there was a short breathing space between closure of the line and arrival of the scrap merchants; in the case of the Talyllyn, this was enough. The first preservation movement secured the Talyllyn and its locomotive stock; few in 1951 would have been prepared to bet on there being any more successes.

If the Talyllyn was first in the 'amateur' list of preserved railways, with a small but significant batch of locomotives, then it was not first in the field by any means; *Rocket* had survived by the slenderest of threads to become part of the infant Science Museum collection. *Locomotion No1*, *Puffing Billy* and *Derwent* all survived intact due to the foresight of the Stockton and Darlington Railway and its successor, the North Eastern. This trend was continued in the nineteenth century, with the sole exception of the Broad Gauge, where the last survivor was cut up at Swindon works, after supposedly being preserved. A series of museum exhibits was thus inherited, preserved, and added to by the 'Big Four', to the extent that the LNER had enough to fill a small museum at York, as well as mount the original Stockton and Darlington locomotives on plinths at Darlington Bank Top station.

The centenary of the steam railway was celebrated at Shildon in 1925 with a cavalcade that included many of the oldest locomotives still fit to run on rails; some of them in steam. These locomotives were the basis of the British Transport Commission's museum at Clapham, expanded after nationalisation by a series of individual locomotives specifically targeted to represent a significant cross-section of the engines that ran on the rails of this island. Merging of the Clapham collection and the York museum exhibits generated the core of the National Railway Museum at York. While steam continued to grace the tracks of the nationalised railway, these locomotives were given occasional outings, events that were to end abruptly in 1968.

Meanwhile, on the narrow gauge, two events were to turn the infant preservation movement into an unstoppable force. The first was the formation of the Ffestiniog Railway Society in 1951, the second, Mr Alan Pegler using the very considerable resources provided by his family firm to buy a controlling interest in the Ffestiniog Railway Company in 1954. Up to this point, the preservation movement had relied on enthusiasm. The Ffestiniog Railway Company and the Ffestiniog Railway Society rapidly displayed a level of professionalism that equalled, and after 1960 exceeded, the professionals on the nationalised railway. On the narrow gauge, this professionalism, and the lower scrap value of small engines, led to numbers of locomotives being rescued from being cut up over the next twenty years. The Corris locomotives were bought and moved elsewhere, a fate mirrored on the Penrhyn and Dinorwic railways, as they too closed and the rails went for scrap.

If the preservation movement cut its teeth on the narrow gauge in Wales, then it was not to be long before it was realised that the rural standard gauge branch line was an endangered species. Locomotives to run the Bluebell Railway, first of the new genre, were initially the 'small and cheap' variety, as the new attraction opened its doors in 1960. Short, indirect and little used lines fell to the British Transport Commission hatchet with regularity in the 1950's, with 1953 and 1959 seeing whole rounds of railway closures. Railways with severe structural problems or high operating costs were closed rather than repaired or given modern traction; for these lines there was to be no rescue. As yet the steam locomotive *proper*, the core of the nationalised railway motive power, was both unaffected by mass withdrawal and, seemingly, beyond the pocket of individual enthusiasts. In two years that whole premise was to be turned on its head.

If the 1950s had seen a thinning in the number of locomotive classes, and the elimination of significant numbers of locomotives, this had been balanced to a degree with the introduction of numbers of 'Standard' locomotives. The railways still brimmed with locomotives forty, fifty and sixty years old. By 1960, though, deliveries of diesel locomotives and multiple units had reached the point where there was no need to store unwanted steam stock, and withdrawals and scrapping started in earnest. Whole classes started to disappear; the 'K3s' were withdrawn en masse, their compatriots on the east coast, the 'B16s', soon followed. The speed at which locomotives went for scrap exceeded the capacity of the works, and hundreds were sold to outside contractors, of which only one put aside more than the odd engine before turning the rest into furnace feedstock. By the end of 1962 the writing was on the wall for every class.

Numbers of individuals started to apply to British Railways to buy their favourite locomotive, led, almost inevitably, by Alan Pegler, who bought *Flying Scotsman* in 1963, and unlike the rest, he also had the foresight to buy the right to run it on the nationalised railway. In a similar fashion a number of the largest express engines were sold to those individuals who could convince the authorities that they had the resources to complete a purchase; this was not easy, as British Railways were not in any great hurry to sell locomotives. Strange as it might now seem, many people in railway management were not at all enthused about selling steam engines: rather, they wanted to rid the railway of these anachronisms, and scrapping them meant that they would be rid of them for good. The effect of this on the engines that were ultimately to be preserved was to distort the past in no small way; only one each of LNER classes 'A3', 'A2', 'V2', 'B12' and 'Director' survived. No survivors of LNER classes 'A1', 'B16', 'B17', 'K3', 'V3', 'L1', to name a few of many, and only two 'B1's and 'D49's. Distaste for the past and only a few individuals wealthy enough to purchase more than one engine, meant that by the end of steam in 1968, all but a few hundred engines had been scrapped, and very few indeed were safe in private hands, or so it seemed.

The exceptions to this gloomy picture appeared limited: Billy Butlin had bought a handful of engines as attractions for his holiday camps; Alan Bloom a small number for exhibition at Bressingham Gardens; eight 'A4' Pacifics had gone to various owners; Bulmer's had bought a 'King', and half a dozen 'Castles' had been sold, to add to *Caerphilly Castle's* place of honour in the Science Museum. Then there was the national collection, which included single examples, from a Bowen Cooke 'G2', to the '9F' *Evening Star*, of a wide cross-section of post war traction, added to those collected by the 'Big Four'. Those groups of enthusiasts who had set out to preserve an engine by buying one from British Railways had on the whole fared very badly; the 'dash to diesel' had been so fast that fundraising and establishing suitable credentials had just taken too long, and there was a further problem, buying a railway to run the engines on.

As steam vanished from the national network, it became increasingly clear that, Alan Pegler apart, there was going to be no steam allowed after the final farewell run of 11 August 1968 (three 'Black Fives' and the sole serviceable 'Britannia', *Oliver Cromwell* taking turns). If you owned an engine there was no prospect of being able to run it, except on a private railway. Those railways in 1968 were pitifully short; not a single line had five miles of track with a light railway order allowing them to run passenger-carrying trains, and most were no more than extended sidings. Bulmer's 'King' was restricted to a private siding in Hereford, and was considered fortunate. If there was double trouble for steam enthusiasts in 1968, then partial relief emerged in 1970 with the realisation by a South Wales scrap merchant that he was now the owner of all the extant ex-British Railways locomotives not sold for preservation and had, by default, cornered the market.

David Woodham had set up in business as a scrap merchant in Barry, South Wales, and bought a large number of locomotives in the

1960s. The variety was significant: No LNER types, but good numbers of many classes from the other three regions, and a fair number of post-war nationalisation engines as well. Woodham's (his company) had also bought large volumes of unbraked freight wagons, and it was these that he cut first, before making a start on the locomotives. Finding himself with a market corner, cutting of engines ceased and sales began. These locomotive sales were to continue for fifteen years, and included two 'Kings', 'Merchant Navy's', 'Halls', a variety of tank engines, and a fair selection of other Southern Railway, Great Western and LMS types.

The condition of these scrapyard escapees varied wildly; there were no cab fittings at all, many were missing all the side and valve rods, one of the 'Kings' had a wheelset cut, and most of the thinner plates on cabs and boiler cladding were rusted through. All the later engines had to be stripped of asbestos, and tenders were often little better than wheels and a frame. When the low loader departed from Barry with ten thousand pounds worth of rusty metal aboard, the purchasers were faced with at least that many hours' work, and ten times the cost in pounds, before there would be a firebox that they could light a fire in.

In spite of this, with time now on the enthusiast's side, Dai Woodham eventually sold almost all of the engines that graced his sidings in 1971. One or two engines were scrapped in the 1970s to keep up the pressure on purchasers. The last ten were sent to further storage at Cardiff Bute Road. Escape from a fate close to death by no means meant a speedy return to life.

Less than half of those engines rescued from the scrapyard have been returned to steam in the thirty three years since 1968. Many engines have been standing idle for longer than their working lives, one or two much longer. Those that made a quick return to steam are famous primarily because they are so few; the 'Jubilee' *Leander* made the return via British Railways works, a route that vanished with astonishing rapidity as works and the skills to handle steam locomotives evaporated in the 1970s. Both the 'Kings', *King Edward I* and *King Edward II* had been withdrawn in 1962, twenty years later rescue was achieved though neither had been completely restored. A return to active service before the end of the twentieth century was the exception rather than the rule.

The 1970s represented a turning point for the preservation movement; rising incomes left numbers of people with significant resources to indulge their hobbies in a manner previously the preserve of the few. The attractions of an interesting hobby to offset a boring job meant that the preserved railways began to thrive. Most of the railway preservation movement had set their sights modestly on short lengths of line, but a few had much grander strategic plans up their sleeves. Two of these, the Severn Valley Railway and the North Yorkshire Moors Railway, planned from the off in the 1960s to have lines on which it was both possible to operate a proper service, and have numbers of locomotives in service at a time. That vision spread in the 1970s but only one further line, the West Somerset, set its sights on a full length railway, and currently runs one. Others are still trying.

One of the reasons for the preserved railways not realising the vision of running a proper railway, and being restricted very much to short branch line type shuttles, was the end of the 'steam ban' in the 1970's on the nationalised railway. Vacillation on the part of British Railway's management, ending of the steam ban and a quite enthusiastic approach to the 'Shildon 150' celebrations that saw numerous historic engines steamed, gave a lease of life to those preserved set-ups that had not gone for broke and acquired, or built, a railway. This left the preservation movement with two options: steam on private metals, and, for those with enough noughts on their bank balances, certification to run on the main line.

End of the steam ban also meant that the managers of the National Collection determined that they were going to have some fun as well, and it was not long before all manner of rare or unique locomotives were in steam and back on the tracks. The problem this generated was one of professional facilities and expertise; British Railways made it clear that their workshops could do much, but only at a price many found both exorbitant and beyond their pockets. Facilities that had been underused or not used at all since the last works overhauls of 1966 were coming under the microscope as losses on the nationalised railway showed no signs of ameliorating; halving the network had merely shown that there was *no* profitable core.

What British Rail did not wish to provide, others found that they could, and make money also. Steam in the 1970s might well have been yesterday's technology, but many people realised that, weight and size apart, there was no real reason why a modest engineering establishment could not repair the steam locomotive. There was also no reason why this new band of engineers should not adopt new methods to keep old engines in running order, and that is what happened. The preservation movement thus adopted a number of strategies to substitute for the facilities that the 'works' had provided. Firstly, there was almost no demand for drawings; what drawings were needed could be recovered from archives, and only rarely was a new detail required. Secondly, facilities to handle quantities of molten metal, for casting new parts, were absent. If parts needed casting, then they had to be purchased commercially, patterns obtained or made, and the cash stumped up. Casting remains outside the mainstream 'preservation engineering' sector. Thirdly, there grew up a small number of specialist commercial engineers, who provided services, such as boilersmiths, where quality standards have to rely on techniques that are dictated by others; in the case of boilers this means the insurers.

The bulk of the rest of the general engineering; fitting, turning, the 'grubby' tasks of component stripping and refitting, setting up motion and painting, the preservation movement set to and provided the facilities for itself. All of the larger preserved railways established workshops able to handle, with the necessary outside assistance, a full works overhaul. So too did a number of the centres that had no lines to run. Until the health and safety killjoys discovered that they could ban visitors on the grounds that these workshops were dangerous places, there was much that the casual visitor could learn by a brief tour. In practice, most of the preserved workshops are idle when their railway is busy, and the biggest risk was tripping over an abandoned connecting rod, or missing a footing by an inspection pit. Not really to be compared with a trip across an uncontrolled occupation crossing on the east coast main line.

Having both facilities and rails to run upon, and the human resources to man the works and crew the engines, meant that after 1971 a new era of steam locomotive running dawned. Commencing with dawdles down branch lines, and moving quite quickly to intensive weekend rosters, preserved locomotives eventually graduated to long distance excursions on the nationalised railway. The stresses and strains of this sort of intermittent operation meant failures in service were fairly common: boilers suffered major thermal stresses as they were not steamed regularly, and had to be warmed from cold by lighting the fire; bearings distorted and ran hot after sitting still for long periods; glands, stuffing boxes and auxiliary equipment suffered likewise. Finding experienced firemen and drivers became a challenge as the mutual improvement system, that had sufficed for a century and a half, disappeared. Keeping up to date those who did have the knowledge, and passing it on to the next generation, nearly slipped off the agenda.

Life was not made any easier by the almost complete absence of coaling and watering facilities on the nationalised railway. Ad hoc arrangements using fire tenders and loading shovels gave decidedly mixed results. Scarcely a turntable remained serviceable, leading to long treks running backwards, either to find a suitable triangle of lines, or because there wasn't one. That seamless co-ordination on the footplate was compromised by lack of practice, and an absence of supplies of consistently *the same* coal meant a new firing challenge every trip. All of these factors took their toll, both on reliability and on intervals between works overhauls. The tendency for preserved engines to spend long intervals out of traffic awaiting repair is not just due to a lack of cash; the steam locomotive was designed for more or less continuous operation, and does not take kindly to semi-fossilisation.

If preservation was a mixed bag for privately-owned locomotives, the stresses and strains on the unique locomotives in the national collection soon brought an end to regular running of those engines that could be steamed. In its place was substituted a policy of running engines that were fairly 'modern', and not the sole representatives of their type, notably *Evening Star*, *Duchess of Hamilton*, *Mallard*, and a handful of others. Enthusiasts live in hope, but not expectation, of ever seeing the Midland 'Compound' or Stirling's 'Single' in steam again.

Over the last three decades of the twentieth century, owners of preserved locomotives have had a field day in being able to choose what colour their engines should be painted. Inevitably this led to some paint jobs notable only for their lack of any sort of good taste. Efforts to recreate the 'Crimson Lake' livery of the Midland usually ended in an aesthetic disaster, if only because the effort of applying multiple layers of paint, rubbing down between coats, and then doing the same with many coats of varnish, was usually beyond the facilities available, if not the skills. Applying Great Western green showed just how much easier it was to do a presentable job with something the right colour in the first place. Liveries remain an area of much debate.

With forty years' experience of restoring, running, maintaining and overhauling steam locomotives, it is perhaps inevitable that the preservation movement should seek to move on to altering them and building new. Proposals for altering locomotives had an early start with *Duke of Gloucester*. Restorers on this expensive project commenced with the knowledge that if all they did was put the bits back that had been cut off (the valve gear), then they would have an engine that would not go very well. Restoration thus included alterations to the locomotive draughting, with addition of a Kylchap blastpipe kit, and was judged a success. At the other end of the scale, the project to build an 'A1' Pacific is nearing the halfway point in construction. Between these successes come a wealth of proposals that have not yet achieved their objectives: turning a 'Hall' back into a 'Saint', or recreation of a streamlined 'Duchess', to note just two examples. On the narrow gauge, the challenge of building new was one the Festiniog Railway accepted, replacing the 'double Fairlie' *Livingston Thompson* with a new one, *Earl of Merionydd.* Most of that work was executed in the company's own Boston Lodge works.

With the dawn of the new millennium, we can record both the appearance of women on the footplate, and the continued popularity of the steam locomotive. The problems of intermittent steaming remain, ameliorated by preserved railways running full seven day timetables in the summer months, and by regular services (Fort William to Mallaig) on Railtrack metals. The manual skills needed to run the steam locomotive survive (as distinct from the technical ones that are common to modern traction), and the so far successful keeping at bay the health and safety and environmental Scrooges who would ban the steam locomotive as dangerous and polluting, means that the experience of noise, spectacle, smells, danger and smuts in your eyes is still to be widely found. Long may that happy state of affairs remain.

Chapter Thirty-Three:

Staybolts and Stretcher Plates: The Technology Explained

Whilst every effort has been made in the text to prevent technojargon staging a take-over, it has to be admitted that every technology has its own vocabulary. If care is not taken to avoid the abyss of incomprehension and the ivory tower of superiority, then the drift into these realms can be a proverbial slippery slope. Here then is the place for all that jargon.

Adhesive Weight

Proportion of locomotive weight resting on the coupled wheels, and available to assist in transmission of engine thrust to the rail. Engineers designing four, six, eight and ten coupled units went to some considerable effort to ensure that the load on all the coupled wheels was equalised as far as possible. The maximum tractive effort that could be exerted by a locomotive was equal to the total adhesive weight multiplied by the coefficient of friction, the latter usually being between 0.1 and 0.3, depending on rail conditions.

Anti-Vacuum Valve

Automatic valve set in the superheater header, normally held closed by the pressure of steam in the superheater, but falling open when the regulator was closed to prevent a vacuum being formed in the superheater that could lead to overheating of the elements and burning away of the metal. Function rendered redundant by the adoption of the regulator positioned in the smokebox, allowing the superheater to remain full of steam at all times.

Axle, Cartazzi

Axle for leading or trailing wheels (i.e. non-driving) that automatically controlled the amount of lateral play by adoption of inclined axlebox guides.

Axle, Crank

Solid-forged or built-up axle upon which are formed one (in a three cylinder locomotive) or two (in two or four cylindered engines) cranks on which the pistons drive via the big end and connecting rods. With the need also for one, two or three sets of eccentrics in a distance of not more than four feet, and the need for adequate bearing surfaces, inside cylinders and their motion were always cramped and difficult to access.

Axle, Radial

Attempts to improve the vehicular characteristics of locomotives by making their running steadier and entry into curves smoother led to development of the radial axle. As the name implies, the object was to keep the axle, usually the leading axle, aligned with the track through curves, rather than having the outer flange press upon the rail.

Balancing of Motion

As train speeds increased in the middle of the nineteenth century, the issue of locomotive stability was recognised as being multi-factorial rather than just associated with the engine centre of gravity or piston thrust, and balancing of the motion became normal practice. The problem this presented the designer was that there were parts, such as the crank axles, that rotated and could thus be completely balanced, and connecting rods and side rods that displayed non-uniform motion. The motion of the side rods is both up and down, and fore and aft. This movement can be balanced by adding weights to the wheels at 180deg. out of phase, although not on the same line as the rods, but the connecting rod centre of gravity moves up and down a distance equal to half of the piston stroke. Any balance weight added to the driving wheel(s) had to make due allowance for this, and it was normal for 50% of the reciprocating masses to be balanced.

Bearings

Locomotives from first to last relied heavily on plain bearings, as opposed to roller or ball: big and little ends were always of plain form. Roller bearings came into use after the First War, in parts of the valve motion, and eventually in wheel bearings. Plain bearings need oil as lubricant, hence the use of mechanical oil feeds; roller
and ball bearings could use grease lubrication.

Bogie

Four wheel leading (occasionally trailing) truck designed to carry some loads and assist in the task of making the locomotive travel smoothly round curves. Bogies were an early development to assist in fast running, becoming standard for many express engines by 1880. Originally swivelling about a centre ball and socket joint, later developments included side bearers and control springs.

Boiler Washing Plant

Owing to the prevalence of impurities in boiler feed water in much of England (Scotland and parts of Wales have much better boiler feed water) even with treatment of water to remove impurities, regular, usually weekly boiler washouts were needed. Washing plant developed between the wars was designed to ease and speed this process, and hot water plants were developed for this purpose. Locomotives would have their fires dropped and then be connected to the plant to have the boiler steam and water, still at 40-50psi, drained off and the heat recovered. This draining off removed the impurities in the boiler that would otherwise result in priming when in service. Once this was complete the boiler would be washed down with hot water at about 180degF, removing sludge and scale from the firebox plates and boiler tubes. When finished, the boiler would be filled with fresh water at as close to boiling as practicable.

The plant needed to service this comprised one or two locomotive type boilers, providing the heating water, two large tanks holding several thousand gallons each of hot water, one for washing out and one for hot filling of the clean boilers. The washing out tank would normally be used to condense the locomotive steam, gaining much of its needed heat thereby. Filtering and settlement allowed the washout water to be recycled. Most larger sheds were able to handle several locomotives at once, and a hot wash cycle would last five or six hours, depending on engine size. Hot washing reduced the thermal stress on the locomotive boiler, leading to reduced maintenance, but occasional cold washouts were needed to remove the more recalcitrant boiler scale.

Brake Rigging

Locomotive brakes, usually confined to the coupled wheels, are operated by a series of rods and levers, known as rigging, to minimise on the use of steam cylinders.

Brick Arch

Literally an arch of firebrick fitted across the inside of the firebox, above the fire and serving two principal purposes: firstly to provide the necessary high temperature surface to assist in combustion of volatile elements of the fuel that might otherwise be discharged unburnt out of the chimney; and secondly to ensure that combustion products circulate round the firebox rather than pass straight into the boiler tubes.

Buffers and Buffer Beams

Buffers were designed originally to cushion the impact of minor collisions when coupling up and when running, and were originally 'dumb', that is unsprung, usually large blocks of wood. Steel sprung buffers rapidly replaced dumb buffers on passenger trains, but some small shunting tank engines retained them until well into the twentieth century. Buffers were mounted on a buffer beam, which was riveted across the front and rear ends of the locomotive main frames. The location of the buffer beam is approximately in the plane of the centre of gravity of the locomotive and of the carriages and wagons being hauled, avoiding the generation of substantial forces that would lead to buffers being overridden during braking.

Clack Box

Non-return valve for the boiler feed from the injectors.

Clearance

Distance between the piston and cylinder end, usually $1/8$th inch or thereabouts, to allow for slight overrunning when in service. Steam admitted to this space did no useful work, neither did steam in the rest of the clearance volume, which included the ports between the cylinder and piston or slide valve.

Combination Brake Valve

Driver's brake valve that blended the application of the engine steam brake with the vacuum brake on the coaches, allowing both brakes to do the right amount of work.

Compensation Bars

Suspension springing is said to be compensated if the ends of adjacent springs, instead of being hung on the frames, are attached to the end of compensation bars, themselves attached to the frames at the mid point. This arrangement transfers weight between adjacent axles when the engine is in motion, theoretically at least smoothing the ride.

Cut-Off

The point in the stroke of the piston at which steam admission is stopped and expansion commences, expressed as a percentage of the piston stroke. In full gear most link motions allowed about 75% cut-off. As cut-off reduces, the expansion period increases, and at the other end of the cylinder, compression increases as the exhaust port closes earlier. Actual travel of the valve decreases as cut off is shortened, in direct proportion with Stephenson's Link, and much less with Walschaerts' gear.

Coupled Wheel

A wheel that is connected to the driving wheels by means of coupling rods, but is not driven directly.

Dampers

Adjustable plates at the front and rear of the ashpan, controlled by the fireman from the footplate, used to regulate the air supply to the grate. Originally dampers were also fitted to the ends of the superheater flues to prevent overheating when steam was shut off. These dampers were ultimately found to be unnecessary.

Deflector Plate

Steel plate over the firehole in the firebox, to direct air into the firebed and enable coal to be burnt 'smokelessly'.

Derived Motion

The practice of using the motion of one set of valve actuation rods to operate a second valve 180deg. out of phase, by the use of a rocking lever. Used on all Great Western four cylinder locomotives, where inside motion operated the outside valves, and on LMS 'Duchess' Pacifics, where outside motion operated inside valves. The system on three cylinder engines is known as conjugated motion, Gresley-Walschaerts or Holcroft-Gresley motion (see below).

Drain Cock

Manual or automatic valve to allow water to drain from cylinders.

Drawbar

Metal link that connects engine to tender on tender engines (absent on tank engines) the point at which the engine pull is measured, hence the term 'Drawbar Horse-Power', dbhp. On tender engines the drawbar is fixed to the rear cross stay of the frames, behind the firebox and under the footplate.

Eccentric

Machined circular bearing on a crank axle offset from the centre of the axle and encircled by a strap-type bearing to which an operating rod for valve gear or feed pumps (for boiler feed, oil feed or brake air/vacuum) are attached. The rod movement is twice the distance of the eccentric centre from the axle centre.

Ejector

Vacuum pump for generating brake vacuum, based upon the air entrainment principle and using a steam jet in the same way as the blastpipe.

Electric Light

Some of the later classes of steam locomotives, notably the Southern Railway 'Merchant Navy' Pacifics and the LNER/BR 'A1' Pacifics, were fitted with generators to produce electricity for lighting (carriages had their own batteries and generators). Most engines relied upon oil lamps for light, and these classes were unusual, but not unique.

Fire Bars

Short cast iron bars fitted into carrier plates, and holding up the fire above the ashpan. Firebars were usually arranged to have fairly precise gaps between them to allow air into the base of the fire. The passage of the combustion air through the grate kept the bars cool, but burnt bars were a regular maintenance item, much depending on the way the fire and ashpan were managed when in service. Rocking grates allowed part of the fire to be dropped while on the road, to rid the fire of clinker.

Fire or Smoke Tube

Copper, brass or steel boiler tube in which the combustion gases pass through the inside, as opposed to the water tube, where the gases pass round the outside.

Footplate

Where the driver and fireman stand, hence the term 'Footplatemen'.

Foundation Ring

At the base of the firebox the inner and outer shells are riveted to a hooped spacer of metal known as the foundation ring. This ring holds the two plates together and apart and determines the width of the firebox water spaces.

Frames, plate and bar

While early locomotives used the boiler barrel as the main structure, this was soon found limiting, and a separate frame to carry wheels and motion was developed. Ultimately two types of frame came to the fore: plate frames, used almost exclusively in Britain, and bar frames, preferred in the United States. Plate frames comprise two thick iron or steel plates up to two feet deep and running the whole length of the engine, connected by the buffer bar, cylinder castings, and stays and stretchers at intervals along their length. The plates carry all static and dynamic loads and are about an inch thick. Bar frames are similar in principle, but are formed as a space frame of square bars with diagonal bracing, the bars being two or more inches thick.

Frame Stretcher

Iron or steel plate acting as a distance piece between frame plates, and as a mounting block for boiler mountings.

Guard Irons

A pair of steel blades mounted in front of the leading wheels on a locomotive to deflect any obstruction on the track and prevent derailment.

Holcroft-Gresley Motion

A form of link motion developed by Herbert Holcroft and adopted by Nigel Gresley (and almost no-one else) to provide for driving the inside valve of three cylinder locomotives with Walschaerts' outside gear, without the need for inside valve gear. The gear is a derived motion arrangement, where the inside valve spindle is driven by both outside gears via rocking shafts and a floating link. The principal defect of this type of gear is the different motion of the inside valve (see text). The reason why it was not widely adopted, is that the drive, unlike the Great Western derived motion, is taken from the tail rod of the piston valve, where thermal expansion of the outside valve rods affects the setting of the inside valve. The result is variable and unequal distribution of power output between the cylinders, and maintenance of accurate valve settings was rendered a near impossibility. Most locomotives with this valve arrangement emitted a syncopated beat from the exhaust after they had run a reasonable mileage from overhaul, and when in poor condition sounded positively ill.

Horn Blocks

The driving and coupled wheels of an engine are fitted with bearings that slide in slots in the main frames. These slots are fitted with wearing faces known as horn blocks, held in position by flanges on the frames and secured at their lower end by a keep or clip, fixed after the wheels are placed in their running position. To allow for easy fixing and removal, the bearings on the axle were in two parts, avoiding the problem of obstruction by the wheels. When roller bearings were introduced, the wheels had to be pressed on to the axles after the bearings, and bearing removal involved taking the wheel off again.

Hot Box

A perennial problem that has only gone away with the advent of sealed bearings. Plain bearings oiled by cup and trimming and lacking seals on the axle to hold oil in and keep grit out were always vulnerable to overheating, due to lack of oil or presence of foreign bodies. Tender, leading and trailing axles as well as driving wheels were all vulnerable, and if not spotted and attended quickly, plain bearings' white metal linings melted, running the risk of seizure and/or derailment.

Liners, valve and piston

The modern steam locomotive equipped with piston valves had each cylinder and valve assembly formed from five components: the casting, which incorporated the spaces for the cylinder and valve chambers, and the inlet and exhaust passages; the piston valve assembly; the working piston; and the two cylindrical liners that form the cylinder and valve. The valve liner is slotted in two zones for its full circumference with triangular holes and diagonal 'lands' to avoid scoring of the sealing rings. The width of these zones is the maximum port opening to steam and exhaust. Formed in the casting outside these zones are the two passages that lead to the ends of the working cylinder.

At the two ends of the liner, and in the middle, the valve liner is cut away almost entirely, leaving only enough metal to ensure structural competence. These cut outs are not passed by the moving piston valve, and allow for high pressure steam to enter the valve via the middle opening, and exhaust to exit at the two ends. This arrangement is known as 'inside admission'. Reversing the steam and exhaust ports is known as 'outside admission', a rare arrangement in British practice, but illustrated in the National Railway Museum's sectioned Bulleid Pacific *Ellerman Lines*. Slide valves, in contrast, are designed for outside admission by default.

Mechanical Stoker

General term for a variety of devices that deliver coal onto the grate automatically and distribute it for efficient combustion. The two most popular devices were the chain grate stoker and the Archimedian screw, and it is the latter device that was adopted for mechanical stoking on the '9F' freight locomotive, three locomotives receiving the stokers as an experiment that remained just that, no further work being done.

Motion Plate

Transverse plate set between or outside the engine frames on which are mounted the die block and link rods of the valve gear.

Mud Holes

Access holes in the boiler and firebox for insertion of hoses and cleaning tools for removal of scale and sludge during boiler washouts.

Oil Firing

Heavy fuel oil was substituted for coal in a pilot programme instituted after the Second World War, ostensibly to ease the critical coal supply problem of the time. The programme was a failure owing to a lack of foreign exchange to buy the oil. The fuel oil used needed to be heated (it had a very high viscosity at room temperatures) to flow from the tender tank to the burners, achieved by a steam heating coil in the oil tank. Oil firing has been adopted on the Ffestiniog Railway, and the Vale of Rheidol to mitigate the risk of fires at the lineside in the summer.

Oil, Lubricating

Special formulations of distilled crude oil fractions with known and reliable viscosities were unknown in the nineteenth century, and much of the oil and grease used for lubrication purposes was derived from animals and plants rather than mineral oil. Typical animal oils were tallow, whale, sperm and seal oils, and typical plant oils, rape seed, cotton seed and olive oil.

Piston Rings

Single broad cast iron rings were used from the middle of the nineteenth century to form a seal between piston and cylinder walls, but high rates of wear and steam leakage prompted the search for alternatives. The use of multiple narrow rings became universal in the first decade of the twentieth century, that use quickly extending to piston valves as well as cylinders. Similar external multiple rings were developed to form the stuffing box seals, where the piston and valve rods passed into their respective cylinders and steam chests.

Piston Valve

Modernised variation of the slide valve, avoiding the excessive pressure on the valve block that made the slide valve unsuitable for high steam pressures. The operating principle remained the same, though the valve ports became a series of circumferential slots in a cylinder, and the usual method of admission became 'inside', with the high pressure steam chest in the middle and the two exhaust passages on the ends. This arrangement avoided subjecting the packing or stuffing boxes on the valve rods to high pressure steam.

Pony Truck

Leading pair of wheels mounted in their own frame that was independent of the main locomotive frames, as with the bogie. The pony truck was allowed some spring-controlled movement, and was intended to steer the front of the locomotive and improve the dynamics of the ride.

Poppet Valves

The quest for more effective valves than the slide and piston valves ended, as far as the steam locomotive was concerned, with the poppet valve, though not the classic mushroom type seen in the modern internal combustion engine. The idea of having separate inlet and exhaust valves in order to provide independent timing was appreciated early on, but the problem of how to make it work was only really solved by the Italian, Caprotti, after the First World War. The exhaust valve timing is easy to arrange, as it does not change with throttle or cut off positions, but early attempts with stepped actuation cams for the inlet valves failed due to the lack of precision this gave to the cut off. Caprotti designed an infinitely variable cam action, but the poppet valve did not gain immediate ascendancy over the piston valve because of the greater mechanical complexity and hence cost. Later versions of Caprotti valves were of the springless type, where valves were held against their seats by pressure in the steam chest, falling open when the regulator was shut. This feature made the valve simpler, and avoided the need for snifting valves to prevent compression in the cylinder when coasting.

Poppet Valve Regulator

Increasing steam pressures and high degree superheaters led to difficulties with conventional saturated side regulator valves and superheater flues in the twenties and thirties. High pressures could not be easily regulated by a single valve, as the pressure/flow curve is very steep in the initial opening of the valve, making precise slow speed control difficult. This difficulty accentuated slipping on starting, and the need for considerable physical force to open/close the regulator against boiler steam pressure. The multiple poppet valve regulator, mounted on the superheater header in the smokebox, addressed both the issue of burnt superheater flues (by keeping the flues full of steam) and, by using a series of graduated sized valves opened sequentially, addressed the issues of proportional regulator openings and steam chest pressures. The result was more precise control of the locomotive at low speed.

Power Classification

To assist in the formulation of permitted loads for various routes, locomotives were classified by the LMS as to their suitability for hauling passenger and freight trains, starting at 0F (for the lightest freight engines) and concluding at 8F for the most powerful (British Railways added a further category at 9F). Passenger engines started at 0P and ran through to 8P in the same manner. Locomotives rated the same for freight and passenger were rated 3MT, 4MT, 5MT (Mixed Traffic), or 6P5F, for example, where the ratings differed for passenger and freight haulage. The classifications were nominal in that ratings did not imply that all 8P or 7F locomotives were equal, but were more a guide as to what could be expected when allocating maximum loads or timings

Priming

Carry over of water into the cylinders, leading to damage to cylinders and piston valves, due to the presence of impurities in the boiler water. This problem was addressed by regular boiler washouts, draining off the concentrated impurities usually at weekly intervals, and refilling with a charge of fresh water, and later by the use of continuous blowdown, where part of the boiler water was regularly discharged to remove impurities.

Roundhouse

The idea that a new style of architecture could be developed in honour of the steam locomotive appears to have been invented by the London and Birmingham Railway with the building of the first roundhouse at Chalk Farm, Camden, where engines were attached to trains after they had been hauled out of London Euston on the end of a rope. Many copies followed of which a few survive today (including Chalk Farm). The locomotives were shedded round a central turntable, allowing them to be accessed without moving other engines and turned to point the right way at the same time. Later sheds often ran to several turntables, somewhat destroying the original concept.

Route Availability

Each class of locomotive was given a route availability according to its weight and the damage the civil engineer judged that it would do to certain under-line structures such as bridges. Other factors such as dynamic hammer blow and weight per foot run were also involved. Two systems were devised; by the Great Western Railway, which used a coloured disc on the cab sidesheet, and by British Railways, which used a number code. Other companies issued lists of permitted engines for each section of their routes. British Railway route availability started with RA1, the lightest footed engines which could go almost anywhere, to RA9, whose locomotives were restricted to the main lines only. Great Western (it was independent until after the end of steam, of course) colour codes started at clear (go anywhere) and ran through yellow, blue and red to double red (King class only, restricted to the main lines between Paddington and Wolverhampton, and Bristol/Cardiff/Plymouth).

Running Plate

Plate originally fixed to the top of the outside frame plates to allow access to oil the engine whilst it was in motion. With the adoption of inside frames, the running plate was continued in its original position for crew to carry out maintenance in service.

Slide Bars

External guides to ensure that the piston slides in the cylinder without trying to deflect due to the vertical component of the reactive force between piston and crank.

Smokebox Saddle

Top casting of the cylinders/valves, forming the base of the smokebox and containing the exhaust passages and the blastpipe base/nozzle.

Smoke Deflectors

Exhaust steam and smoke has a tendency to drift into the driver's line of sight, because at speed there is a zone of low air pressure at the side of the boiler. The problem became serious with the adoption of long lap and travel valves, where short cut-offs reduced the pressure of the exhaust steam, leading to a soft blast from the chimney. The parallel boilers of the King Arthur and Royal Scot classes quickly gained side sheets to channel air into the low pressure zones, and deflectors were fitted to most of the express locomotive classes after the Second World War. Sharply tapering boilers were less vulnerable, so the Great Western could flaunt its independence by not needing them.

Snifting Valves

Method of preventing damage to cylinders by running a connecting passage between the two ends and closing it with a valve held shut by the pressure of steam in the steam chest. Shutting the regulator caused the valve to drop open, avoiding excessive resistance due to compression in the cylinders when coasting down hills.

Spark Arrestor

Series of baffles or mesh grids in the smokebox designed to break up burning cinders before they are ejected by the blast; smaller particles have insufficient thermal mass to remain alight for any great length of time.

Stay

Short copper or steel alloy bolt holding the sides and top of the firebox together, usually spaced at about four inch centres.

Steam Chest

Box enclosing the slide valve, acting as a reservoir for steam supply to the cylinders.

Steam Space

That part of the boiler and firebox above the top of the gauge glass.

Stuffing Box

Container for metallic or fabric packing where the piston rod or valve rod emerges from the cylinder or steam chest.

Superheater Header

Pipe from the regulator to the superheater flues, and the collection and distribution pipe for the flue tubes.

Swept Volume

The section of the cylinder traversed by the piston. The remainder is the clearance volume, which also includes the steam ports and passages.

Tail rods

Piston tail rods gained some favour in the nineteenth century as a means of reducing wear on piston and cylinder. The idea was to support the piston at both ends, rather than just one. Tail rods were abandoned with the introduction of narrow multiple piston rings.

Tenders

From a simple four wheel wagon with a water barrel mounted on the rear, locomotive tenders evolved to provide substantial storage space for coal and water, fire irons and water scoop. Tenders also provided as much as half of the brake force, equal to that of the engine. Typical of the nineteenth and early twentieth century tenders was that evolved by the Great Western Railway, six wheeled with straight sides and a sloping wedge-shaped space for the coal, closed by a set of doors above the shovelling plate. The water tank was below and to the rear of the coal space, and fitted with baffles (wash plates) to prevent water sloshing around and derailing the tender. The shovelling plate was located at a height that avoided the need to lift coal into the firebox, and the coal space was meant to be 'self trimming', meaning that the coal worked its way forward to the point of use without assistance. The ability of coal to jam by 'bridging' often meant that self trimming tenders were more theoretical than real, and pulling coal forward a regular feature of the fireman's duties. A few tenders were fitted with steam powered coal pushers to assist the fireman in this arduous task.

Increasing demands for more coal and water space after World War One led to the development of the high sided tender, curved to the loading gauge and allowing the rear of the footplate to be protected to a degree from the elements. Eight wheel tenders made an early (1899) appearance behind the London and South Western Railway 'T9' express engines, and were standard for the LNER Pacifics. Coal capacities ranged up to ten tons, water to over 5500 gallons. Some small tank locomotives were semi-permanently attached to a four wheel wagon that carried their coal, and since preservation, the Ffestiniog Railway has added tenders to some of its tank engines to cope with the demands of hauling passengers against the grade. Some companies designed tenders with coal rails, of which the Great Northern Railway are perhaps the best known.

Tenders generally were designed for various duties; coal and water capacities varied, and different tenders could be used on the same class of engine (as with the LNER corridor tenders, which were only needed on the non-stop Edinburgh services).

Thermic Siphon

Tubes that were inserted into the firebox to assist in circulation of water. Their purpose was twofold: to improve heat transfer, and to reduce thermal stress, thus increasing firebox life.

Top Feed

Boiler feed in the nineteenth century was usually through a clack valve into the side of the boiler to mitigate the effect of thermal stress by allowing some mixing of hot and cold water; the bottom of the boiler received little heat and would be cold if water was fed at that point. Churchward led the way to reduced wear and tear by using the steam space to heat the feed water and deposit sludge in trays to protect the tubes, and the top feed was the way to do this.

Track and Structure Gauge

In its efforts to mitigate the cost of over-line structures, the companies that constructed the railways after 1830 in Britain did so to a series of track and structure gauges that made life difficult for their successors. Apart from the rail gauge of four feet eight and a half inches, the only other gauge stipulation for the premium engine at Rainhill was a maximum height of fifteen feet. Over subsequent decades rail gauges coalesced to standard, broad and two or three widths of narrow, but virtually every company decided upon a different structure gauge, with the inevitable result that when mergers took place, the composite structure gauge was based upon the smallest envelope rather than the largest. Three dimensions were critical to the steam locomotive: the available width at platform height, the total height to the top of the chimney, and the point at which the top curve of the roof profile commenced, the cantrail height.

Of these, the overall height of just over thirteen feet meant that the British steam locomotive was smaller than both its European and American cousins, and that the ultimate dimensions of the locomotive were more or less equivalent to a machine that could just about be fired by hand. In power output, gross horsepower/ton ratios were higher in Britain than the rest of the world, even though maximum oomph was double elsewhere (America, where the articulated Mallett Union Pacific 'Big Boys' developed 6000hp).

The other serious limit was the width over outside cylinders; when two cylinders were used outside after 1900, their diameter was limited by the available space outside the wheels. The cylinder centre line being on the centre of the crank, some three to six inches outside the outer wheel face, led to the outer edge of the cylinder being up to fifteen inches outside the wheels, leading to bans on the worst offenders (Great Western 'Halls') away from their home metals. Due to the broad gauge legacy, the Great Western had varying widths to its structure gauge, which was the most generous on this island. Poor tunnel construction on the Hastings line led to the narrowest, but there was a lot of variation between these two extremes.

Tractive Effort

A measure of a locomotive's ability to start a train, and expressed as '26,500lb' (force). For practical purposes the calculation took 85% of the full boiler pressure, this being the maximum that could be expected as 'mean effective pressure' in the cylinder. The formula is as follows:

$$T = \frac{2\,P\,l\,r^2\,n}{D}$$

Where T is the tractive effort in pounds, r the radius of the piston, in inches, n the number of cylinders, l the length of the piston stroke, in feet, P the mean effective pressure in pounds per square inch and D the diameter of the driving wheels, in feet. As can be seen, the formula is an approximation, that allows for two cylinders acting at the same time (a two-cylinder engine gives four exhaust beats per revolution, three cylinders gives six beats, and four cylinders, eight, i.e. four pairs) assumes that the position of the cranks is of no effect, and ignores any back pressure that may be generated. Horsepower, the ability to do work, is not measured with steam locomotives except as recorded on indicator diagrams or drawbar pull.

Table 1:
Changes in weight, tractive effort and heating surface, express passenger locomotives, 1829 to 1954

Date	Locomotive	Tractive Effort (lb.)	Weight (Tons/Cwt)	Power/ Weight Ratio (lb/ton.)	Heating Surface (sq.ft.)
1829	Rocket	818	4T 3C	197	110
1830	Planet	1371	8T	171	370
1833	Patentee	1836	10T	183	410
1845	Crewe Type	3984	16T	249	709
1846	Iron Duke (Broad Gauge)	6885	26T	264	1733
1847	Jenny Lind	6375	24T 2C	264	1138
1870	Stirling Single(GNR No. 1)	11,129	38T 9C	289	1165
1870	Kirtley "800" Class 2-4-0	11,578	40T	289	1097
1873	Precedent, LNWR	10,382	32T 15C	317	1083
1875	Johnson 4-4-0 (Midland)	17,585	53T 7C	329	1313
1882	Webb "Compound"	16,224	37T 15C	429	1083
1903	GWR "City"	17,345	55T 6C	313	1818
1905	Midland "Compound"	21,840	61T 14C	353	1720
1907	Star	25,086	75T 12C	331	2143
1923	Castle	31,625	79T 17C	396	2049
1925	King Arthur	25,320	80T 19C	312	1878
1927	King	40,285	89T	452	2201
1928	A3 Pacific	32,909	96T 5C	341	2635
1933	Princess Royal Pacific	40,285	104T 10C	385	2523
1935	A4 Pacific	35,455	102T 19C	344	2576
1941	Merchant Navy	37,514	94T 15C	395	2451
1946	A2 Pacific	40,430	101T 10C	385	3141
1951	Britannia	32,150	94T 4C	341	3178
1954	Duke of Gloucester	39,080	101T 5C	386	3181

Power/weight ratios, expressed as tractive effort, for express locomotives doubled over a period of a century and a quarter, while engine weights alone increased twenty five fold in the same period, quadrupling in the fifteen years after 1829, and quadrupling again between 1845 and the start of the First War. From 1928, weights hovered around around the hundred ton mark, tractive effort between thirty and forty thousand pounds. While maximum speeds were close to 70mph by 1850, it was to be a further half century before one hundred miles an hour was reached, and not until after 1930 was there a brief period where a single line (the East Coast) saw occasional topping of that speed. Average speeds climbed quickly (at about 10mph/decade) to 50mph by the 1850s and only topped 60mph after 1930. Most of the extra power of locomotives was absorbed by the rapidly rising weights of carriages; few trains had trailing loads over 100 tons in 1860, by the 1930s the heaviest expresses were topping 500 tons.

In terms of heating surface, the Broad Gauge's advantage in 1846 is obvious, with a potential steaming capacity equal to that of many locomotives being built in 1925. Superheating in locomotives built after the First War distorts the picture, and the large heating surfaces of the last express locomotives was not a reflection of their superiority over previous types, quite the reverse.

Table 2:
Changes in weight, tractive effort and heating surface, freight locomotives, 1858 to 1954

Date	Locomotive	Tractive Effort (lb.)	Weight (Tons/Cwt.)	Power/ Weight Ratio (lb/ton.)	Heating Surface (sq.ft.)
1858	DX Goods	11,410	27T	422	1102
1880	LNWR (Webb 0-6-0)	15,995	29T 11C	541	1074
1894	Highland "Big Goods" 4-6-0	24,555	56T	438	1672
1900	Ivatt 0-8-0	27,664	54T 12C	506	1439
1903	2800 2-8-0	35,380	75T 10C	468	1841
1912	G2	28,045	62T	452	1772
1913	Robinson 2-8-0	31,325	73T 4C	428	1501
1913	N. Eastern 0-8-0 (LNER Q6)	28,800	65T 18C	437	1699
1919	N. Eastern 0-8-0 (LNER Q7)	36,965	71T 12C	516	1564
1921	Gresley 2-8-0 (LNER 02)	36,740	75T 16C	484	2084
1922	Midland 0-6-0	24,555	48T 15C	503	1157
1926	LNER 0-6-0 (J39)	25,665	57T 17C	443	1669
1935	LMS 8F	32,440	72T 2C	450	1650
1942	Southern 0-6-0 (Class Q1)	30,080	51T 5C	587	1642
1954	9F 2-10-0	39,670	86T 14C	457	2550

On freight locomotives, power/weight ratios scarcely varied from 1858 to 1954, with weight no more than tripling in the same period. The total heating surface, a reflection of the locomotive's ability to boil water, increased by a factor of 2.5. This serves to emphasise the lack of forces of change in freight movement in a hundred years, and why the steam freight railway was swept into the dustbin of history in little over two decades after the Second World War. The contrast between the 'DX' and the Midland 0-6-0 of 1922, the latter being heavier and with more tractive effort, but effectively the same steaming ability, illustrates the inertia of freight haulage after 1860.

As a contrast to this, power/weight ratios in the motor car rose tenfold, from about five horsepower/ton (HP/ton), to over fifty HP/ton in the twentieth century. Installed horsepower in the motor lorry saw a proportionately similar rise. On the railway, the first production batch of diesels (the 133 ton English Electric Type 4, later class 40) mustered 15HP/ton in 1958, the 1975 Paxman engined High Speed Train 32HP/ton. At 2000HP at the generator, the class 40 was inferior to the Stanier Pacifics it was meant to replace by over 1000HP, and fifty five tons, or two coaches, heavier than the diesel hydraulics (of the same or greater installed horsepower) the Great Western bought to replace the 'Kings' and 'Castles'. Diesels brought lower running costs but not greater power to the railway, at least not initially. The sole first generation diesels significantly more powerful than the steam locomotives they replaced were the 3300HP 'Deltics', and they raised average rather than top speeds by continuous outputs greater than those possible with one man and a shovel.

Trick Valve

Slide valve in which the valve block contains a passage running from end to end of the valve face, allowing a secondary route for steam to enter the cylinder, making for a fatter indicator diagram. Useful for raising power output at slow speed, but ineffective in addressing the basic issues of economical running.

Turntables

The first steam locomotives demonstrated clearly that while they were able to go backwards just as they could go forward, engines were much more stable when pointing the right way. Turntables thus became an essential for all main lines and most branches, and the idea that much larger locomotives would be needed to haul trains in the not-too-distant future was generally not acted upon. The first turntables were thus only twelve to fifteen feet long, and this led to the use of long overhangs of fireboxes and smokeboxes at the front and rear of engine designs in the 1830s and 1840s. Larger engines begat longer turntables in the 1850s until, eventually, seventy foot turntables enabled the last of the LNER Pacifics to be turned for service.

Later turntables used the vacuum supply from the engine, or were electrically operated. With a well-used and oiled turntable, even the largest engines could be turned by hand if needed, but a lot of shove was needed to get the engine moving in the first place, and a similar amount of effort was required to make the engine stop. Many locomotive depots were served by turntables within the buildings (the roundhouse concept), and failing to set the turntable to the right road led to the occasional event of engines being driven into the turntable pit rather than onto the rotateable track section

Tyres

After plain cast iron wheels were shown to be inadequate for the steam locomotive in 1825-1830, use of wrought iron shrunk-on tyres rapidly became near universal. Wrought iron, however, wore rapidly, and steel tyres displaced iron as soon as the first cost of the former declined after 1875. Shrinking tyres onto the wheel was a bit of a hit and miss affair, and the enormous stresses and resultant heating, as engines started their loads led to slipping of tyre on wheel. This was prevented by riveting or bolting the tyre in place, and eventually by rolling a lock ring over the edge of the tyre, thus offering continuous support. Tyres were made to various profiles, the basic form being conical, with a radiussed curve into the wheel flange, which was part of the tyre. As tyres wore, they were periodically machined back to their new profile until they were too thin to re-profile, at which point they had to be renewed.

Water Treatment

Much water in eastern England was (and is) heavily charged with soluble salts which were deposited in the boiler when used for raising steam. One way to address this, and to avoid the corrosion of steel boiler tubes and barrels, and the wasting of firebox plates and stays, was to treat the water to maintain the correct level of alkalinity. Two methods of treatment, pre- and point of use, were adopted, but boiler washouts to remove water saturated with salts that could not be precipitated out and removed as sludge, remained regular, often weekly, events (the use of continuous blowdown to minimise washouts by regularly discharging a proportion of the boiler water while in service was a late arrival on Britain's railways). The waste hot water was usually utilised to heat the water in the washout process, or the hot fill of fresh water when the locomotive was put back into service.

Weighbar

The weight of the two eccentric rods and the curved link of Stephenson valve gear (two sets for engines with two cylinders, three for three cylinders) had to be moved up and down to adjust the cut off whilst the engine was running. Practically this meant that it was not possible for the driver to adjust the gear without a lot of effort, and the weight of the gear was thus balanced by the use of counterweights on the cross-shaft that connected the two or three sets of gear to the reversing lever or screw, hence the name.

Westinghouse Pump

Westinghouse Brake and Signal developed the air brake as an alternative to the less efficient vacuum brake at the end of the nineteenth century, and the classic way of mounting the steam pump that supplied the high pressure air to the brake system, was to fit it to the side of the smokebox, where it emitted an irregular panting noise when the locomotive was stationary. The pump came to be known by its manufacturer's name.

Wheel Arrangement

British convention in locomotive technology entailed the use of a standard nomenclature for the combination of leading, driving and trailing wheels that the locomotive ran on. The LNER adopted a standard classification letter denoting each wheel arrangement, and some of the layouts also gained names. Names in brackets below indicate that it was not in general British use. (See table on p. 333 opposite.)

Wheel, Driving

Wheel to which the drive from the piston via the connecting rods is connected. Where two axles share the drive (LMS Pacifics, GWR 4 cylinder 4-6-0's), the drive is said to be divided. The remaining wheels that are driven via coupling rods are known as coupled wheels.

Wheel Drop

Section of track that can be lowered to remove a wheelset without having to lift the engine.

LNER Code Letter	Wheel Layout	Standard Notification	Name
A	oo OOO o	4-6-2	Pacific
B	oo OOO	4-6-0	(Ten Wheeler)
C	oo OO o	4-4-2	Atlantic
D	oo OO	4-4-0	(American)
E	o OO	2-4-0	
F	o OO o	2-4-2	
G	OO oo	0-4-4	
H	oo OO oo	4-4-4	
J	OOO	0-6-0	
K	o OOO	2-6-0	Mogul
L	o OOO oo	2-6-4	
M	o OOO oo	0-6-4	(Adriatic)
N	OOO o	0-6-2	
O	o OOOO	2-8-0	(Consolidation)
P	o OOOO o	2-8-2	Mikado
Q	OOOO	0-8-0	
R	OOOO o	0-8-2	
S	OOOO oo	0-8-4	
T	oo OOOO	4-8-0	
U	o OOOO+OOOO o	2-8-0+0-8-2	Garrett (LNER)
V	o OOO o	2-6-2	Prairie (GWR)
W	oo OOO oo	4-6-4	Baltic
X	oo OOOO	4-8-0	
Y	OO	0-4-0	
Z	O oo	0-4-2	

Other Wheel Arrangements:

OOOO	0-10-0	Decapod
o OOOO	2-10-0	
o OOO+OOO o	2-6-0+0-6-2	LMS Garrett

Suffixes:-   T - Tank, PT - Pannier Tank, TT - Tender Tank, WT - Well Tank, ST - Saddle Tank.

Select Bibliography

Prof. Henry Adams. The Engineers Handbook. Waverley Book Co. London.

E. L. Ahrons. The British Steam Railway Locomotive 1825 to 1925. Locomotive Publishing Company 1927.

E. Morton Bell. Locomotives. Virtue & Co, London. 7th ed. 1950.

Bennett College. Engineering. University Press, Edinburgh.

F. A. S. Brown. Nigel Gresley. Ian Allan, London, 1961.

Rankin Kennedy. The Book of Modern Engines And Power Generators. Caxton Publishing Co., London, 1911.

O. S. Nock. The British Steam Railway Locomotive 1925 to 1965. Ian Allan. London 1966.

Loco Profiles Nos 3, 7, 8, 15, 17, 21, 22, 37. Profile Publications Ltd. Windsor. 1974.

Acknowledgements

The author wishes to thank Rob Thewlis for his contributions to the text, which, as always, have been informed and have acted as a restraining influence on some of the more esoteric ideas. The author also wishes to thank John Reid for his memories of life as a fireman at Severn Tunnel Junction, and Tony Telford for his recollections of train spotting in the age of steam, in addition to his assistance with the text. In checking and cross referencing, the author has made use of both Ahron's and Nock's work on the British steam locomotive, and has seen fit to disagree at times with both. For technical references, various volumes of *Loco Profiles* have been consulted, and have always proved accurate, as has E. Morton Bell's *Locomotives*.

For matters of engineering in the nineteenth and early twentieth century, the author has drawn upon Professor Henry Adam's prodigious one thousand four hundred and ninety six section *Engineer's Handbook*, a slightly slimmer tome on *Engineering* by the Bennett College, and, largest of them all, Rankin Kennedy's six volume *The Book of Modern Engines and Power Generators*. As less than light reading, none of these deals exclusively with the steam locomotive, but all are excellent in providing background.

The author has been fortunate to have had comprehensive tours of inspection of Derby Works, and Doncaster "Plant", British Railways, and has drawn extensively on those experiences. Thanks are also due to the "open shed" policy pursued by the Dinting Railway Society and Severn Valley Railway in the 1970s and 80s, wherein much minutiae was revisited.

Finally, thanks are also due to Maisie Robson for her kind reading of the initial manuscript, and of course to Chris White for his illustrations.